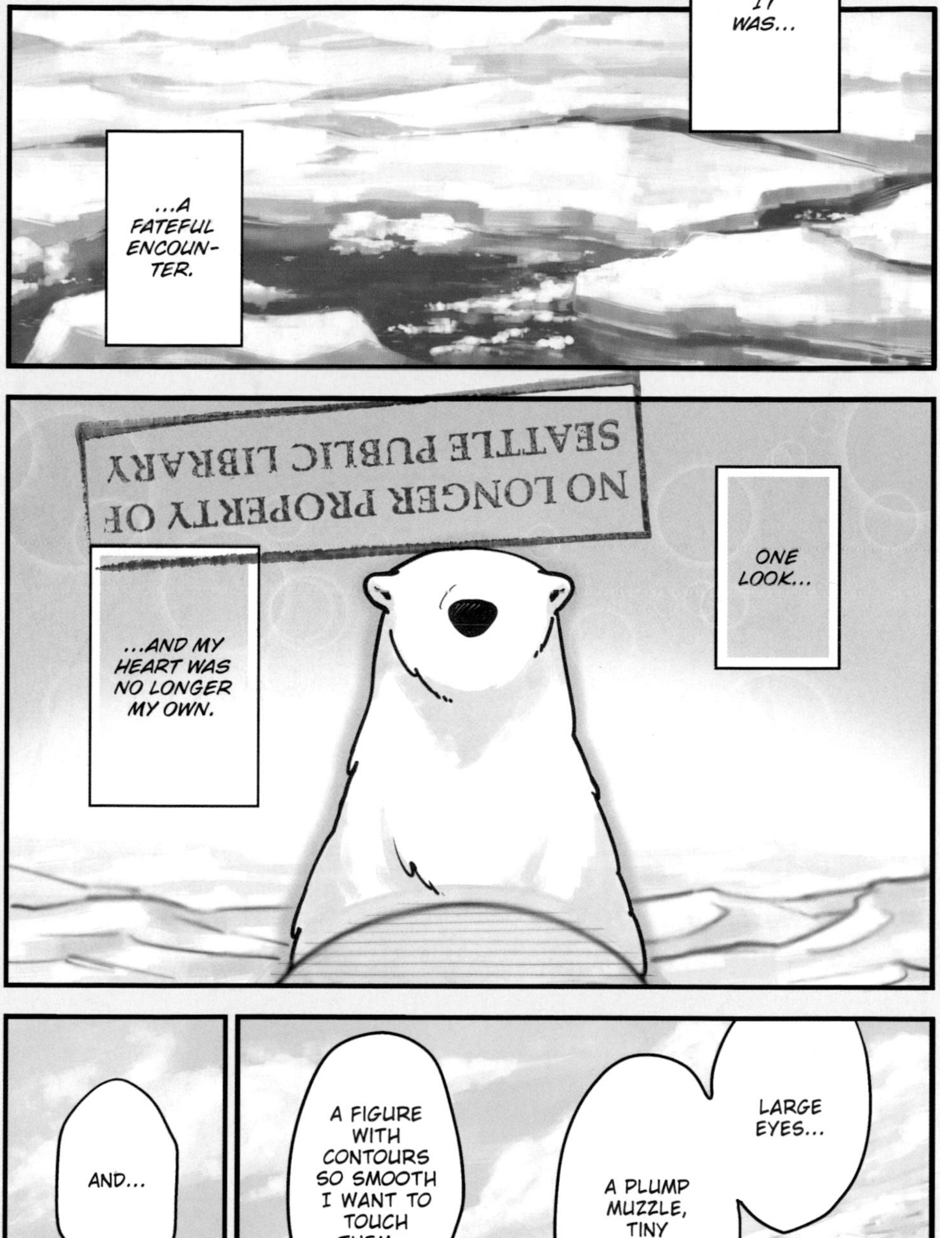
IT WAS...
...A FATEFUL ENCOUN-TER.
ONE LOOK...
...AND MY HEART WAS NO LONGER MY OWN.
LARGE EYES...
A PLUMP MUZZLE, TINY HANDS...
A FIGURE WITH CONTOURS SO SMOOTH I WANT TO TOUCH THEM...
AND...

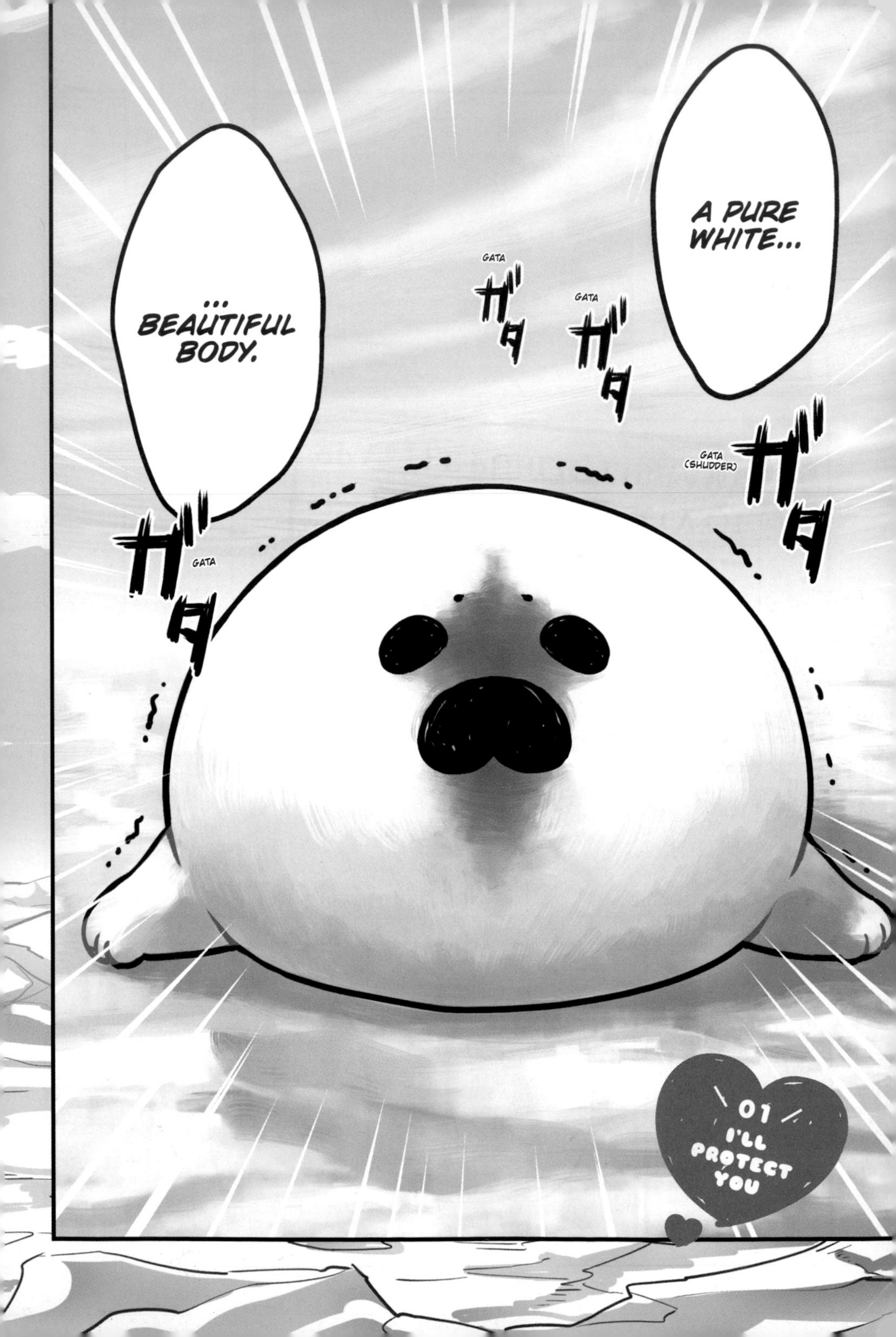
A PURE WHITE...
GATA
GATA
GATA (SHUDDER)
...BEAÜTIFUL BODY.
GATA
01
I'LL PROTECT YOU

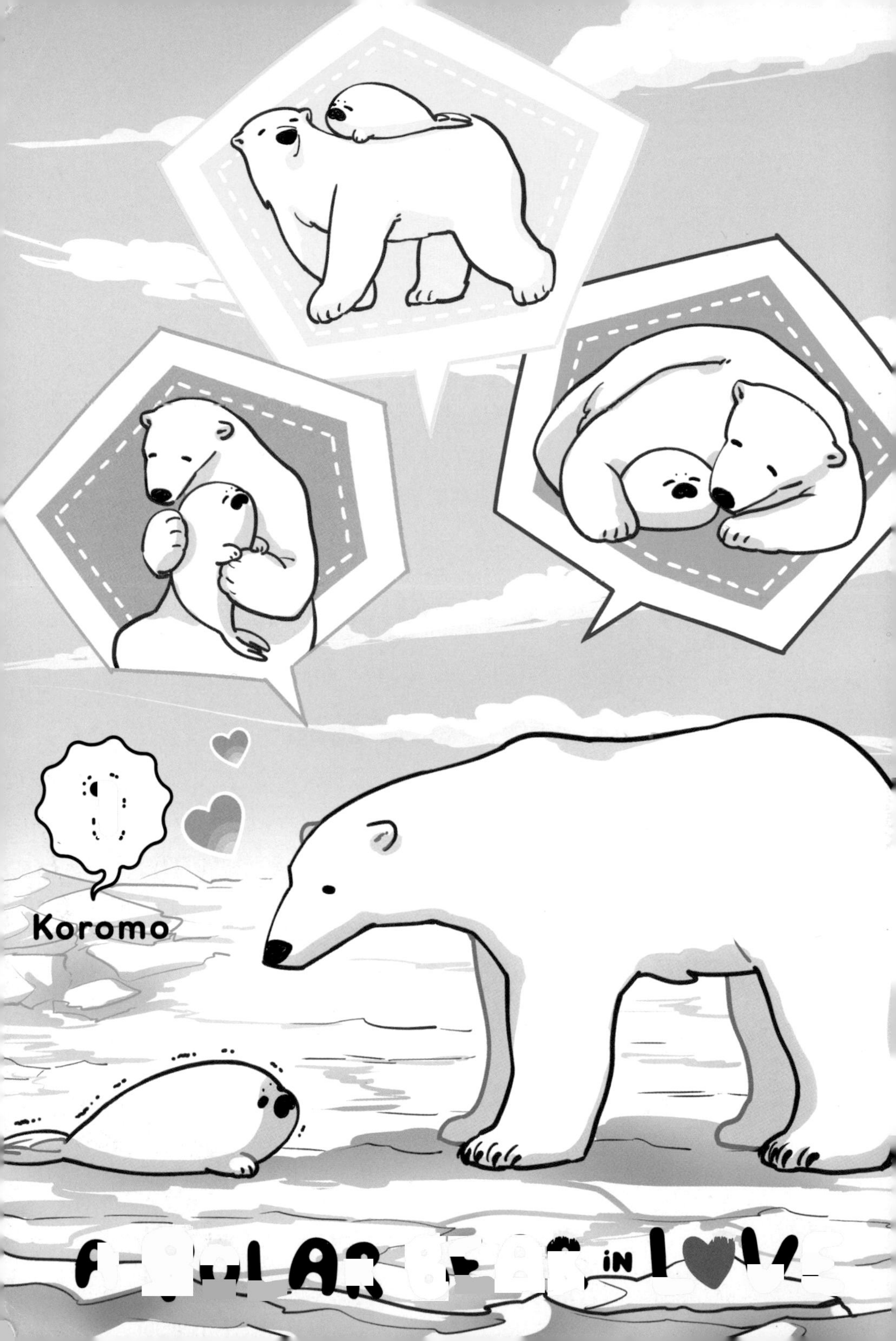

9
Koromo
A POLAR BEAR IN LOVE

c o n t e n t s

THE SECRET OF WHITENESS

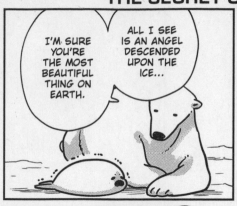

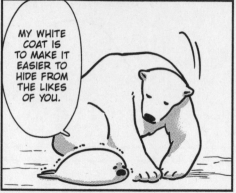

MY WHITE COAT IS TO MAKE IT EASIER TO HIDE FROM THE LIKES OF YOU.
ALL I SEE IS AN ANGEL DESCENDED UPON THE ICE...
I'M SURE YOU'RE THE MOST BEAUTIFUL THING ON EARTH.
I STILL HAVE A LONG WAY TO GO, BUT...
...SOMEDAY, I'LL BECOME A SPLENDID MALE AND PROTECT YOU—EVEN IF IT COSTS ME MY LIFE.
CHU (KISS)
ARE YOU LISTENING TO ME?
AND...
SU (SHFF)
...I PROMISE I'LL MAKE YOU HAPPY.
ONCE YOU GROW UP, LET'S GET MARRIED.
BUT I'M MALE TOO.
GATA (TREMBLE)
ガタ
GATA
ガタ

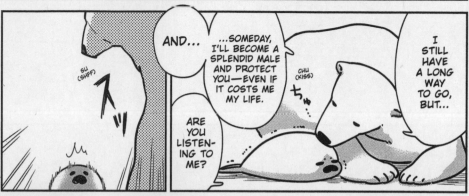

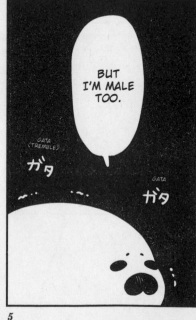

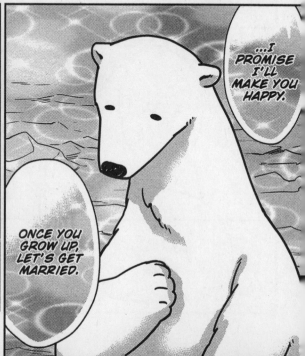

I MIND

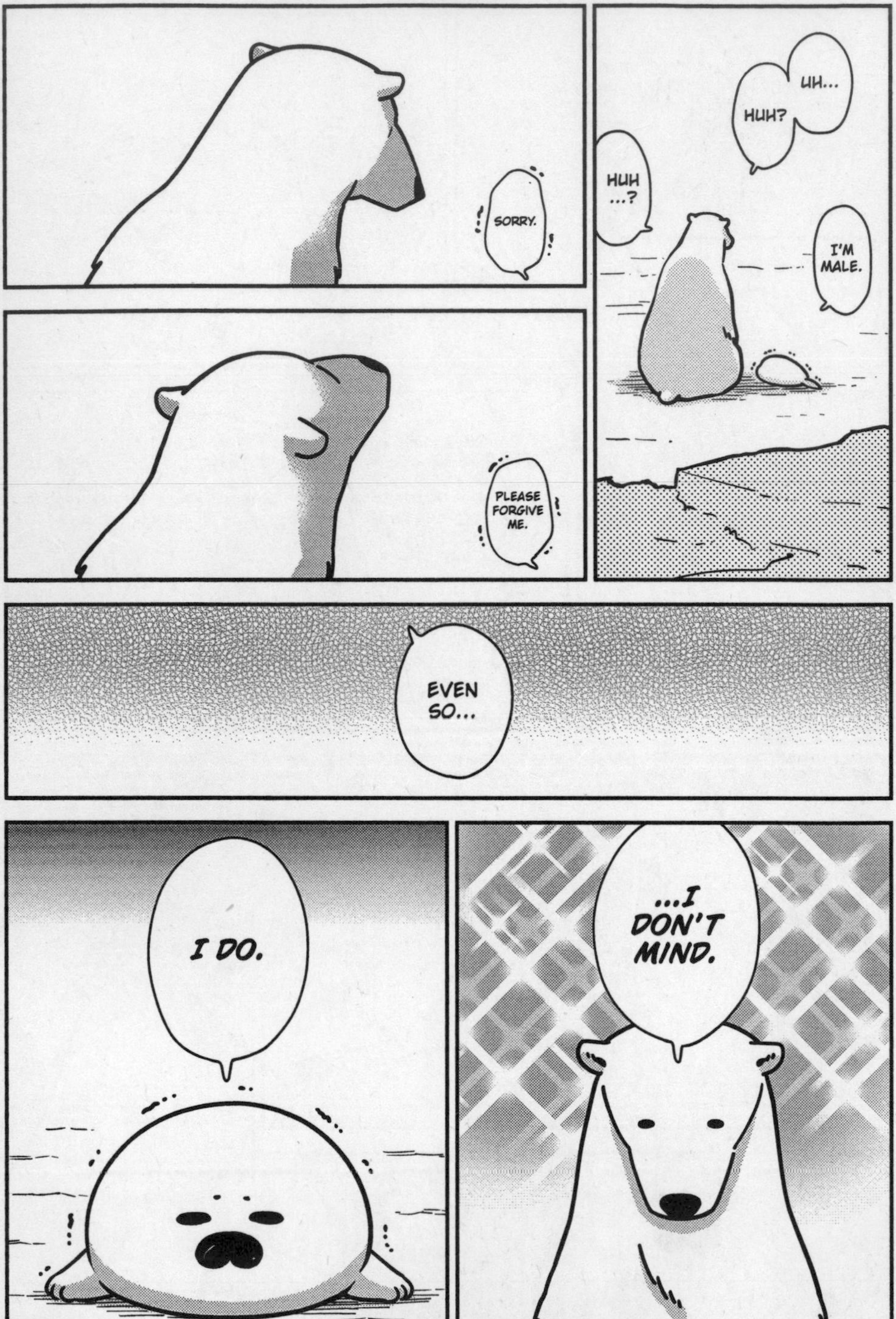
UH...
HUH?
HUH ...?
I'M MALE.
SORRY.
PLEASE FORGIVE ME.
EVEN SO...
...I DON'T MIND.
I DO.

DRAWN TO YOU

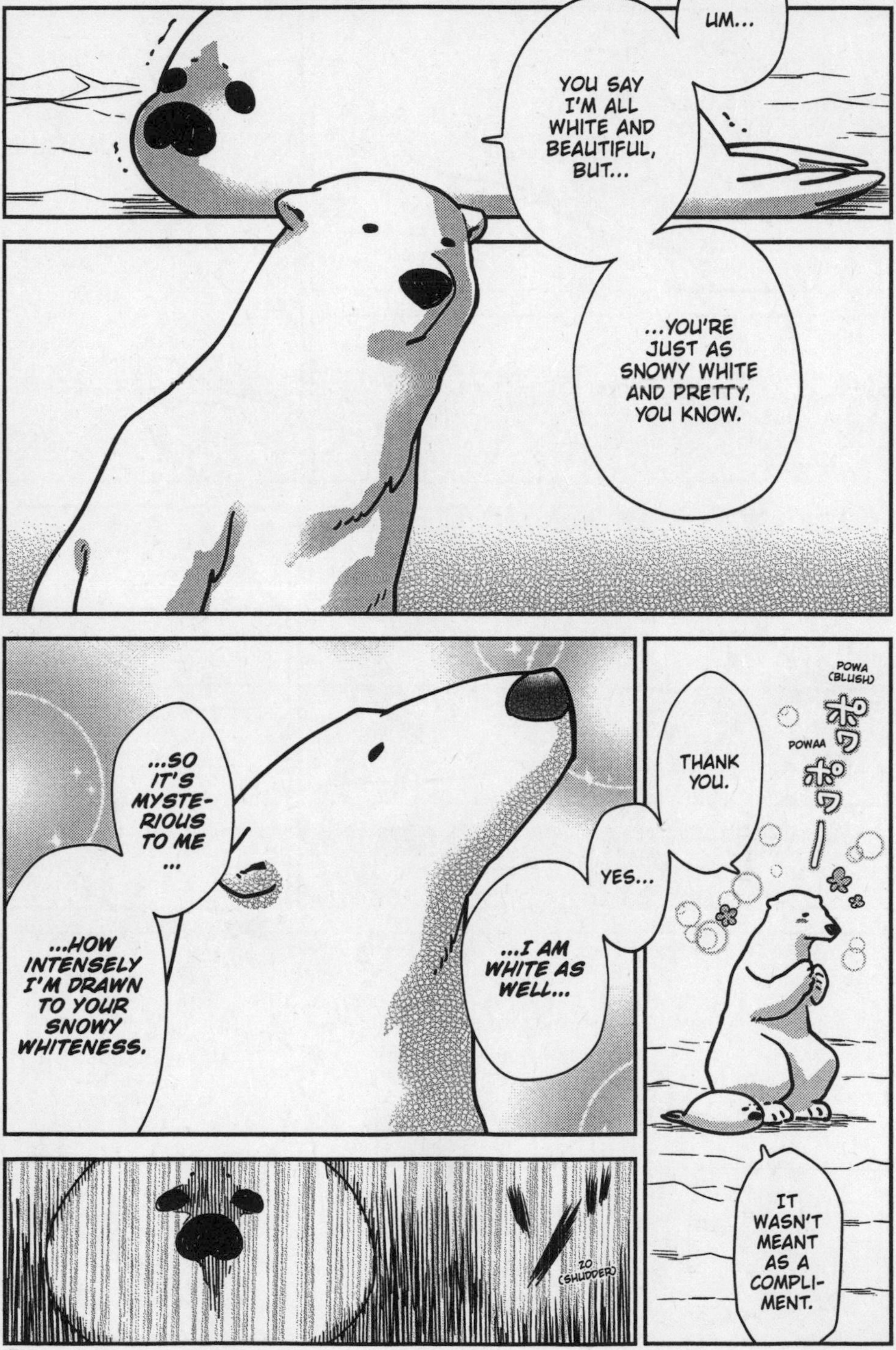
UM...
YOU SAY I'M ALL WHITE AND BEAUTIFUL, BUT...
...YOU'RE JUST AS SNOWY WHITE AND PRETTY, YOU KNOW.
YES...
...I AM WHITE AS WELL...
...SO IT'S MYSTERIOUS TO ME ...
...HOW INTENSELY I'M DRAWN TO YOUR SNOWY WHITENESS.
THANK YOU.
POWA (BLUSH)
ポワ
POWAA
ポワー
IT WASN'T MEANT AS A COMPLIMENT.
ZO (SHUDDER)

MATCHING

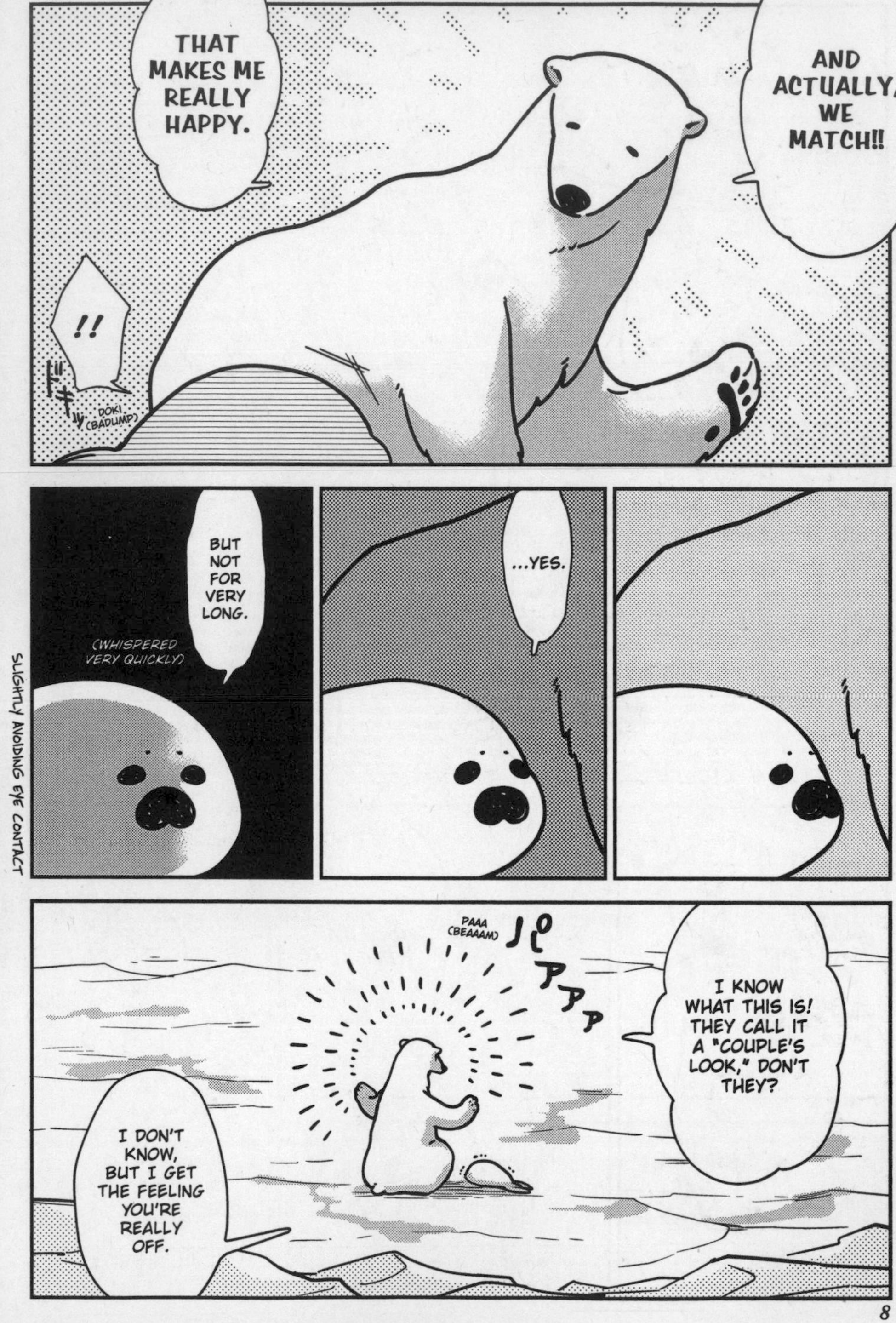
AND ACTUALLY, WE MATCH!!
THAT MAKES ME REALLY HAPPY.
!!
DOKI (BADUMP)
...YES.
BUT NOT FOR VERY LONG.
(WHISPERED VERY QUICKLY)
SLIGHTLY AVOIDING EYE CONTACT
PAAA (BEAAAM)
I KNOW WHAT THIS IS! THEY CALL IT A "COUPLE'S LOOK," DON'T THEY?
I DON'T KNOW, BUT I GET THE FEELING YOU'RE REALLY OFF.

CALL ME

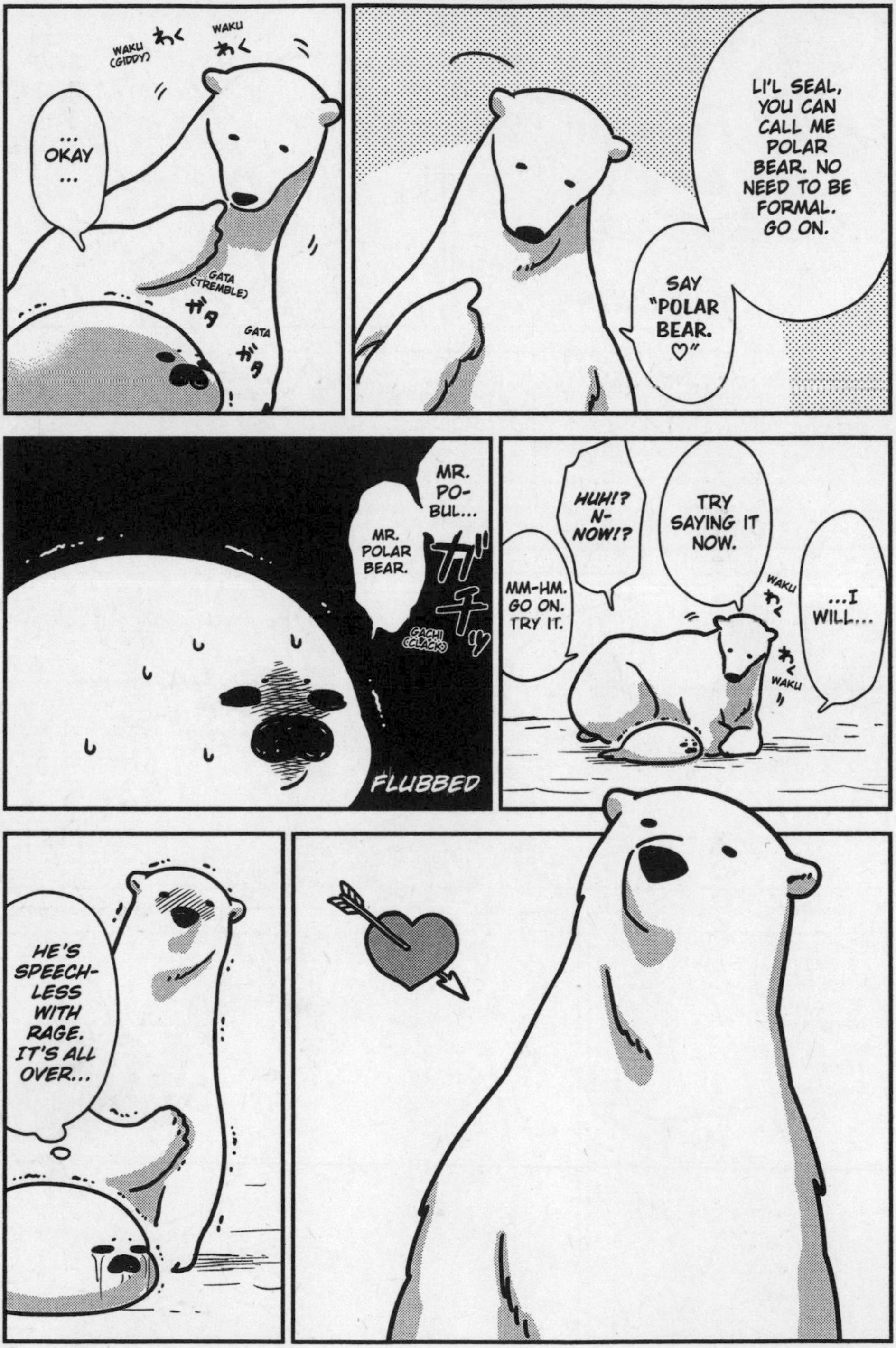
LI'L SEAL, YOU CAN CALL ME POLAR BEAR. NO NEED TO BE FORMAL. GO ON.
SAY "POLAR BEAR. ♡"
WAKU わく
WAKU (GIDDY) わく
...OKAY...
GATA (TREMBLE) ガタ
GATA ガタ
...I WILL...
TRY SAYING IT NOW.
WAKU わく WAKU わく
HUH!? N-NOW!?
MM-HM. GO ON. TRY IT.
MR. PO-BUL...
MR. POLAR BEAR.
ガチッ GACHI (CLACK)
FLUBBED
HE'S SPEECHLESS WITH RAGE. IT'S ALL OVER...

CALL ME 2

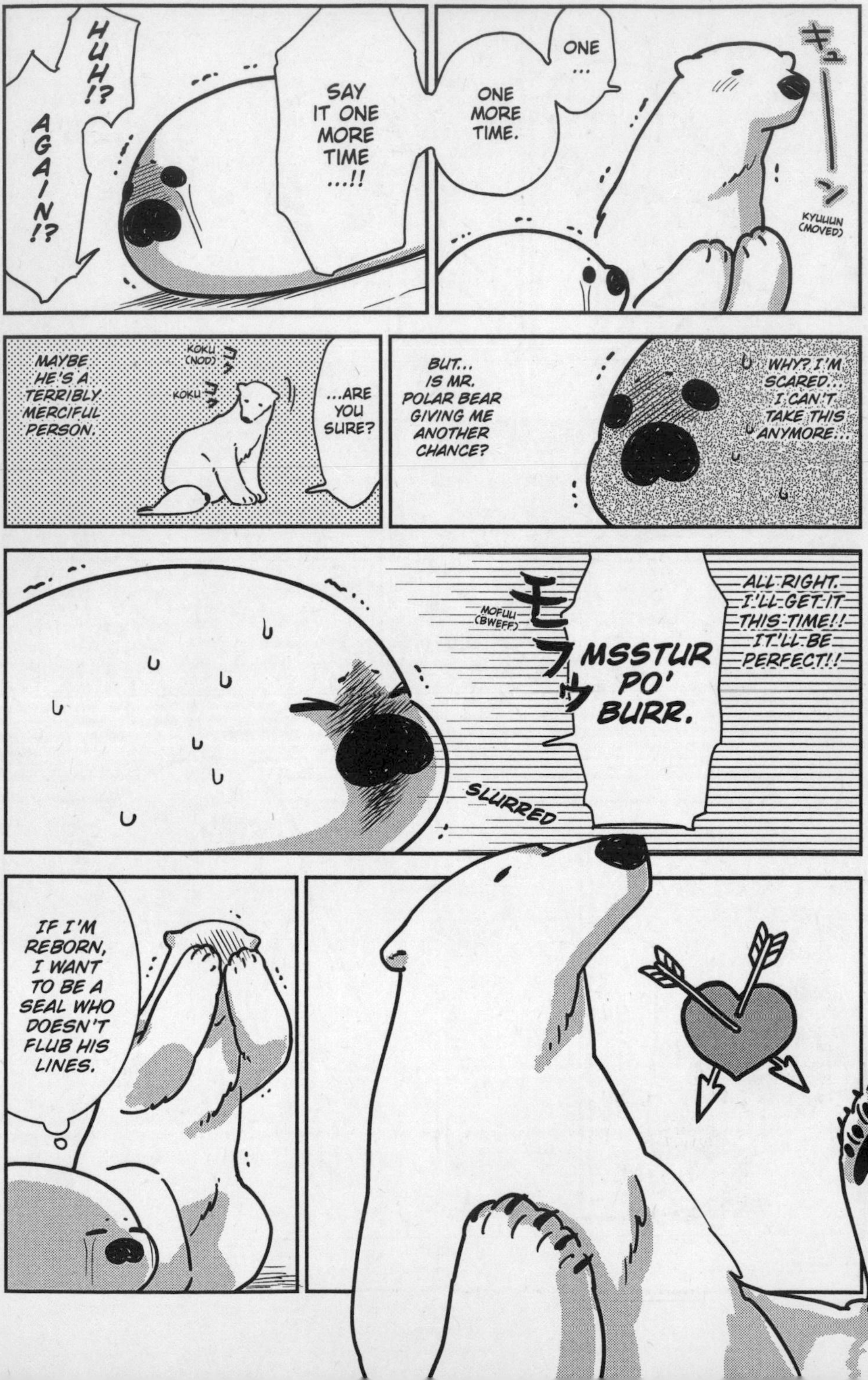
ONE ...
ONE MORE TIME.
KYUUUN (MOVED)
SAY IT ONE MORE TIME ...!!
HUH!? AGAIN!?
WHY? I'M SCARED... I CAN'T TAKE THIS ANYMORE...
BUT... IS MR. POLAR BEAR GIVING ME ANOTHER CHANCE?
...ARE YOU SURE?
KOKU (NOD)
KOKU
MAYBE HE'S A TERRIBLY MERCIFUL PERSON.
ALL RIGHT. I'LL GET IT THIS TIME!! IT'LL BE PERFECT!!
MSSTUR PO' BURR.
MOFUU (BWEFF)
SLURRED
IF I'M REBORN, I WANT TO BE A SEAL WHO DOESN'T FLUB HIS LINES.

YOINK, CHOMP

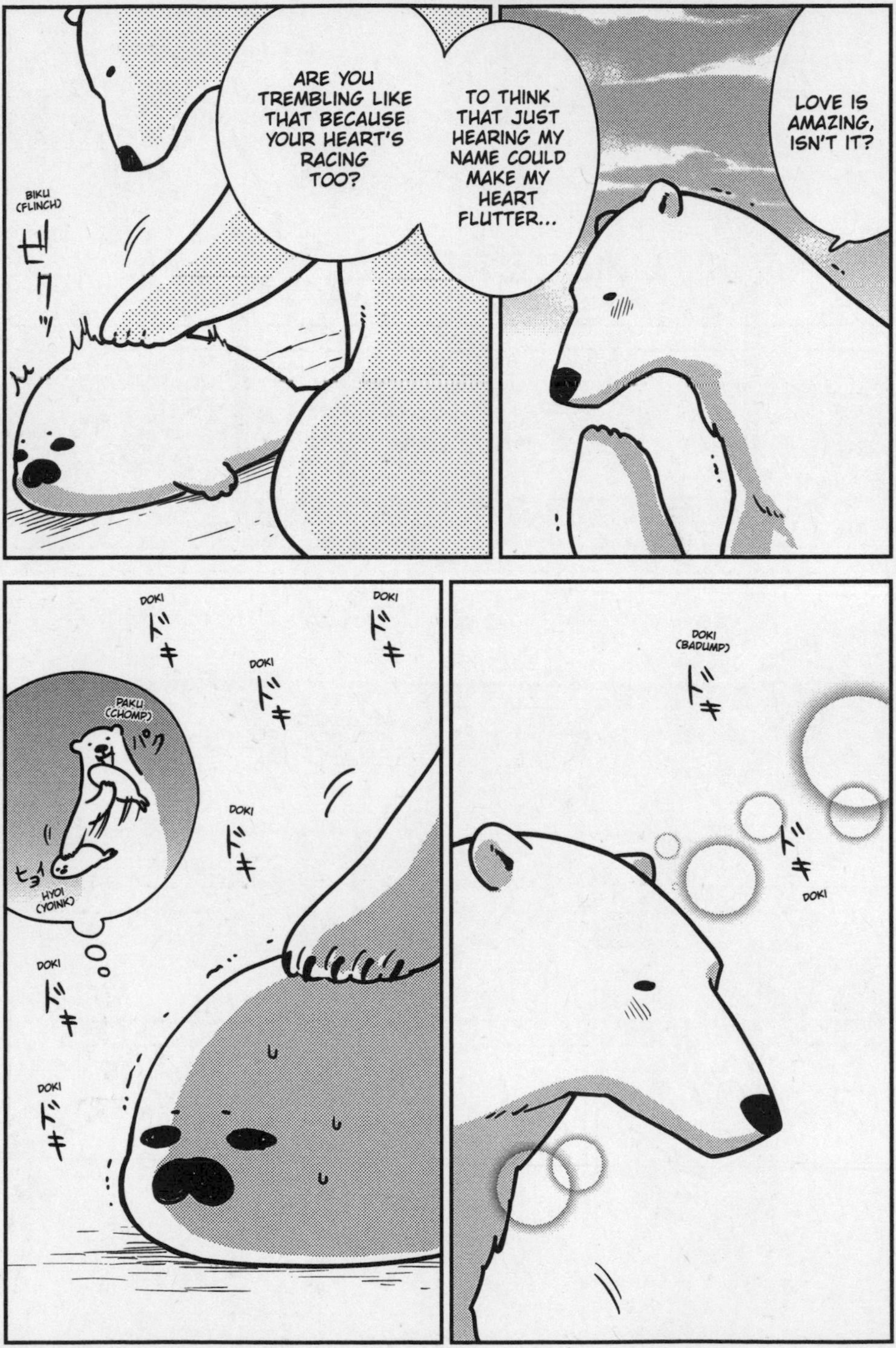
LOVE IS AMAZING, ISN'T IT?
TO THINK THAT JUST HEARING MY NAME COULD MAKE MY HEART FLUTTER...
ARE YOU TREMBLING LIKE THAT BECAUSE YOUR HEART'S RACING TOO?
BIKU (FLINCH)
DOKI (BADUMP)
DOKI
DOKI
DOKI
DOKI
PAKU (CHOMP)
DOKI
HYOI (YOINK)
DOKI
DOKI

IN THE FIRST PLACE

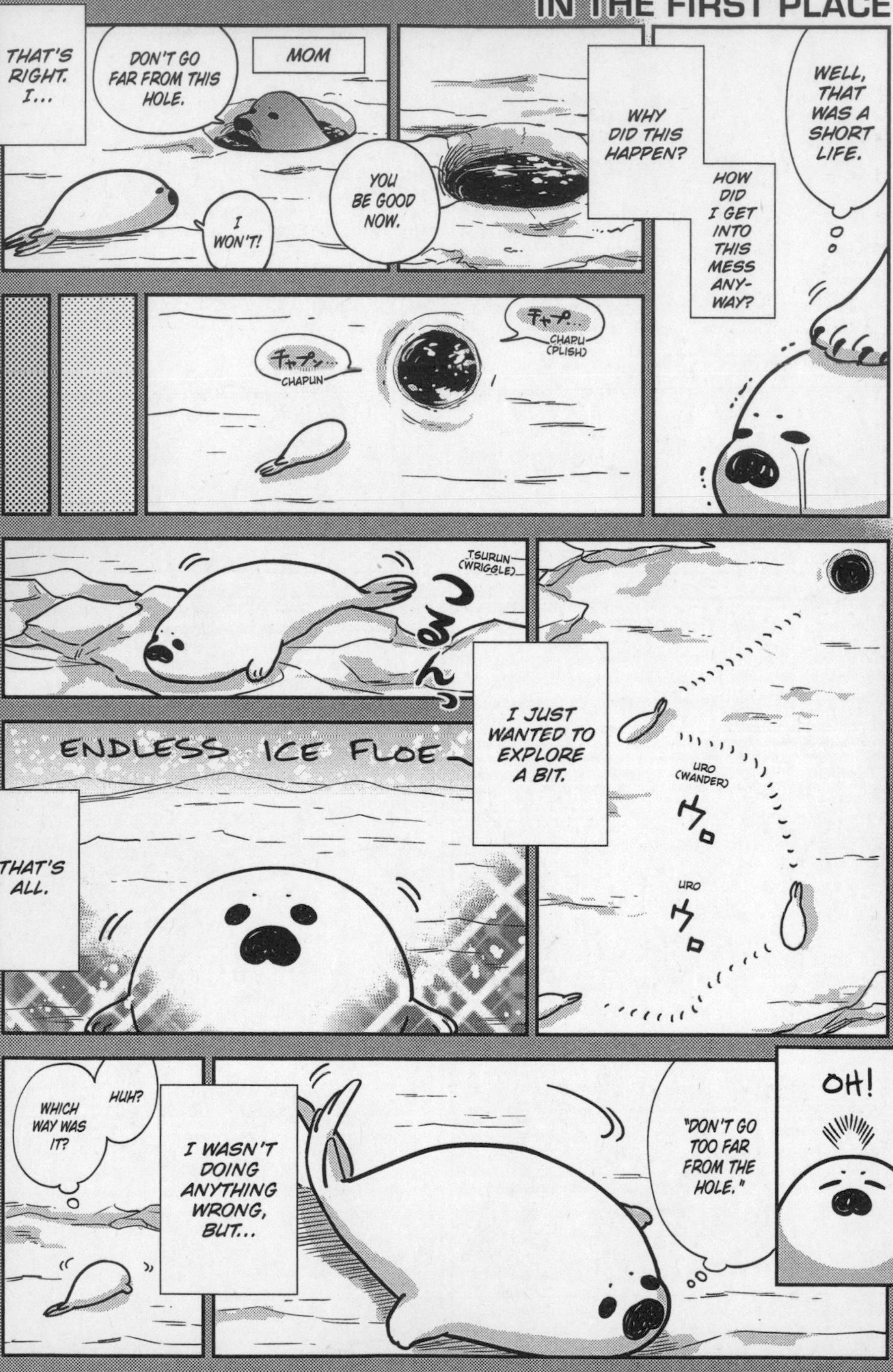
WELL, THAT WAS A SHORT LIFE.
WHY DID THIS HAPPEN?
HOW DID I GET INTO THIS MESS ANYWAY?
THAT'S RIGHT. I...
MOM
DON'T GO FAR FROM THIS HOLE.
I WON'T!
YOU BE GOOD NOW.
チャプ…
CHAPU (PLISH)
チャプン…
CHAPUN
I JUST WANTED TO EXPLORE A BIT.
URO (WANDER)
ウロ
URO
ウロ
TSURUN (WRIGGLE)
つるん
ENDLESS ICE FLOE~
THAT'S ALL.
OH!
"DON'T GO TOO FAR FROM THE HOLE."
I WASN'T DOING ANYTHING WRONG, BUT...
HUH?
WHICH WAY WAS IT?

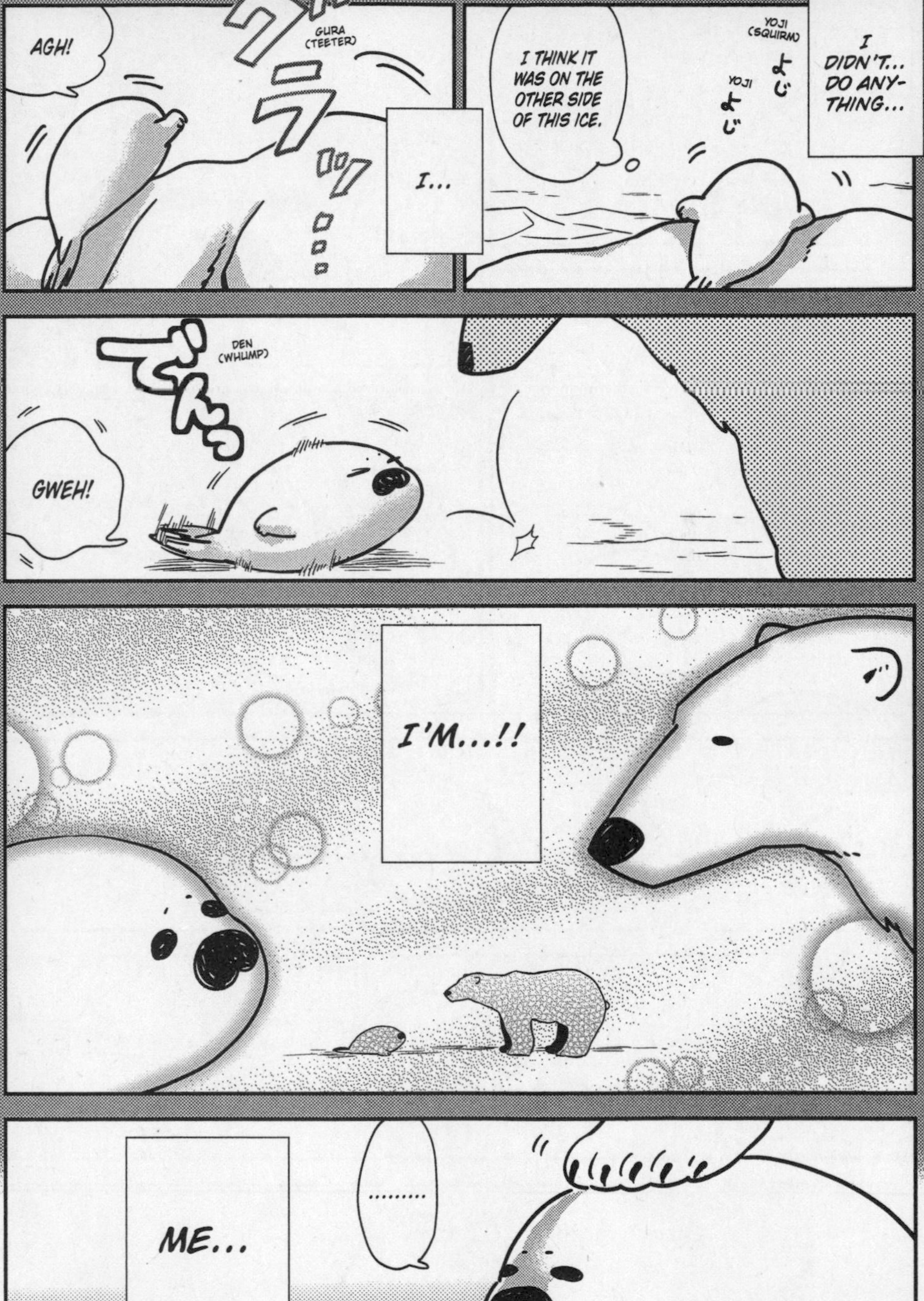
I DIDN'T... DO ANYTHING...
YOJI (SQUIRM)
よじ
YOJI
よじ
I THINK IT WAS ON THE OTHER SIDE OF THIS ICE.
GURA (TEETER)
AGH!
I...
DEN (WHUMP)
GWEH!
I'M...!!
....
ME...

?

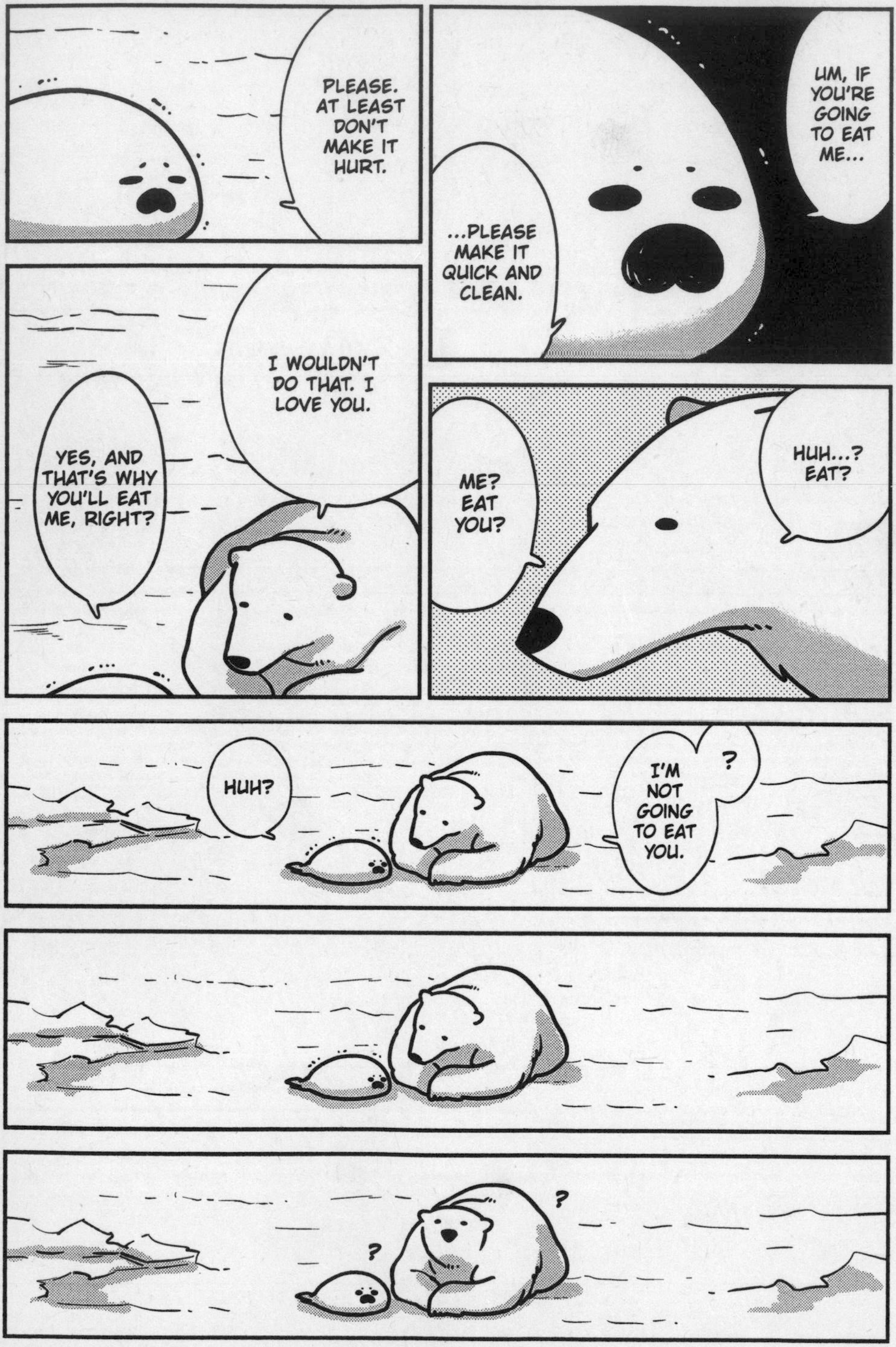

UM, IF YOU'RE GOING TO EAT ME...
...PLEASE MAKE IT QUICK AND CLEAN.
PLEASE. AT LEAST DON'T MAKE IT HURT.
HUH...? EAT?
ME? EAT YOU?
I WOULDN'T DO THAT. I LOVE YOU.
YES, AND THAT'S WHY YOU'LL EAT ME, RIGHT?
?
I'M NOT GOING TO EAT YOU.
HUH?
?
?

KENNY AND JULIE

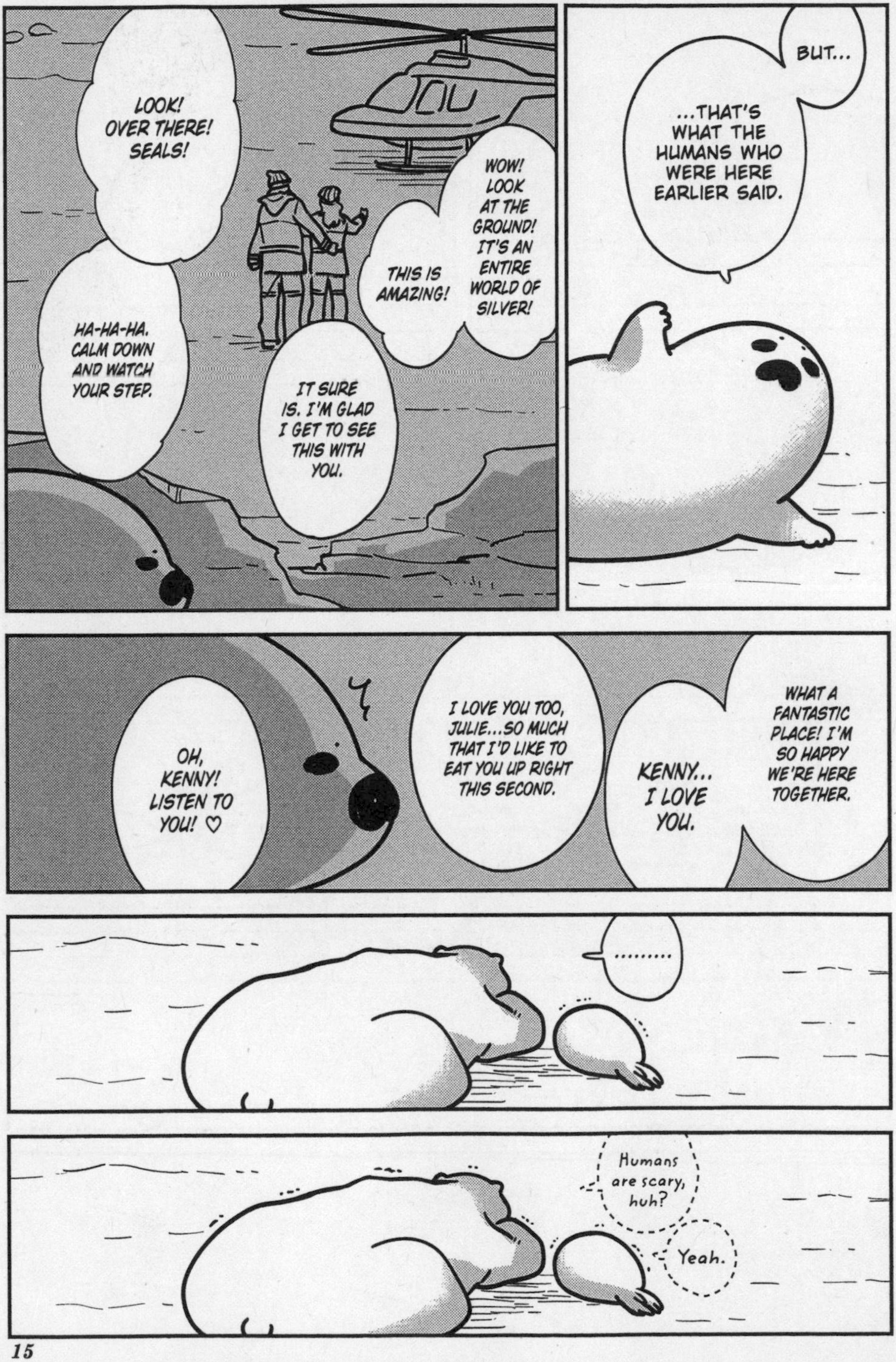
BUT...
...THAT'S WHAT THE HUMANS WHO WERE HERE EARLIER SAID.
WOW! LOOK AT THE GROUND! IT'S AN ENTIRE WORLD OF SILVER!
THIS IS AMAZING!
LOOK! OVER THERE! SEALS!
IT SURE IS. I'M GLAD I GET TO SEE THIS WITH YOU.
HA-HA-HA. CALM DOWN AND WATCH YOUR STEP.
WHAT A FANTASTIC PLACE! I'M SO HAPPY WE'RE HERE TOGETHER.
KENNY... I LOVE YOU.
I LOVE YOU TOO, JULIE...SO MUCH THAT I'D LIKE TO EAT YOU UP RIGHT THIS SECOND.
OH, KENNY! LISTEN TO YOU! ♡
....
Humans are scary, huh?
Yeah.

NOW'S MY CHANCE

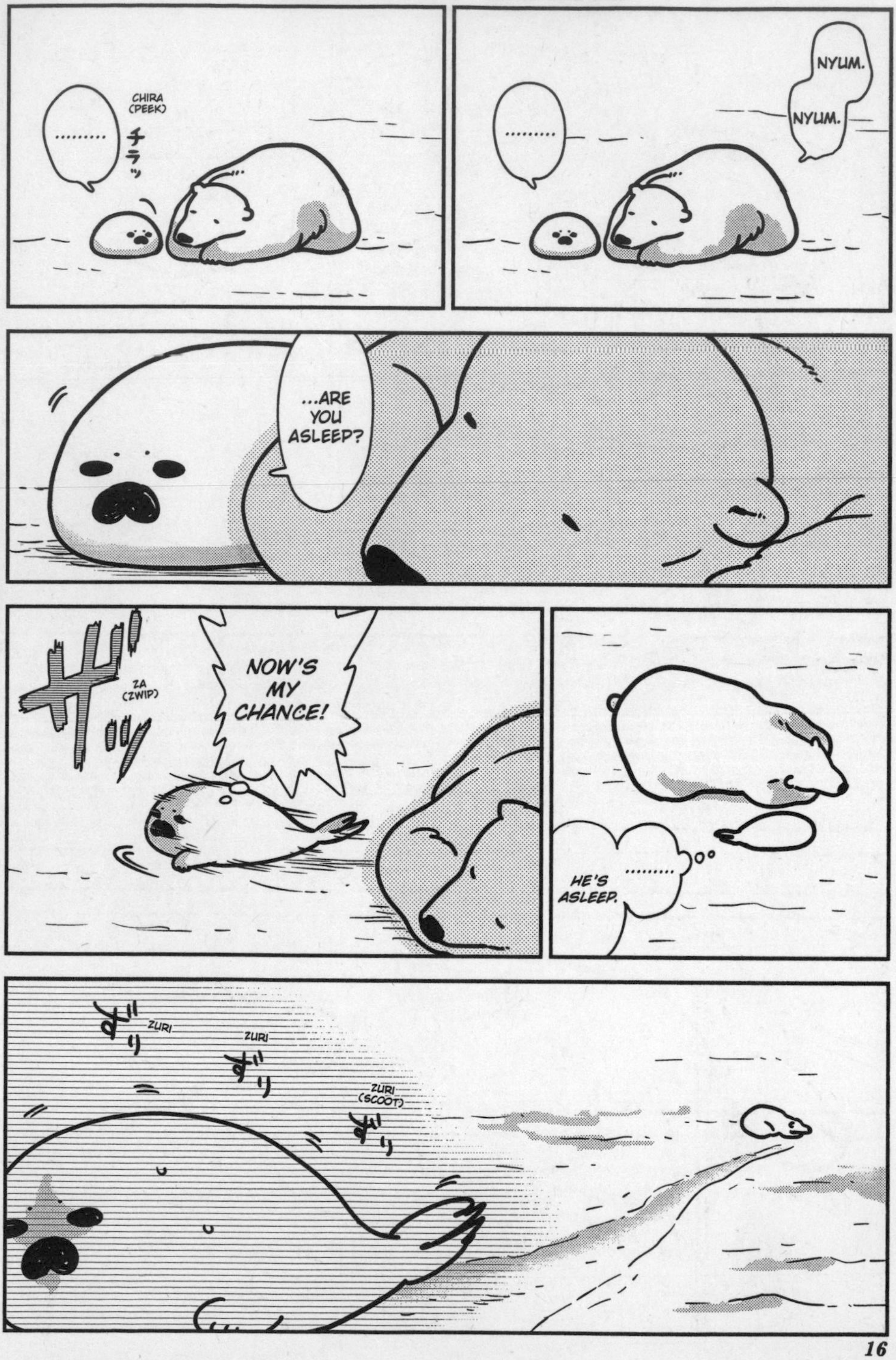
NYUM.
NYUM.
....
....
CHIRA (PEEK)
チラッ
...ARE YOU ASLEEP?
....
HE'S ASLEEP.
ザッ
ZA (ZWIP)
NOW'S MY CHANCE!
ずり
ZURI
ZURI
ずり
ZURI (SCOOT)
ずり

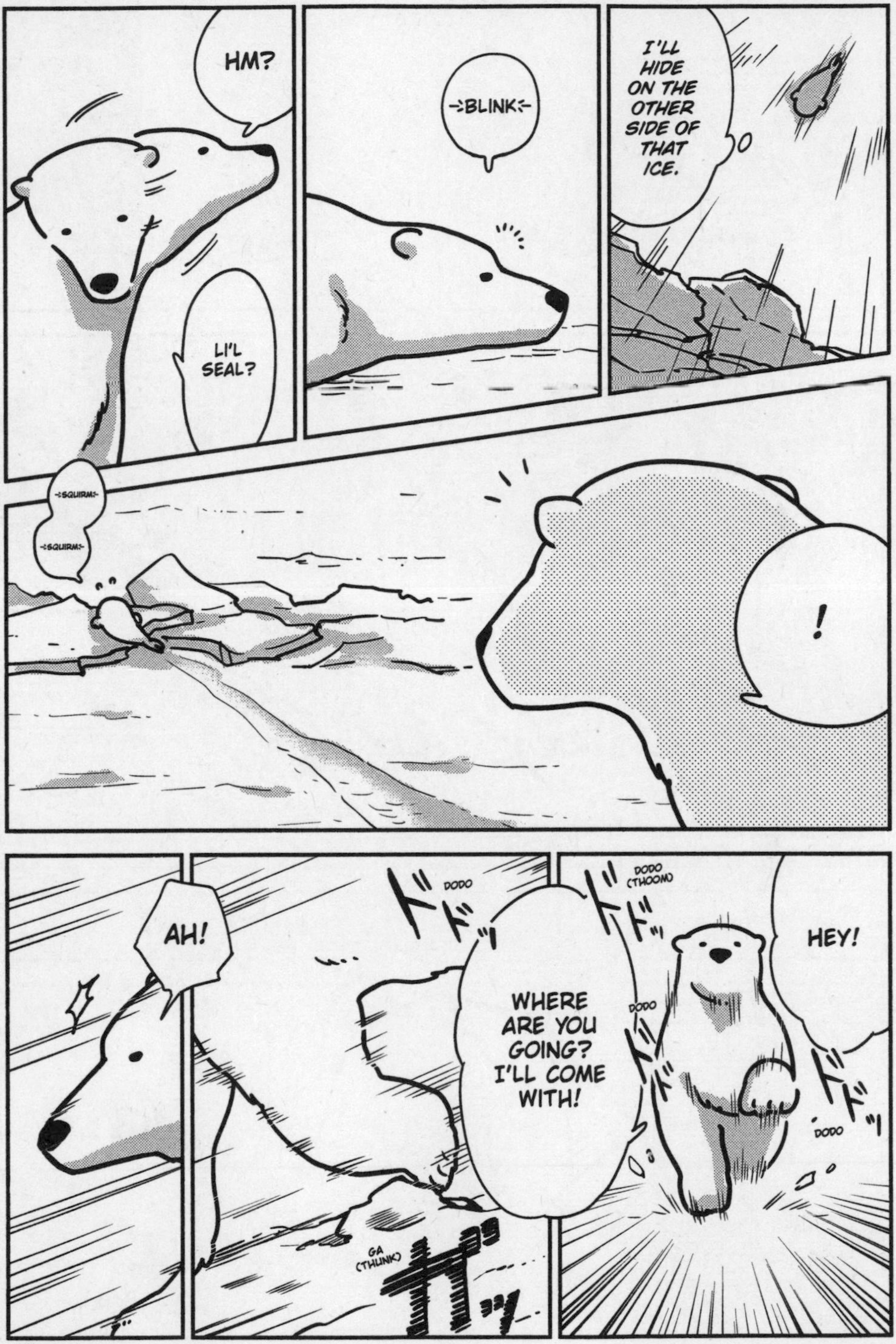
I'LL HIDE ON THE OTHER SIDE OF THAT ICE.
-BLINK-
HM?
LI'L SEAL?
!
-SQUIRM-
-SQUIRM-
HEY!
DODO (THOOM)
DODO
DODO
DODO
WHERE ARE YOU GOING? I'LL COME WITH!
GA (THUNK)
AH!

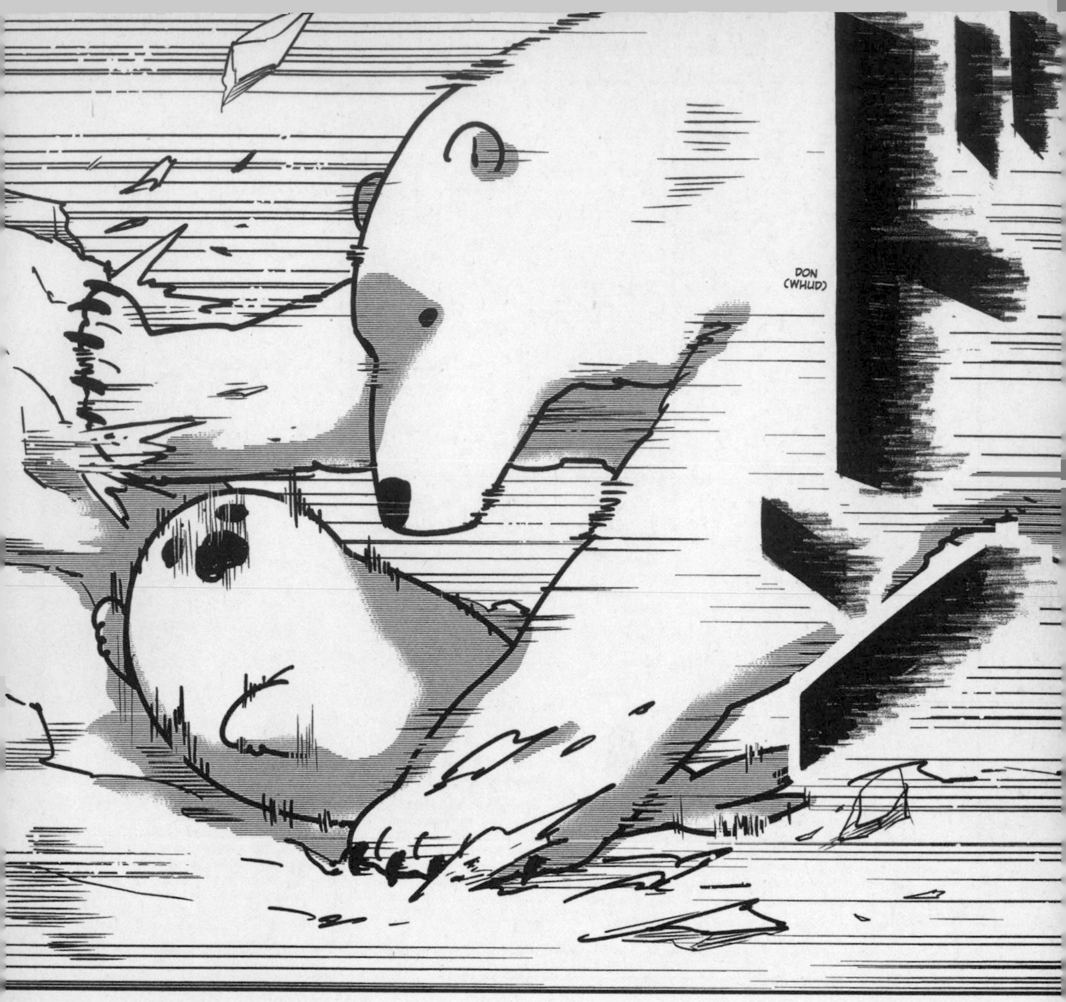
DON
(WHUD)

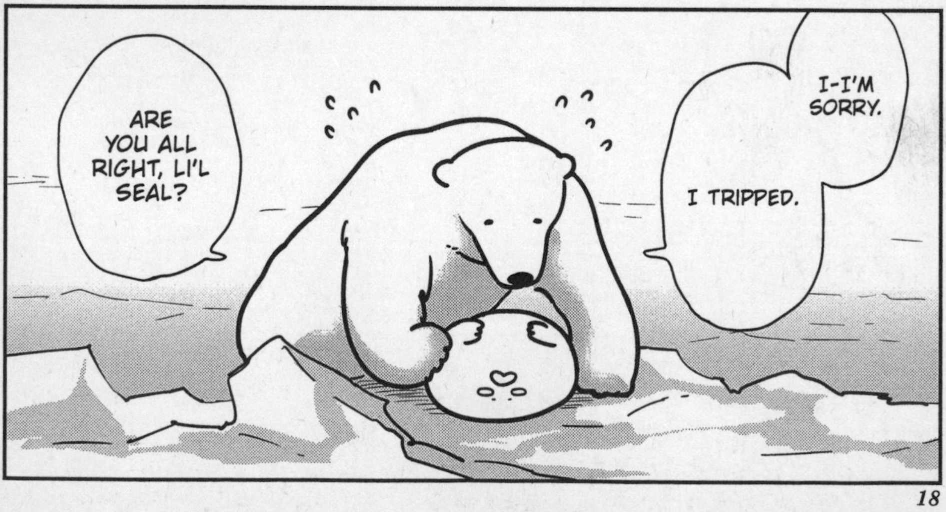
I-I'M SORRY.
I TRIPPED.
ARE YOU ALL RIGHT, LI'L SEAL?

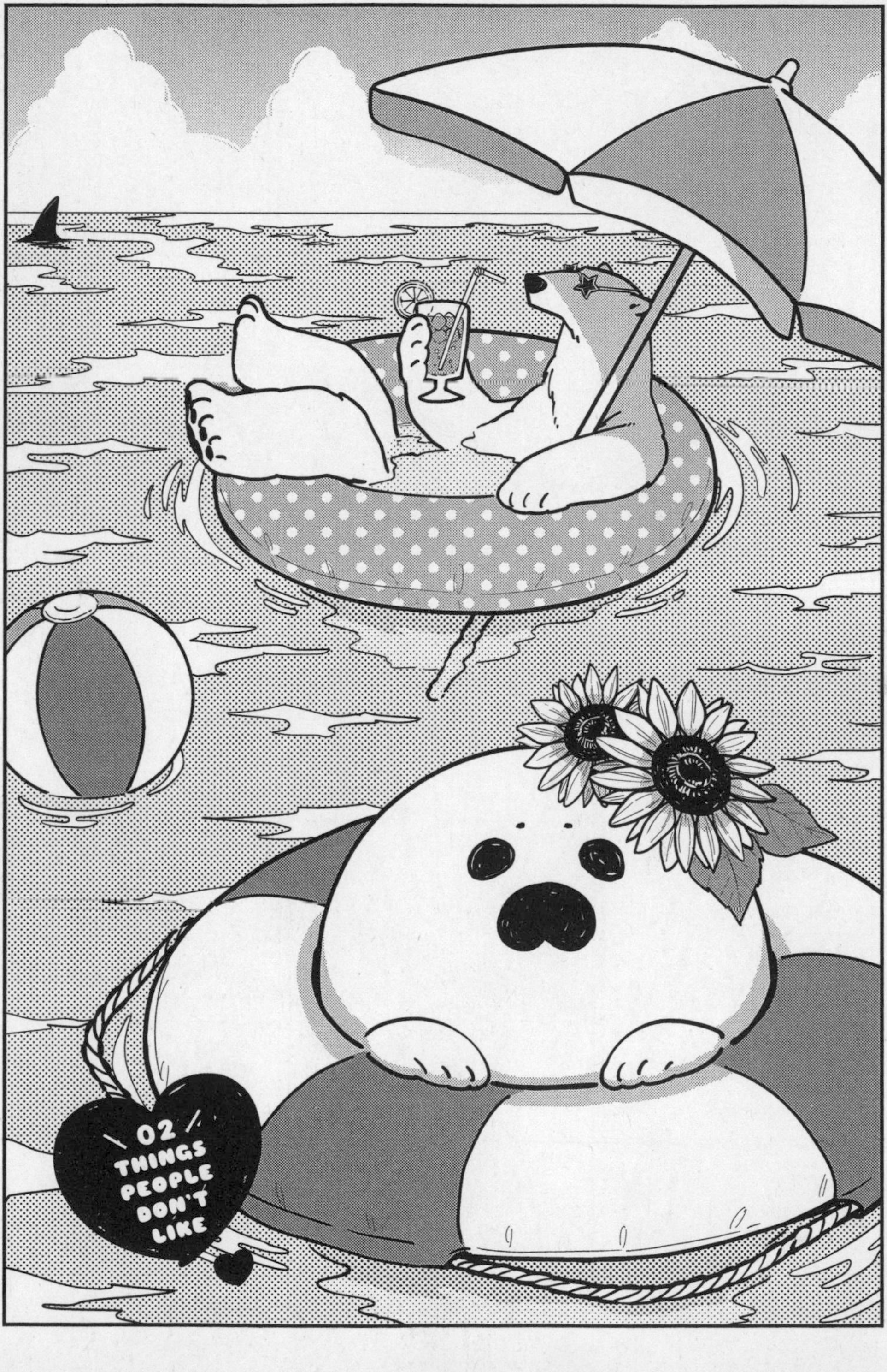
02
THINGS PEOPLE DON'T LIKE

SEAL ECOLOGY

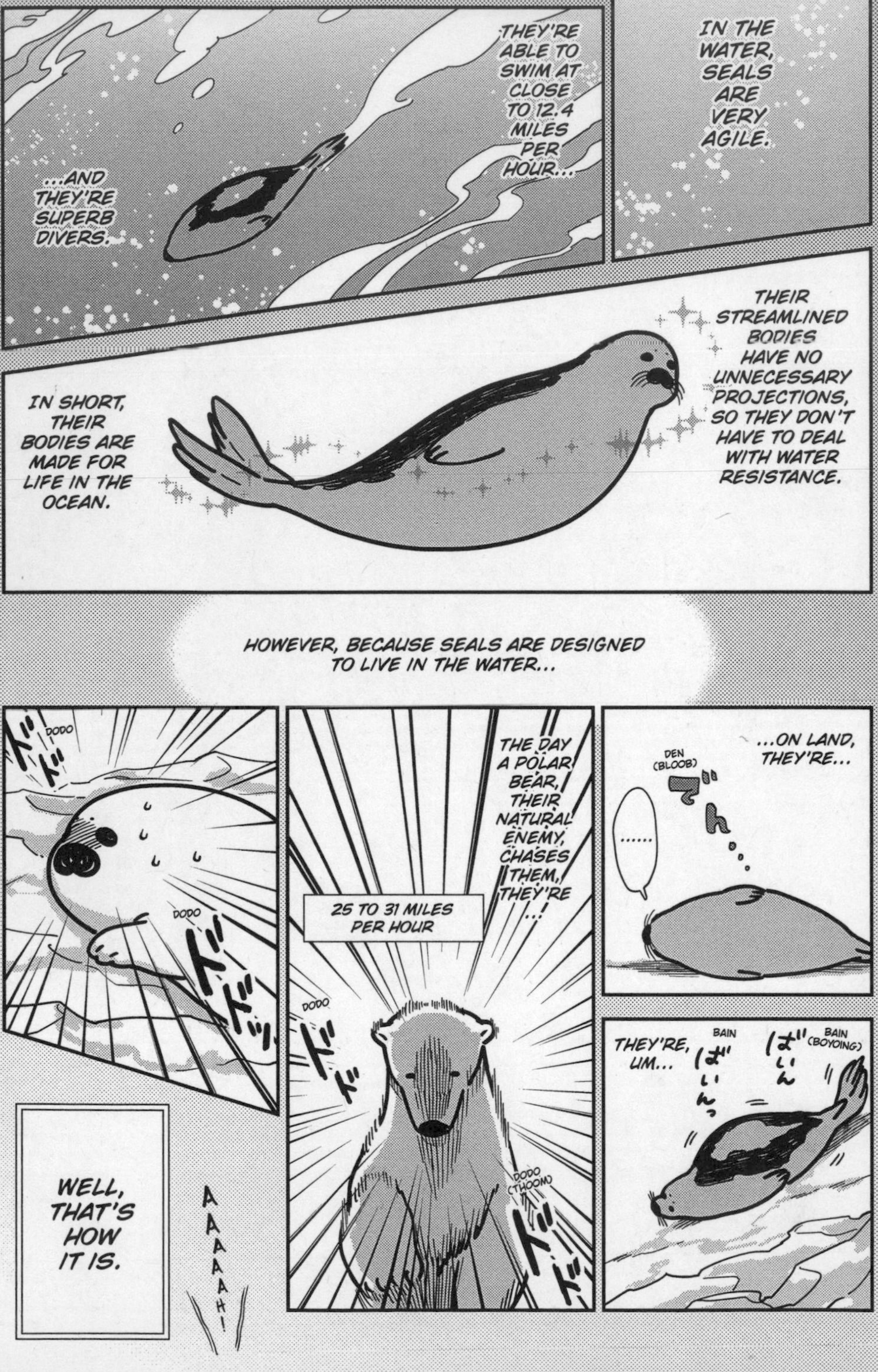
IN THE WATER, SEALS ARE VERY AGILE.
THEY'RE ABLE TO SWIM AT CLOSE TO 12.4 MILES PER HOUR...
...AND THEY'RE SUPERB DIVERS.
THEIR STREAMLINED BODIES HAVE NO UNNECESSARY PROJECTIONS, SO THEY DON'T HAVE TO DEAL WITH WATER RESISTANCE.
IN SHORT, THEIR BODIES ARE MADE FOR LIFE IN THE OCEAN.
HOWEVER, BECAUSE SEALS ARE DESIGNED TO LIVE IN THE WATER...
...ON LAND, THEY'RE...
DEN (BLOOB)
......
THEY'RE, UM...
BAIN
BAIN (BOYOING)
THE DAY A POLAR BEAR, THEIR NATURAL ENEMY, CHASES THEM, THEY'RE ...
25 TO 31 MILES PER HOUR
DODO
DODO (THOOM)
DODO
DODO
WELL, THAT'S HOW IT IS.
AAAAAH!

SNOOZE...

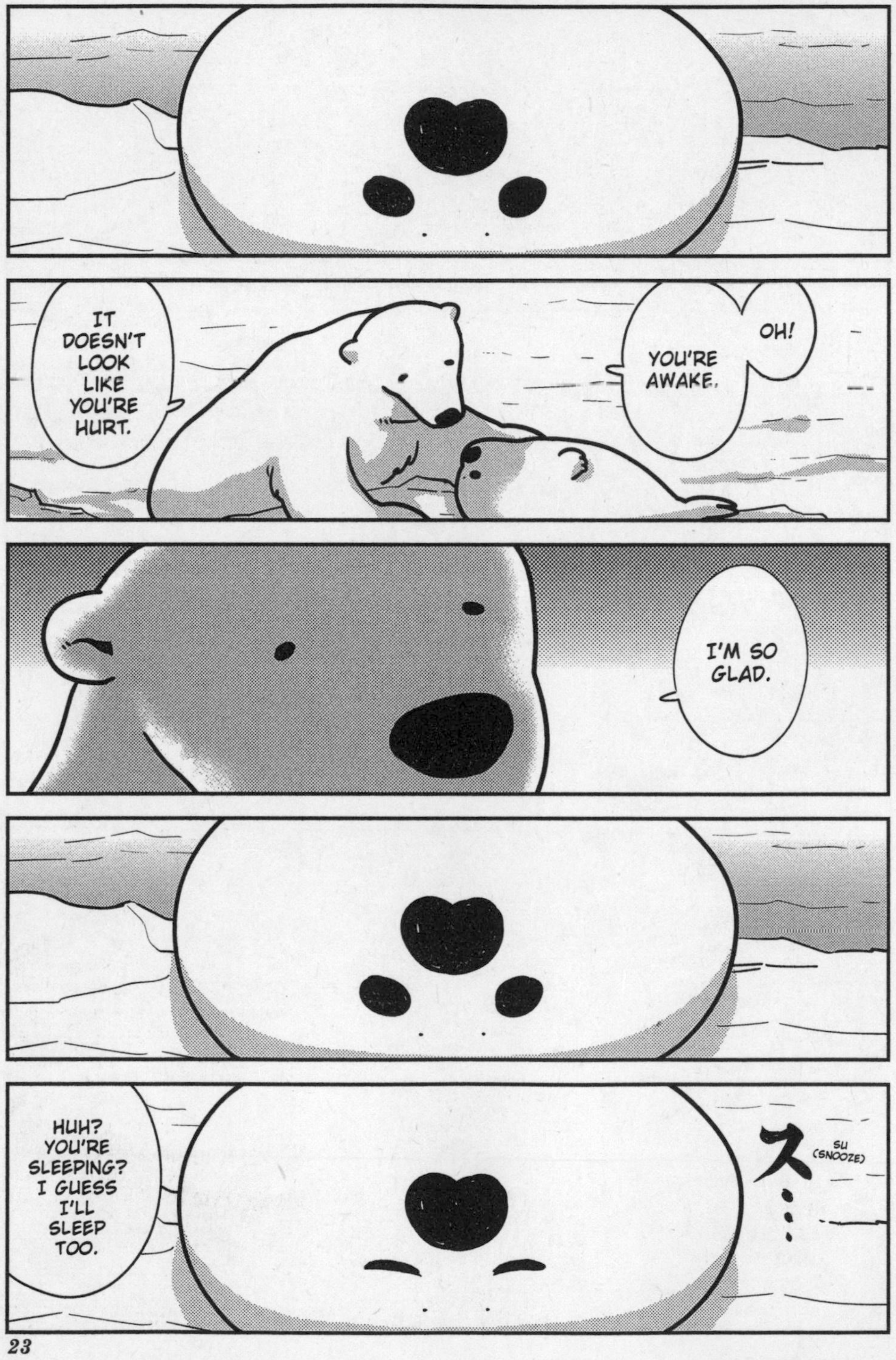
OH!
YOU'RE AWAKE.
IT DOESN'T LOOK LIKE YOU'RE HURT.
I'M SO GLAD.
ス
SU (SNOOZE)
HUH? YOU'RE SLEEPING? I GUESS I'LL SLEEP TOO.

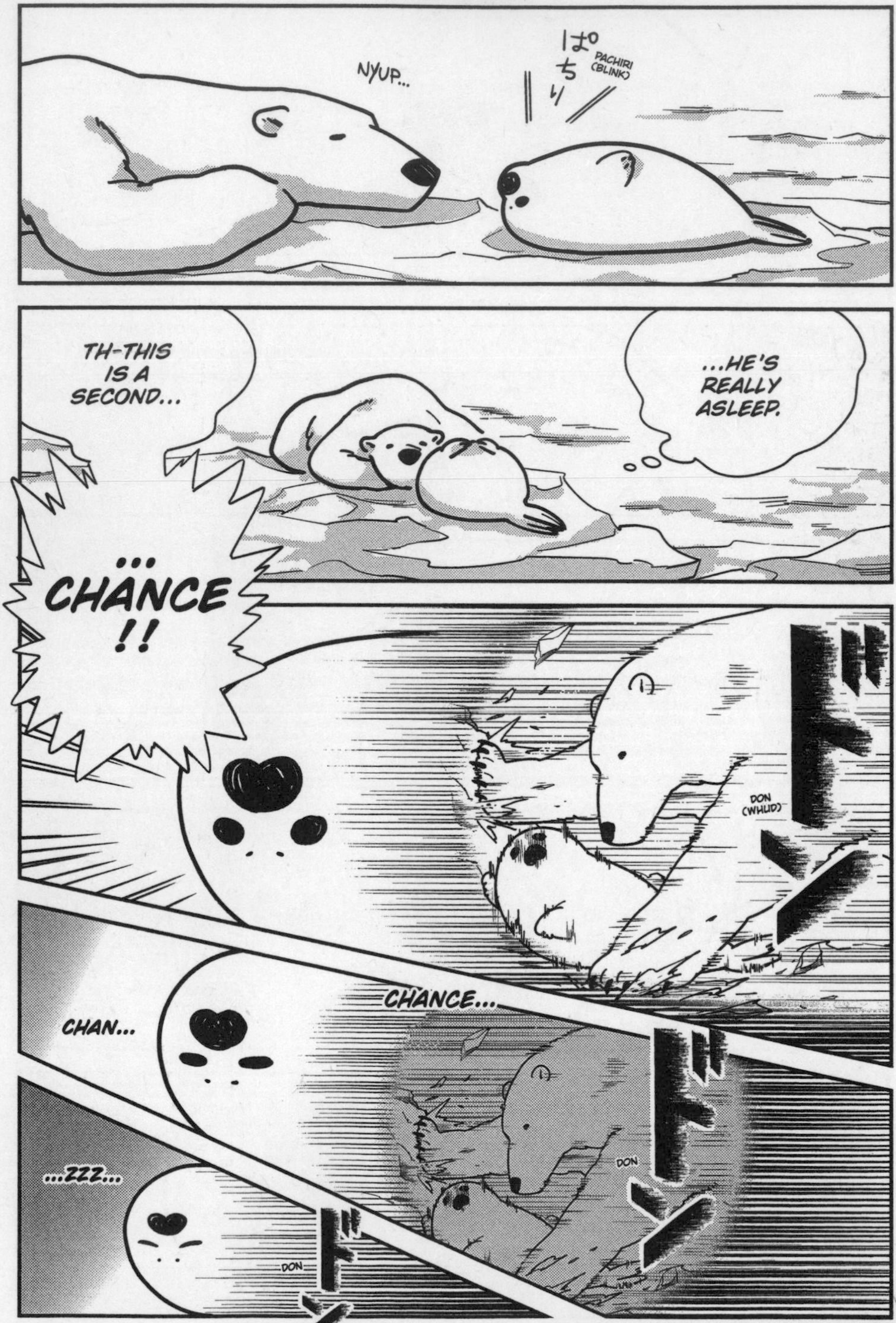
ぱちり
PACHIRI (BLINK)
NYUP...
...HE'S REALLY ASLEEP.
TH-THIS IS A SECOND...
...CHÄNCE!!
DON (WHUD)
CHANCE...
CHAN...
DON
...ZZZ...
DON

YOUR FEELINGS

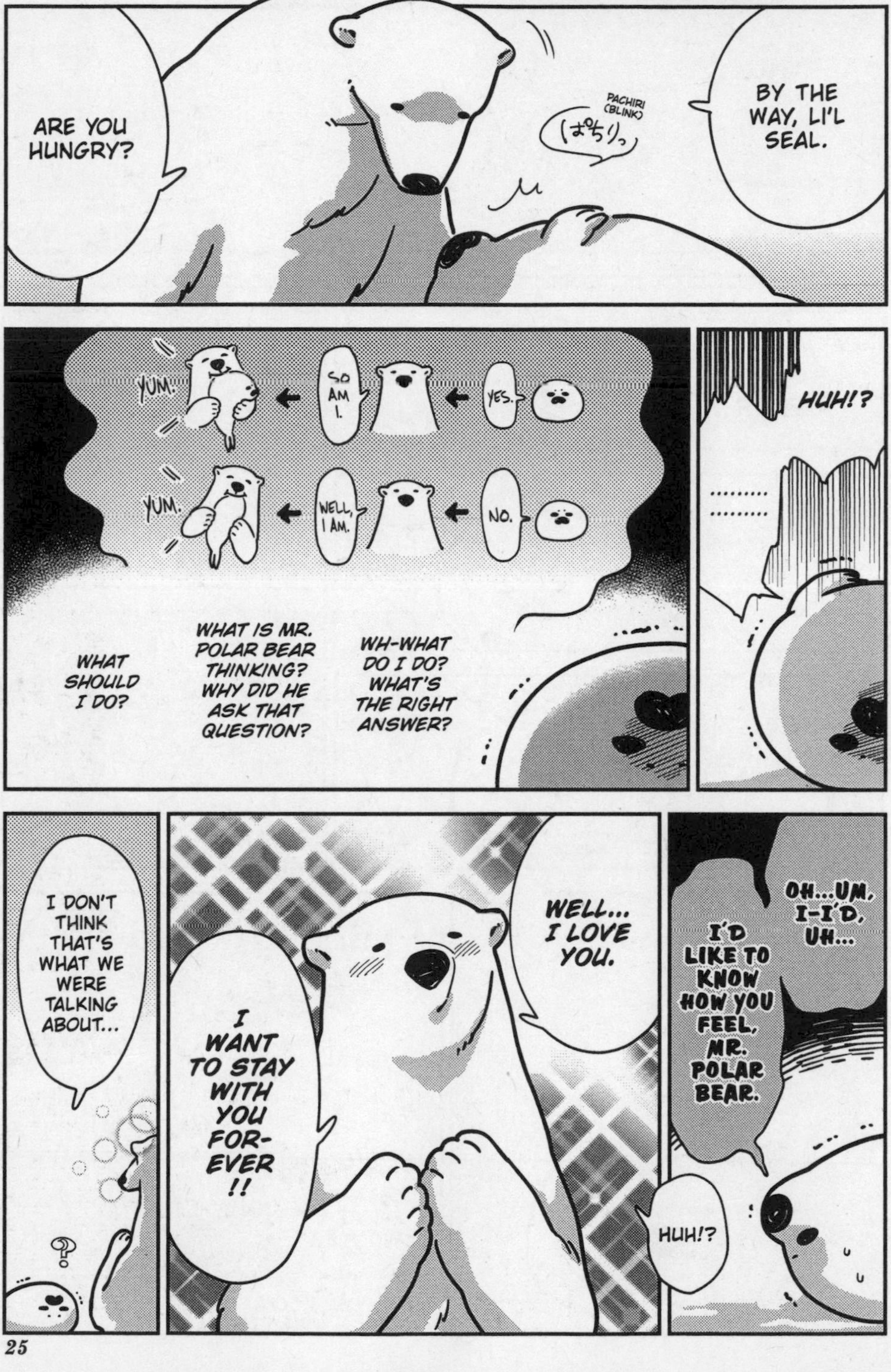
BY THE WAY, LI'L SEAL.
PACHIRI (BLINK)
ぱちりっ
ARE YOU HUNGRY?
HUH!?
....
....
YES.
SO AM I.
YUM.
NO.
WELL, I AM.
YUM.
WH-WHAT DO I DO? WHAT'S THE RIGHT ANSWER?
WHAT IS MR. POLAR BEAR THINKING? WHY DID HE ASK THAT QUESTION?
WHAT SHOULD I DO?
OH...UM, I-I'D, UH...
I'D LIKE TO KNOW HOW YOU FEEL, MR. POLAR BEAR.
HUH!?
WELL... I LOVE YOU.
I WANT TO STAY WITH YOU FOR-EVER!!
I DON'T THINK THAT'S WHAT WE WERE TALKING ABOUT...
?

GUESS

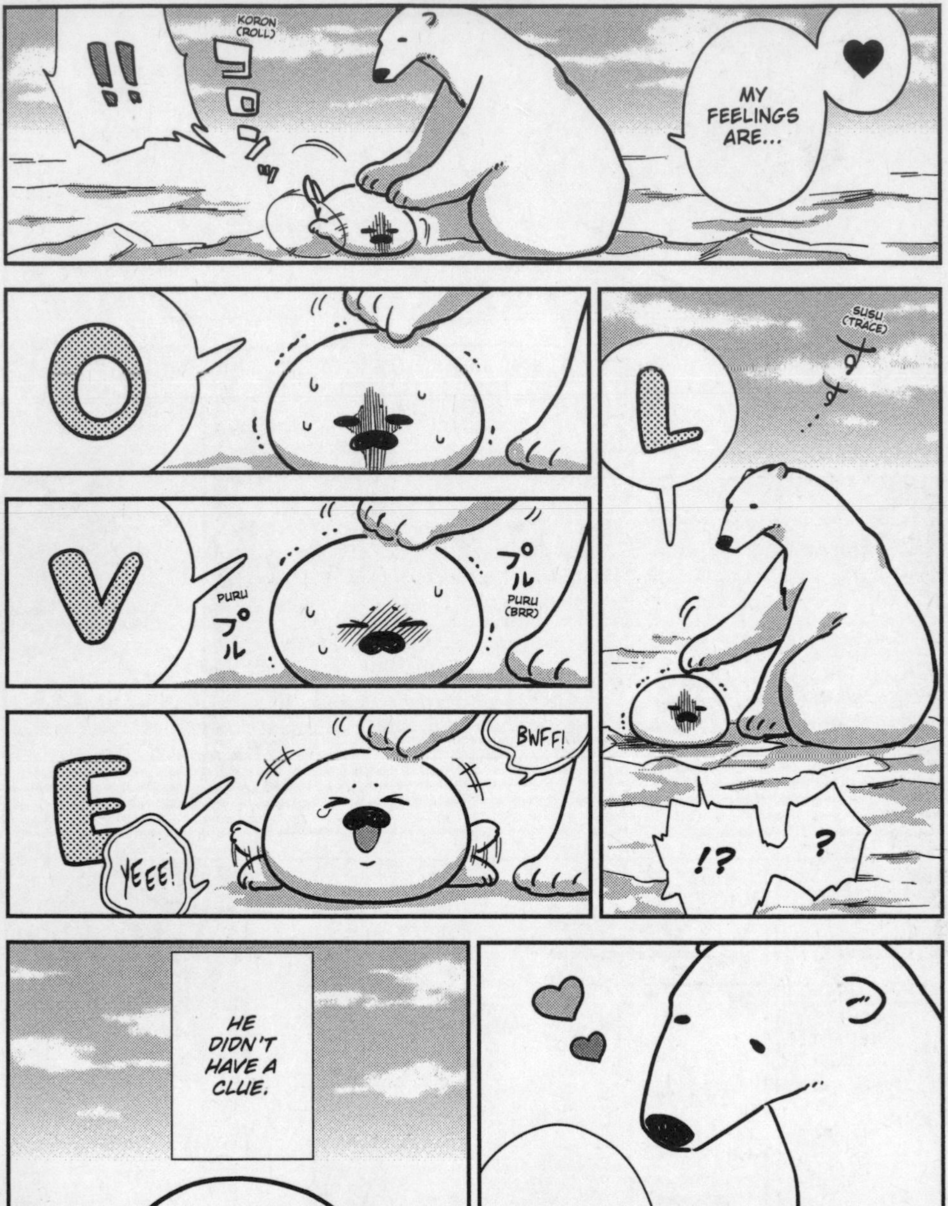
MY FEELINGS ARE...
KORON (ROLL)
!!
SUSU (TRACE)
L
!?
?
O
V
PURU (BRR)
PURU
BWFF!
E
YEEE!
WELL? DO YOU KNOW WHAT I WROTE?
HE DIDN'T HAVE A CLUE.

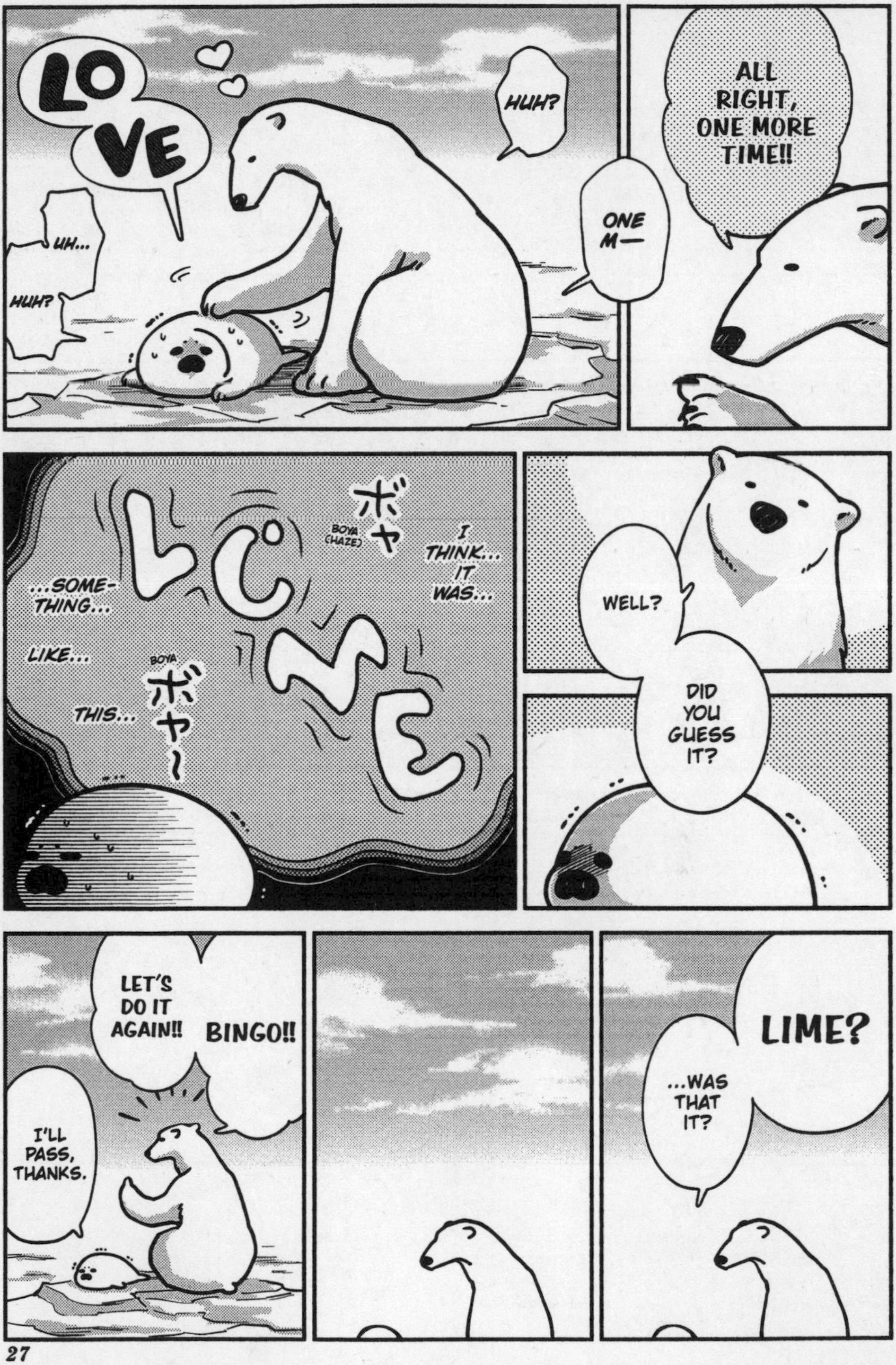
ALL RIGHT, ONE MORE TIME!!
ONE M—
LOVE
HUH?
UH...
HUH?
WELL?
DID YOU GUESS IT?
I THINK... IT WAS...
ボヤ
BOYA (HAZE)
LCME
...SOME-THING...
LIKE...
THIS...
BOYA
ボヤ~
LIME?
...WAS THAT IT?
BINGO!!
LET'S DO IT AGAIN!!
I'LL PASS, THANKS.

AREN'T THE STARS PRETTY?

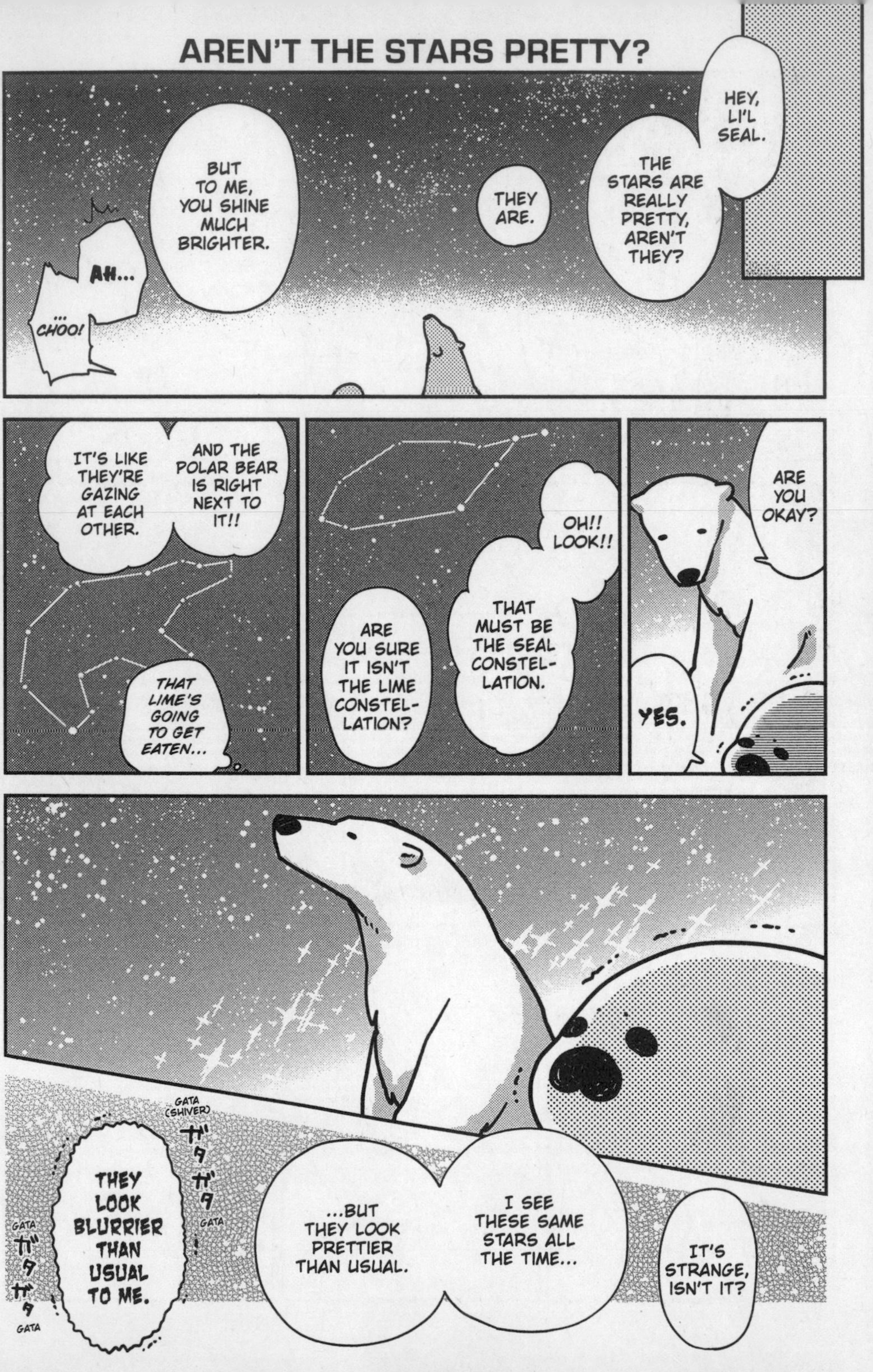
HEY, LI'L SEAL.
THE STARS ARE REALLY PRETTY, AREN'T THEY?
THEY ARE.
BUT TO ME, YOU SHINE MUCH BRIGHTER.
AH...
...CHOO!
ARE YOU OKAY?
YES.
OH!! LOOK!!
THAT MUST BE THE SEAL CONSTELLATION.
ARE YOU SURE IT ISN'T THE LIME CONSTELLATION?
AND THE POLAR BEAR IS RIGHT NEXT TO IT!!
IT'S LIKE THEY'RE GAZING AT EACH OTHER.
THAT LIME'S GOING TO GET EATEN...
IT'S STRANGE, ISN'T IT?
I SEE THESE SAME STARS ALL THE TIME...
...BUT THEY LOOK PRETTIER THAN USUAL.
ガタ GATA (SHIVER)
ガタ GATA
THEY LOOK BLURRIER THAN USUAL TO ME.
ガタ GATA
ガタ GATA

TEARS SPARKLE TOO

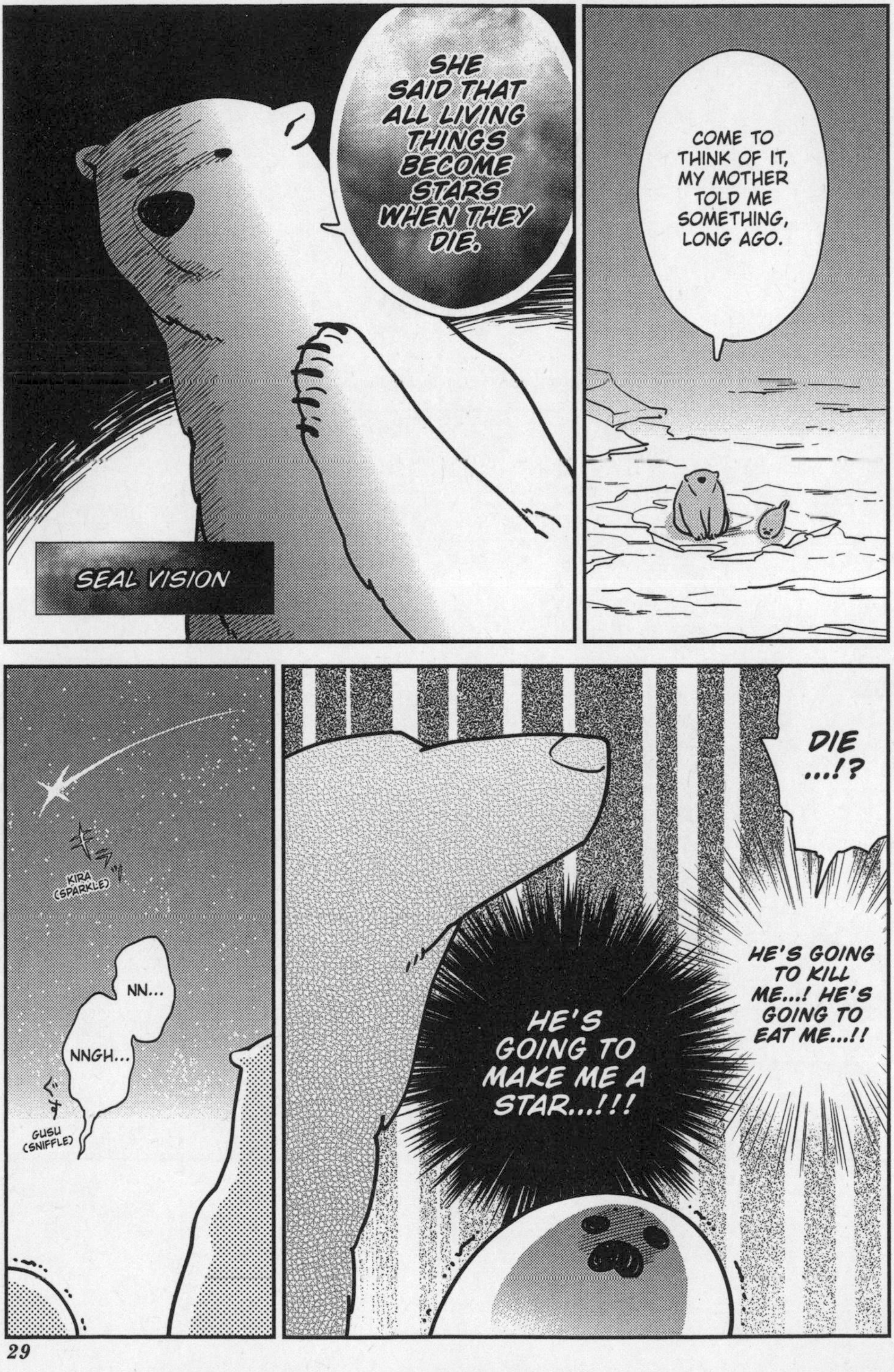
COME TO THINK OF IT, MY MOTHER TOLD ME SOMETHING, LONG AGO.
SHE SAID THAT ALL LIVING THINGS BECOME STARS WHEN THEY DIE.
SEAL VISION
DIE ...!?
HE'S GOING TO KILL ME...! HE'S GOING TO EAT ME...!!
HE'S GOING TO MAKE ME A STAR...!!!
KIRA (SPARKLE)
NN...
NNGH...
GUSU (SNIFFLE)

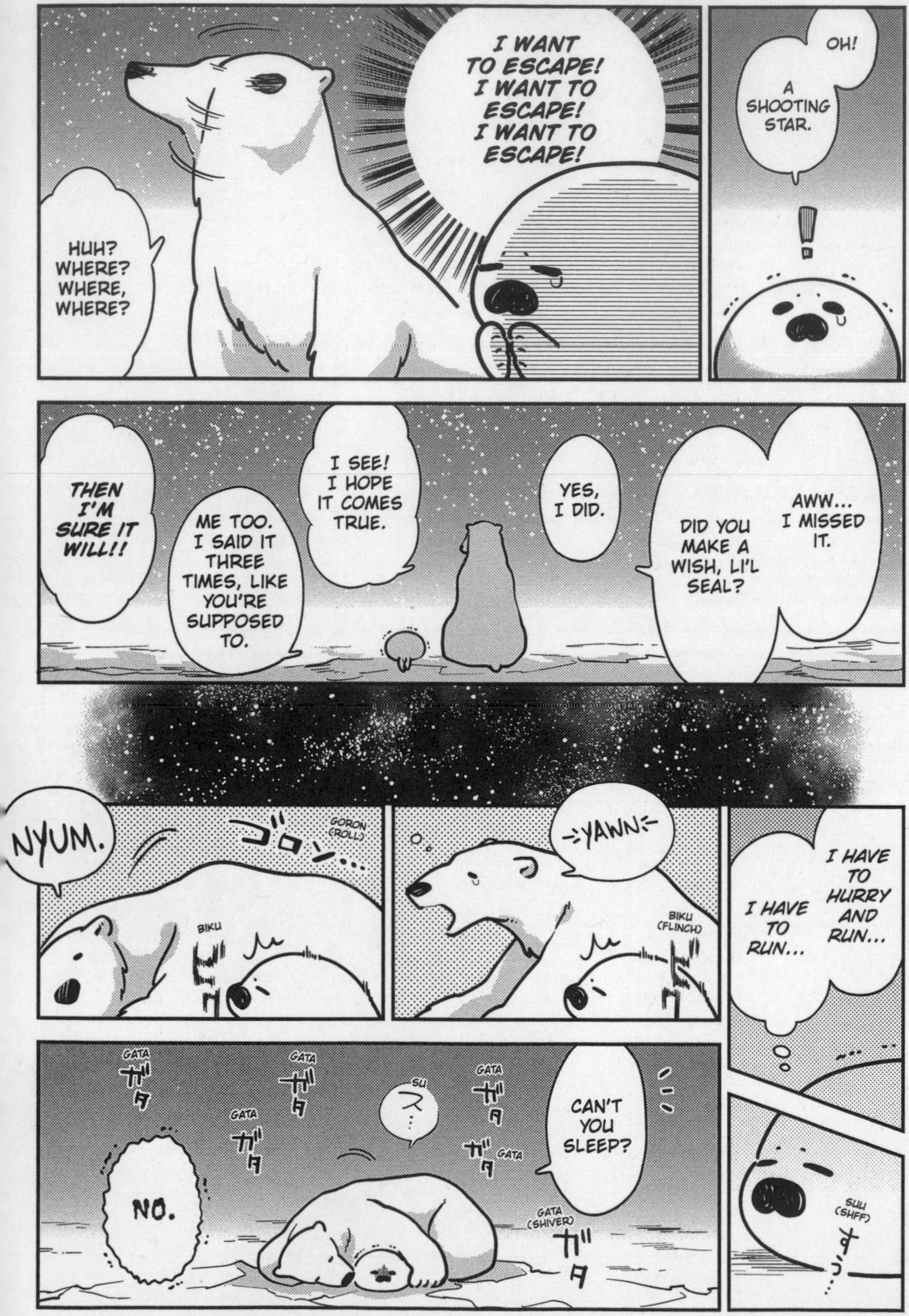
OH!
A SHOOTING STAR.
!
I WANT TO ESCAPE! I WANT TO ESCAPE! I WANT TO ESCAPE!
HUH? WHERE? WHERE, WHERE?
AWW... I MISSED IT.
DID YOU MAKE A WISH, LI'L SEAL?
YES, I DID.
I SEE! I HOPE IT COMES TRUE.
ME TOO. I SAID IT THREE TIMES, LIKE YOU'RE SUPPOSED TO.
THEN I'M SURE IT WILL!!
I HAVE TO HURRY AND RUN...
I HAVE TO RUN...
YAWN
BIKU (FLINCH)
ゴロン...
GORON (ROLL)
NYUM.
BIKU
すぅ
SUU (SHFF)
CAN'T YOU SLEEP?
GATA
ガタ
SU
ス...
GATA (SHIVER)
NO.

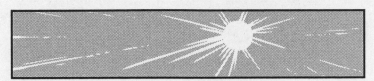

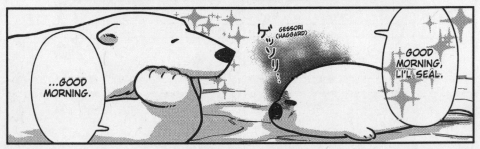

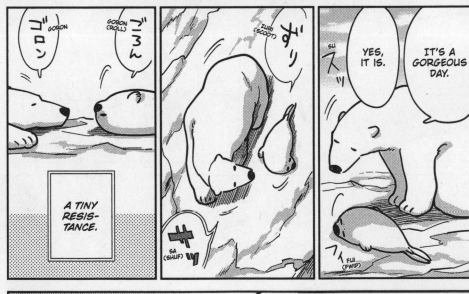

GOOD MORNING, LI'L SEAL.
ゲッソリ…
GESSORI (HAGGARD)
...GOOD MORNING.
IT'S A GORGEOUS DAY.
YES, IT IS.
スッ
SU
フイ
FUI (FWIP)
ずり
ZURI (SCOOT)
サッ
SA (SHUF)
ごろん
GORON (ROLL)
ゴロン
GORON
A TINY RESIS-TANCE.
....

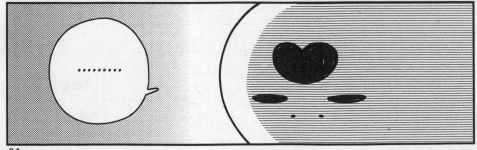

A FRENCH BROTH

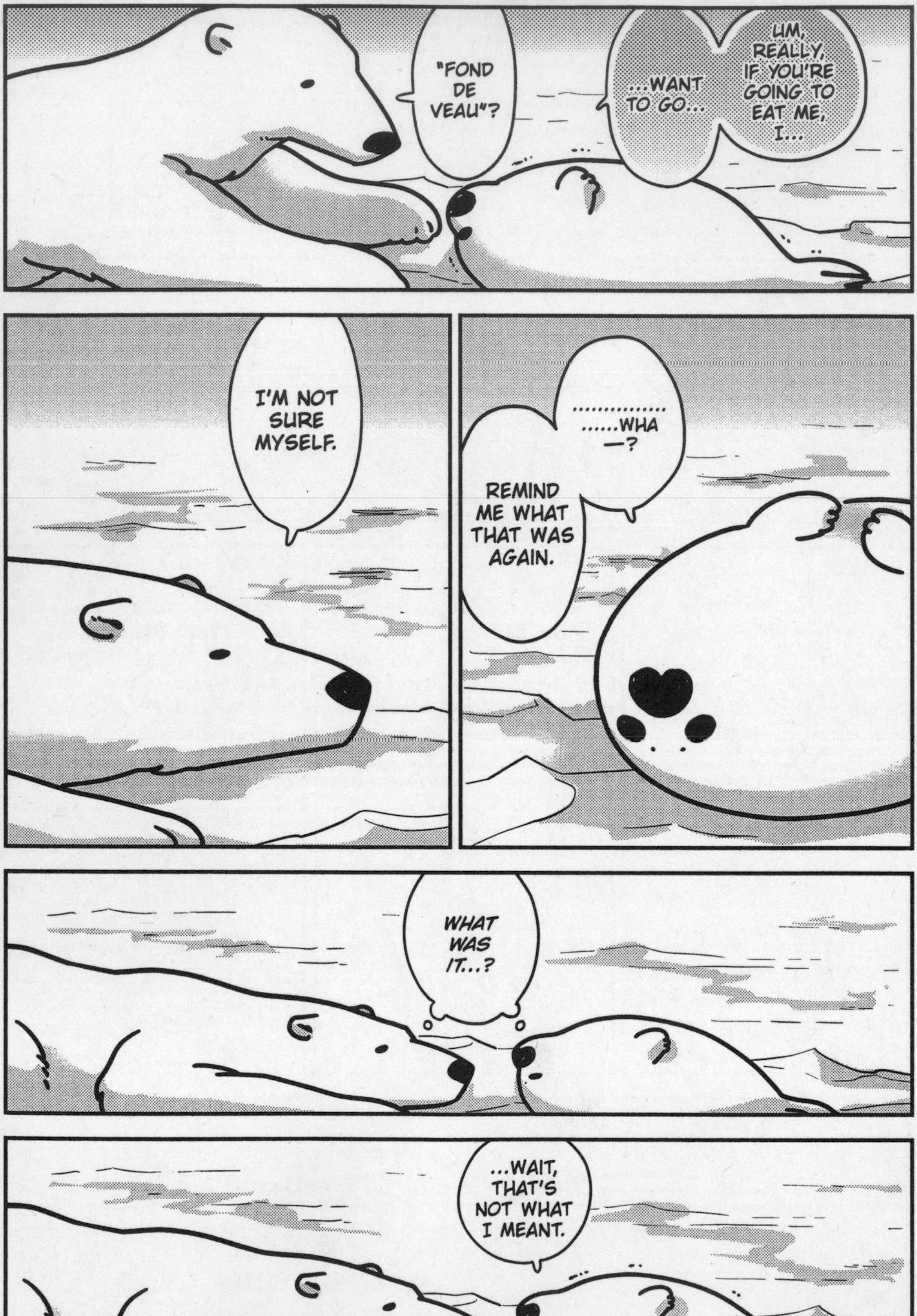
UM, REALLY, IF YOU'RE GOING TO EAT ME, I...
...WANT TO GO...
"FOND DE VEAU"?
....
......WHA—?
REMIND ME WHAT THAT WAS AGAIN.
I'M NOT SURE MYSELF.
WHAT WAS IT...?
...WAIT, THAT'S NOT WHAT I MEANT.

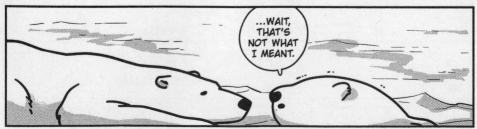

THINGS PEOPLE DON'T LIKE

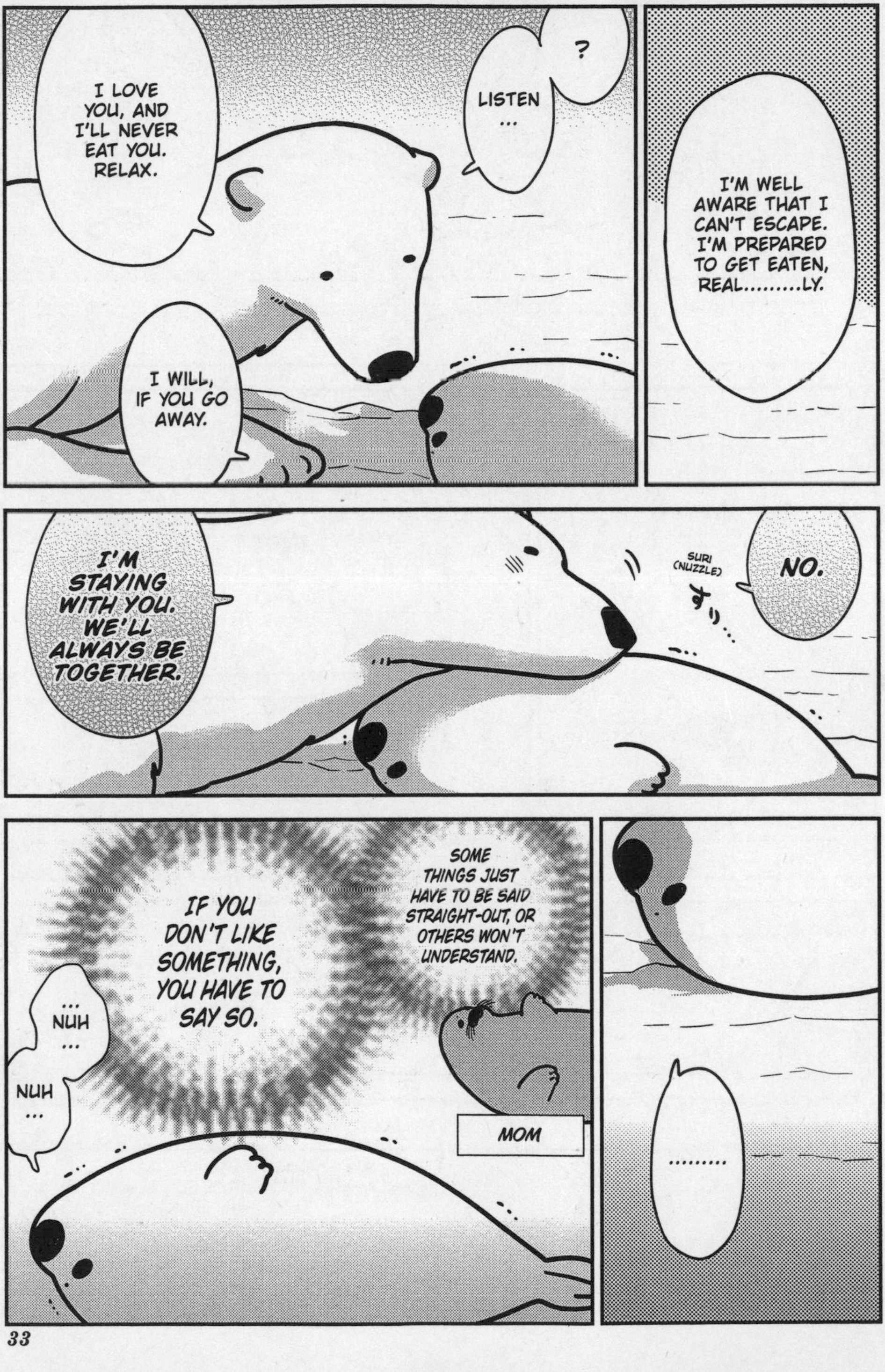
I'M WELL AWARE THAT I CAN'T ESCAPE. I'M PREPARED TO GET EATEN, REAL.........LY.
?
LISTEN ...
I LOVE YOU, AND I'LL NEVER EAT YOU. RELAX.
I WILL, IF YOU GO AWAY.
NO.
SURI (NUZZLE)
すり…
I'M STAYING WITH YOU. WE'LL ALWAYS BE TOGETHER.
....
SOME THINGS JUST HAVE TO BE SAID STRAIGHT-OUT, OR OTHERS WON'T UNDERSTAND.
IF YOU DON'T LIKE SOMETHING, YOU HAVE TO SAY SO.
MOM
... NUH ...
NUH ...

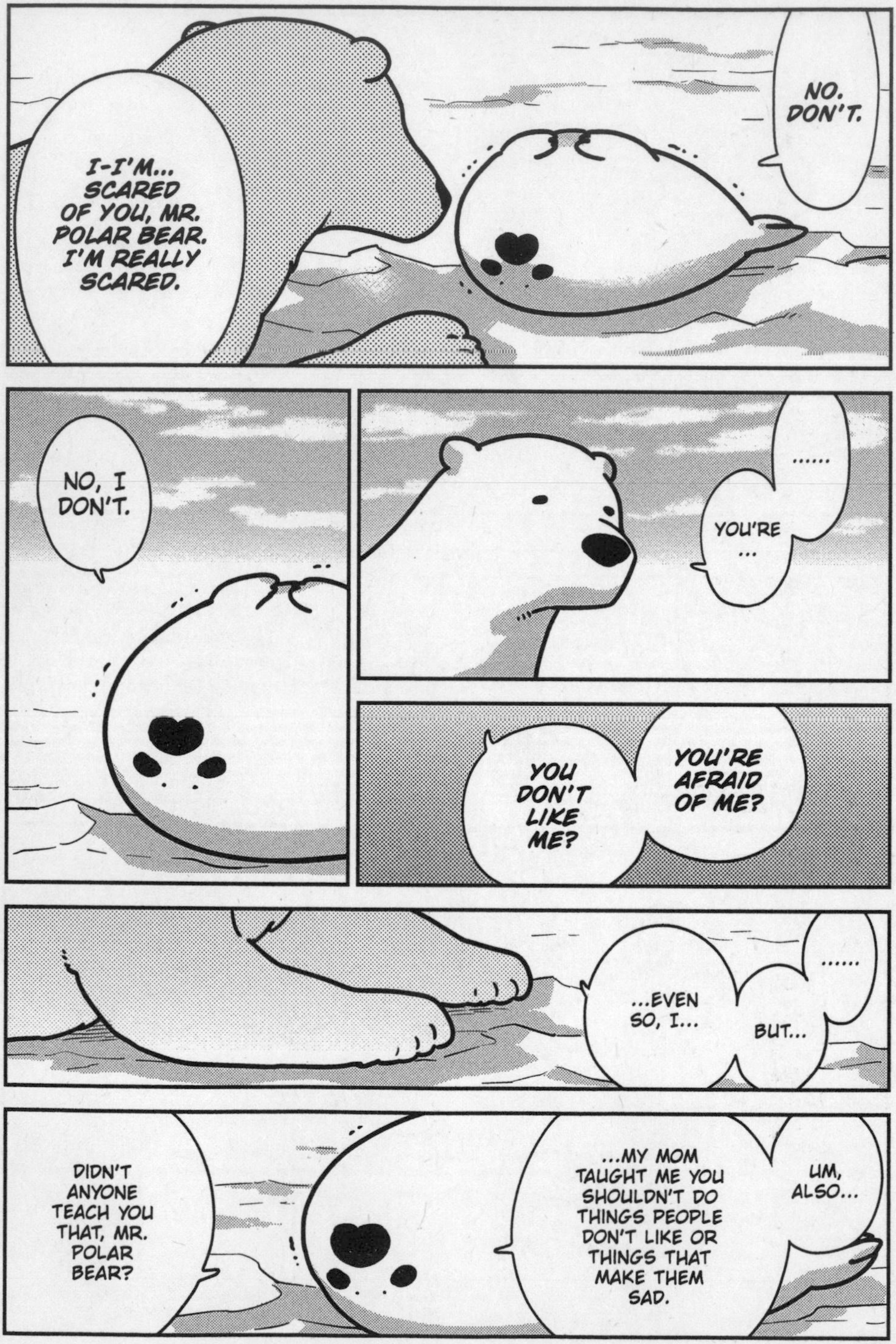
NO. DON'T.
I-I'M... SCARED OF YOU, MR. POLAR BEAR. I'M REALLY SCARED.
......
YOU'RE ...
YOU'RE AFRAID OF ME?
YOU DON'T LIKE ME?
NO, I DON'T.
......
BUT...
...EVEN SO, I...
UM, ALSO...
...MY MOM TAUGHT ME YOU SHOULDN'T DO THINGS PEOPLE DON'T LIKE OR THINGS THAT MAKE THEM SAD.
DIDN'T ANYONE TEACH YOU THAT, MR. POLAR BEAR?

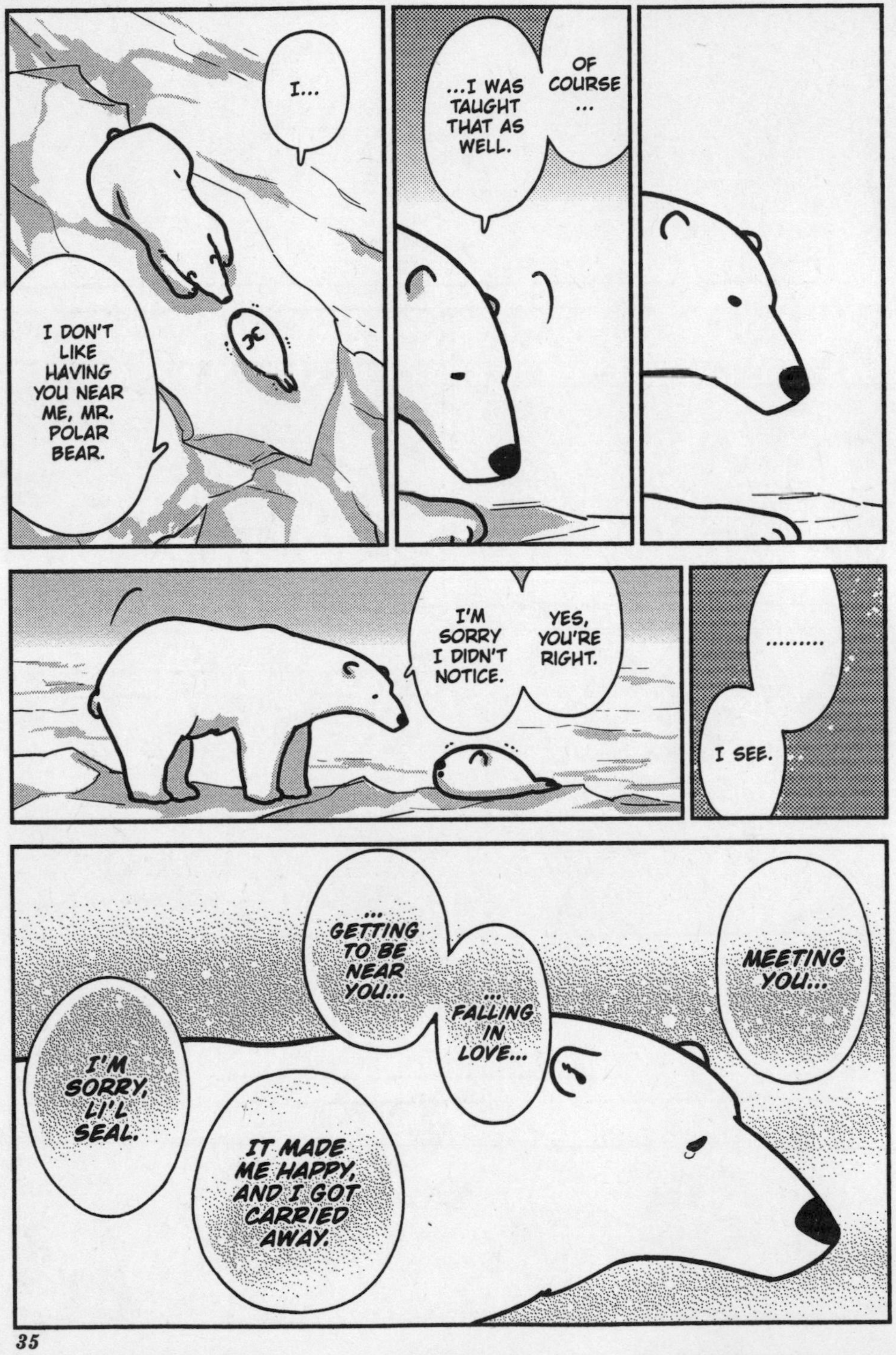
OF COURSE ...
...I WAS TAUGHT THAT AS WELL.
I...
I DON'T LIKE HAVING YOU NEAR ME, MR. POLAR BEAR.
....
I SEE.
YES, YOU'RE RIGHT.
I'M SORRY I DIDN'T NOTICE.
MEETING YOU...
...GETTING TO BE NEAR YOU...
...FALLING IN LOVE...
IT MADE ME HAPPY, AND I GOT CARRIED AWAY.
I'M SORRY, LI'L SEAL.

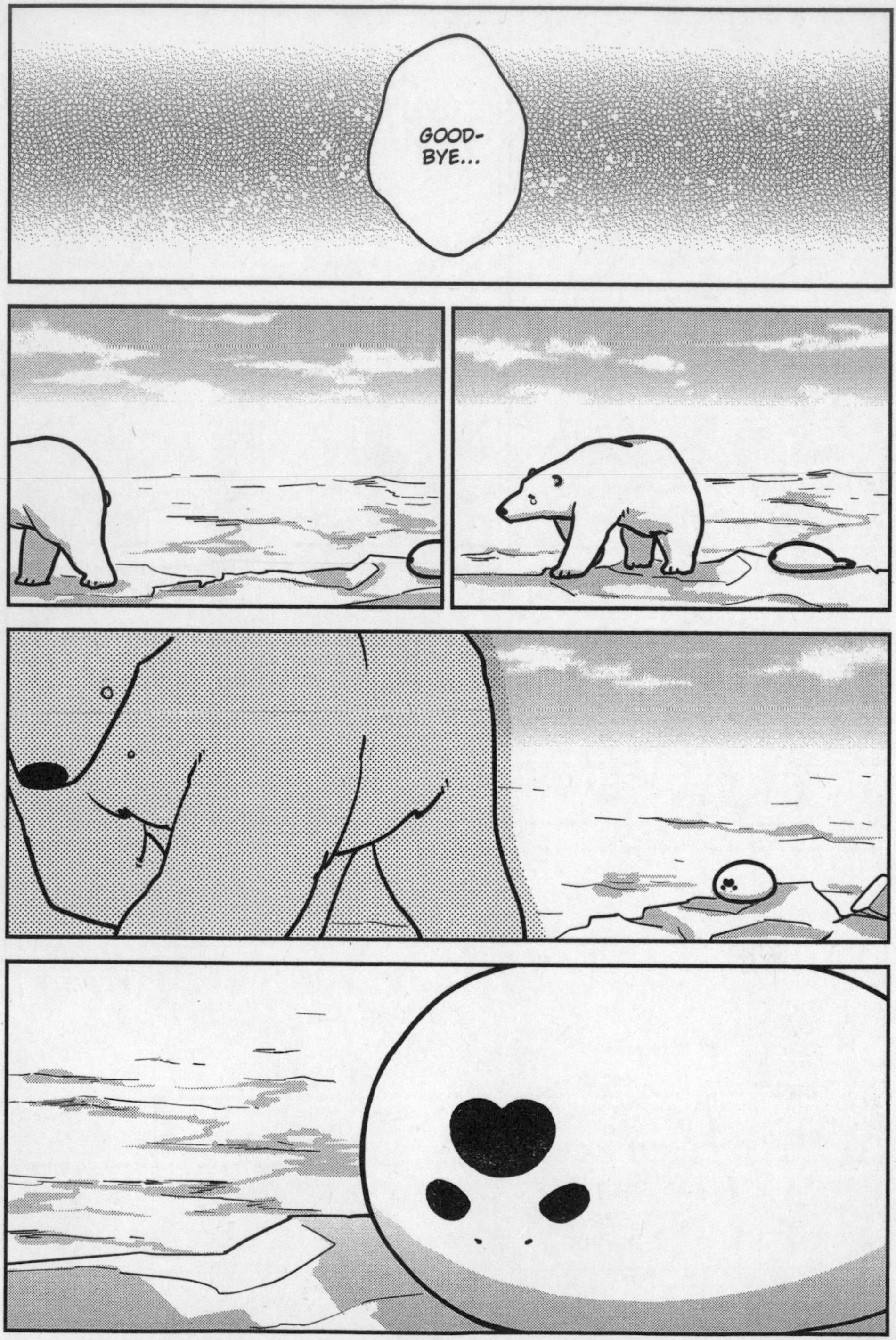
GOOD-BYE...

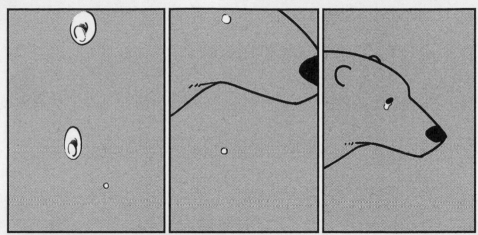

YOU MUSTN'T DO THINGS PEOPLE DON'T LIKE...

GYU
(SQUEEZE)

...OR THINGS THAT MAKE THEM SAD.

MR. POLAR BEAR!!

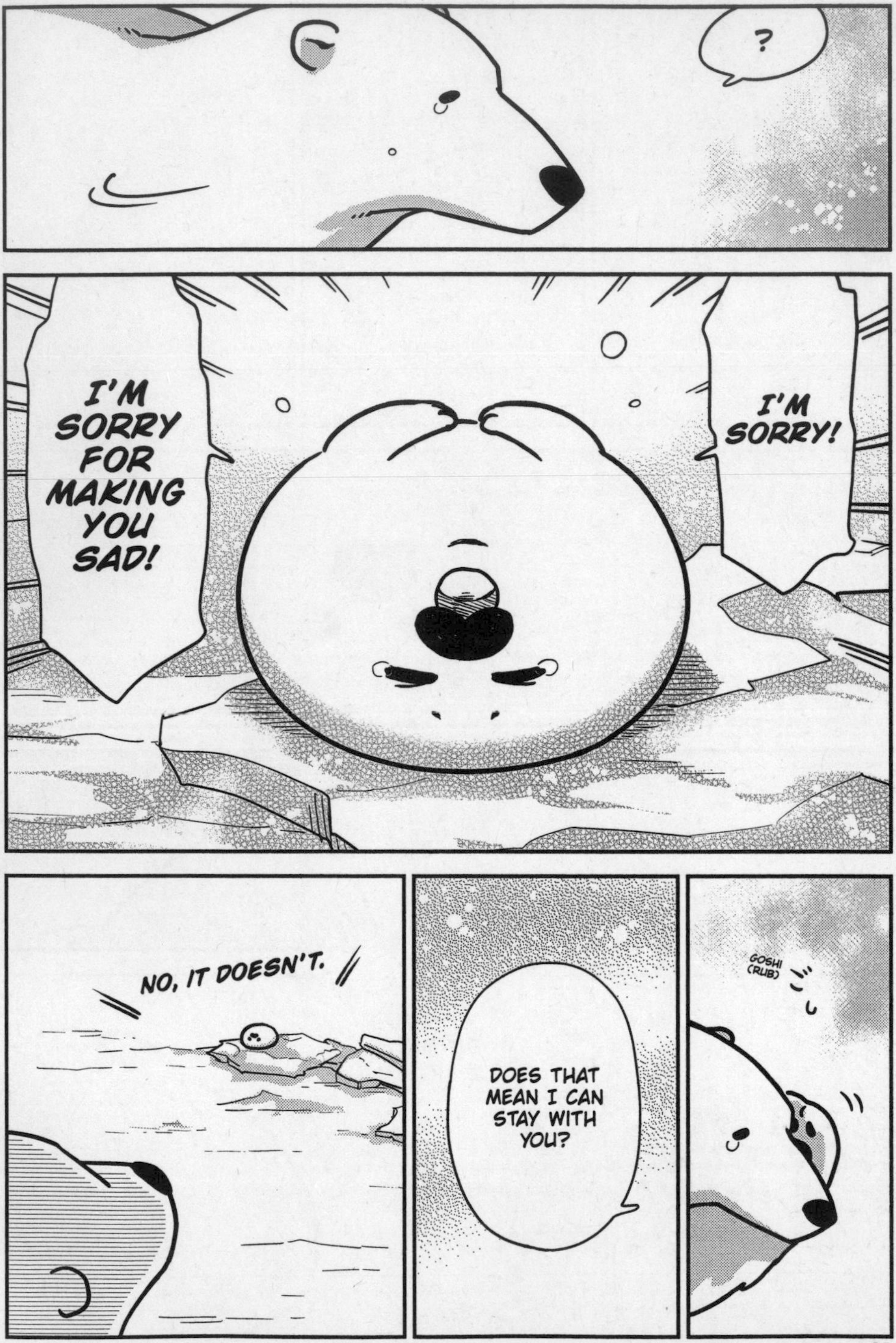
?
I'M SORRY!
I'M SORRY FOR MAKING YOU SAD!
GOSHI (RUB)
DOES THAT MEAN I CAN STAY WITH YOU?
NO, IT DOESN'T.

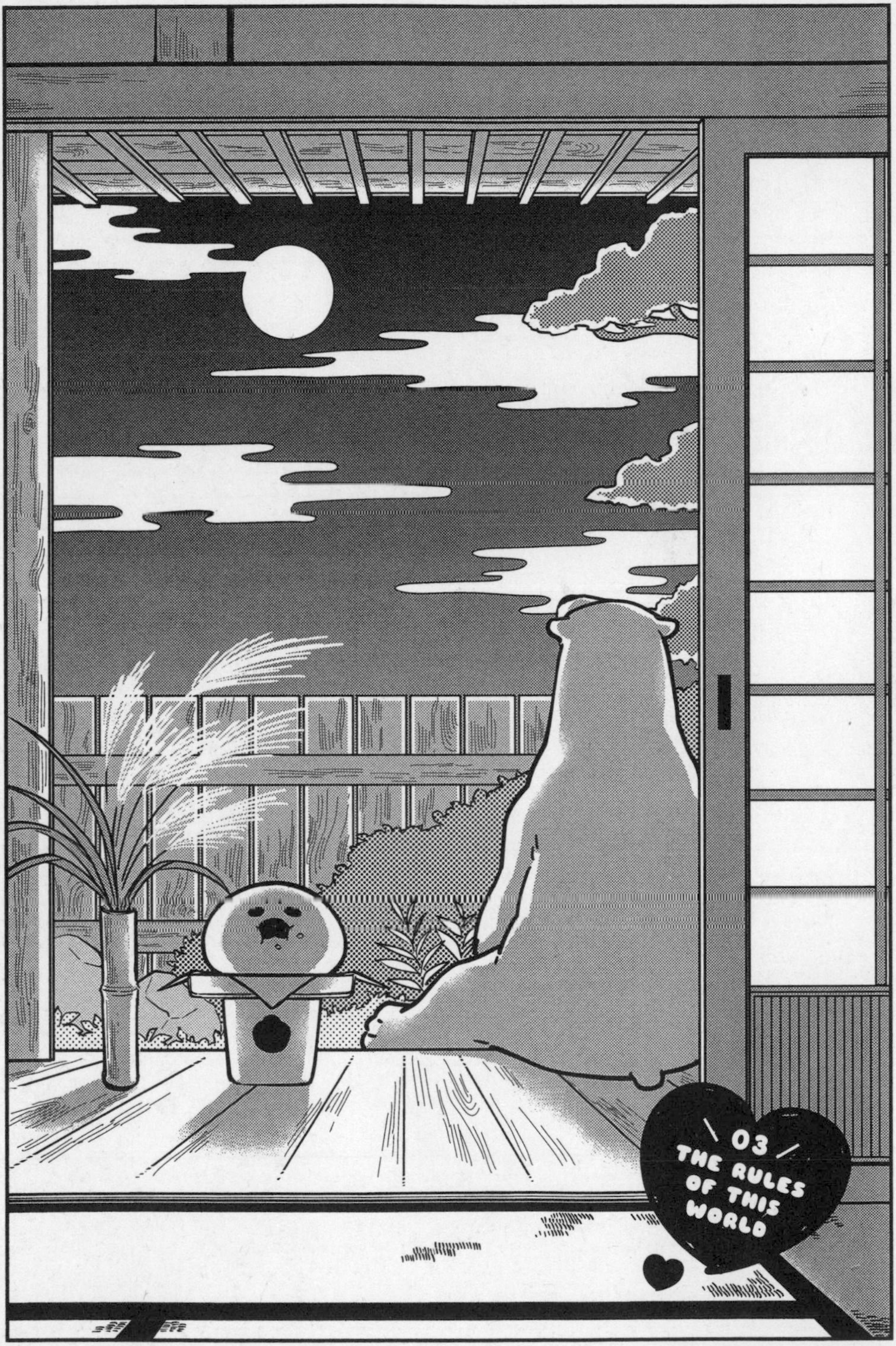
03
THE RULES OF THIS WORLD

FATE

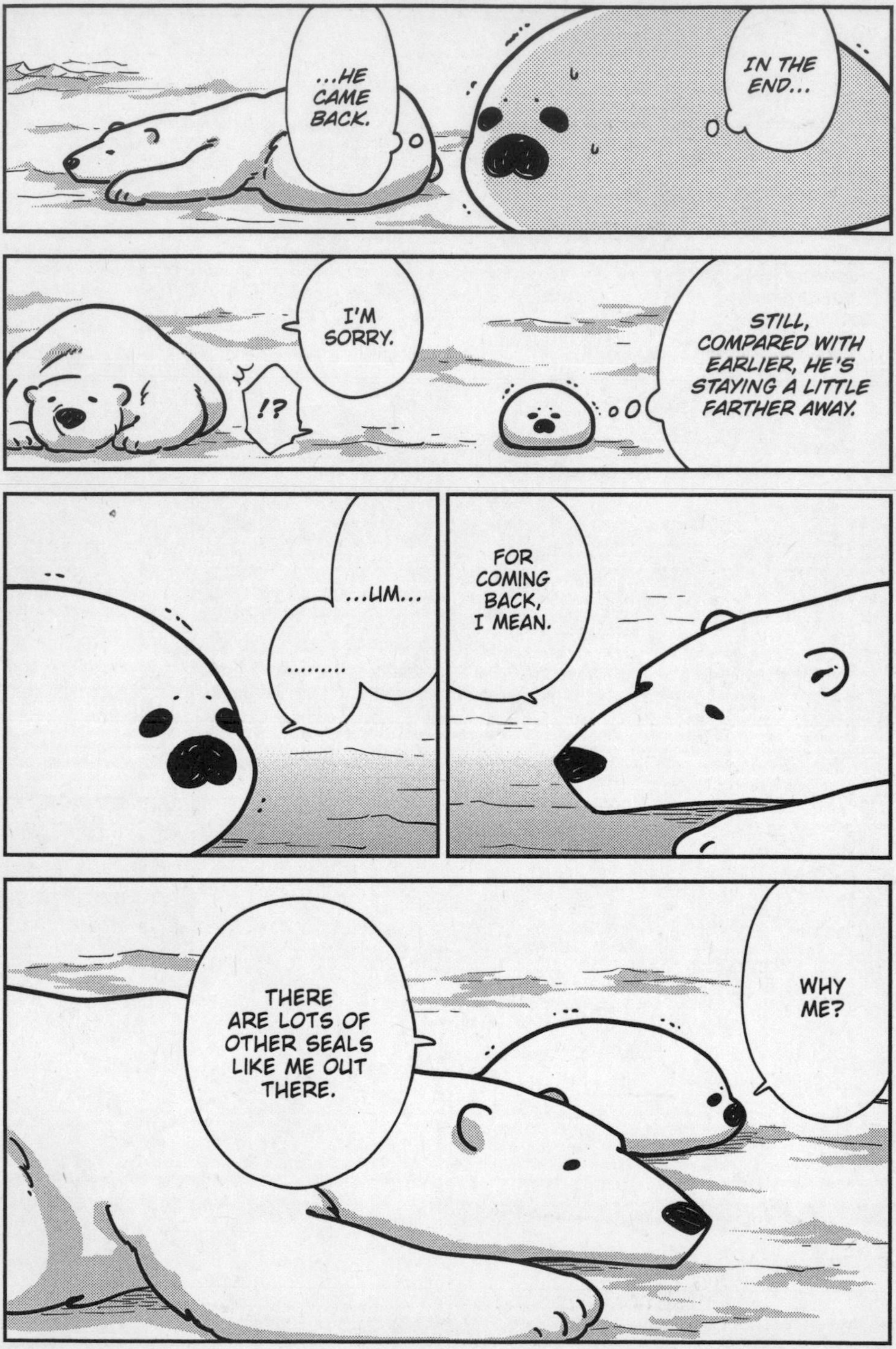
IN THE END...
...HE CAME BACK.
STILL, COMPARED WITH EARLIER, HE'S STAYING A LITTLE FARTHER AWAY.
I'M SORRY.
!?
FOR COMING BACK, I MEAN.
...UM...
....
WHY ME?
THERE ARE LOTS OF OTHER SEALS LIKE ME OUT THERE.

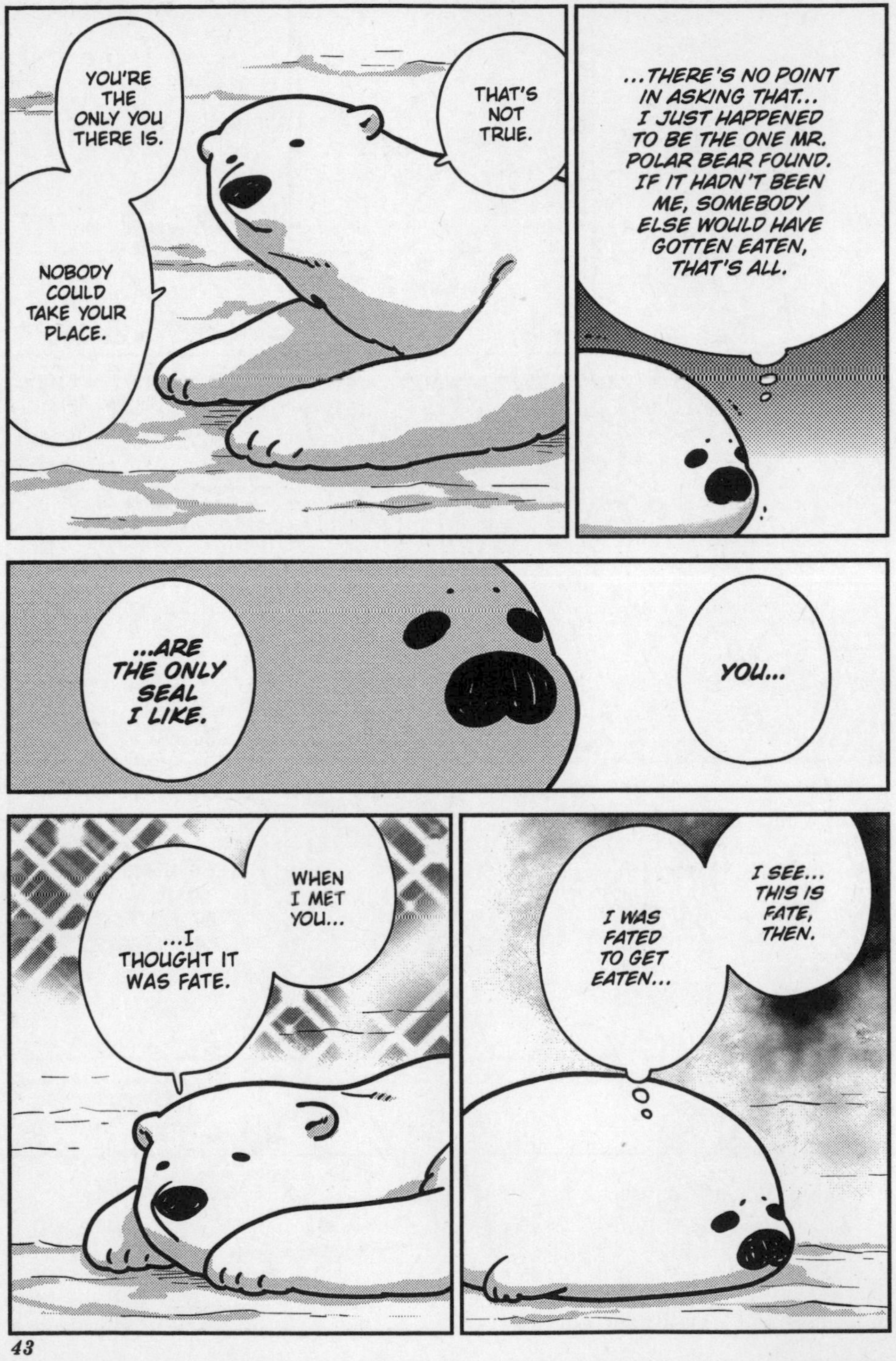
...THERE'S NO POINT IN ASKING THAT... I JUST HAPPENED TO BE THE ONE MR. POLAR BEAR FOUND. IF IT HADN'T BEEN ME, SOMEBODY ELSE WOULD HAVE GOTTEN EATEN, THAT'S ALL.
THAT'S NOT TRUE.
YOU'RE THE ONLY YOU THERE IS.
NOBODY COULD TAKE YOUR PLACE.
YOU...
...ARE THE ONLY SEAL I LIKE.
I SEE... THIS IS FATE, THEN.
I WAS FATED TO GET EATEN...
WHEN I MET YOU...
...I THOUGHT IT WAS FATE.

ZAP, ZAP, ZAP AND BZZ, BZZ, BZZ

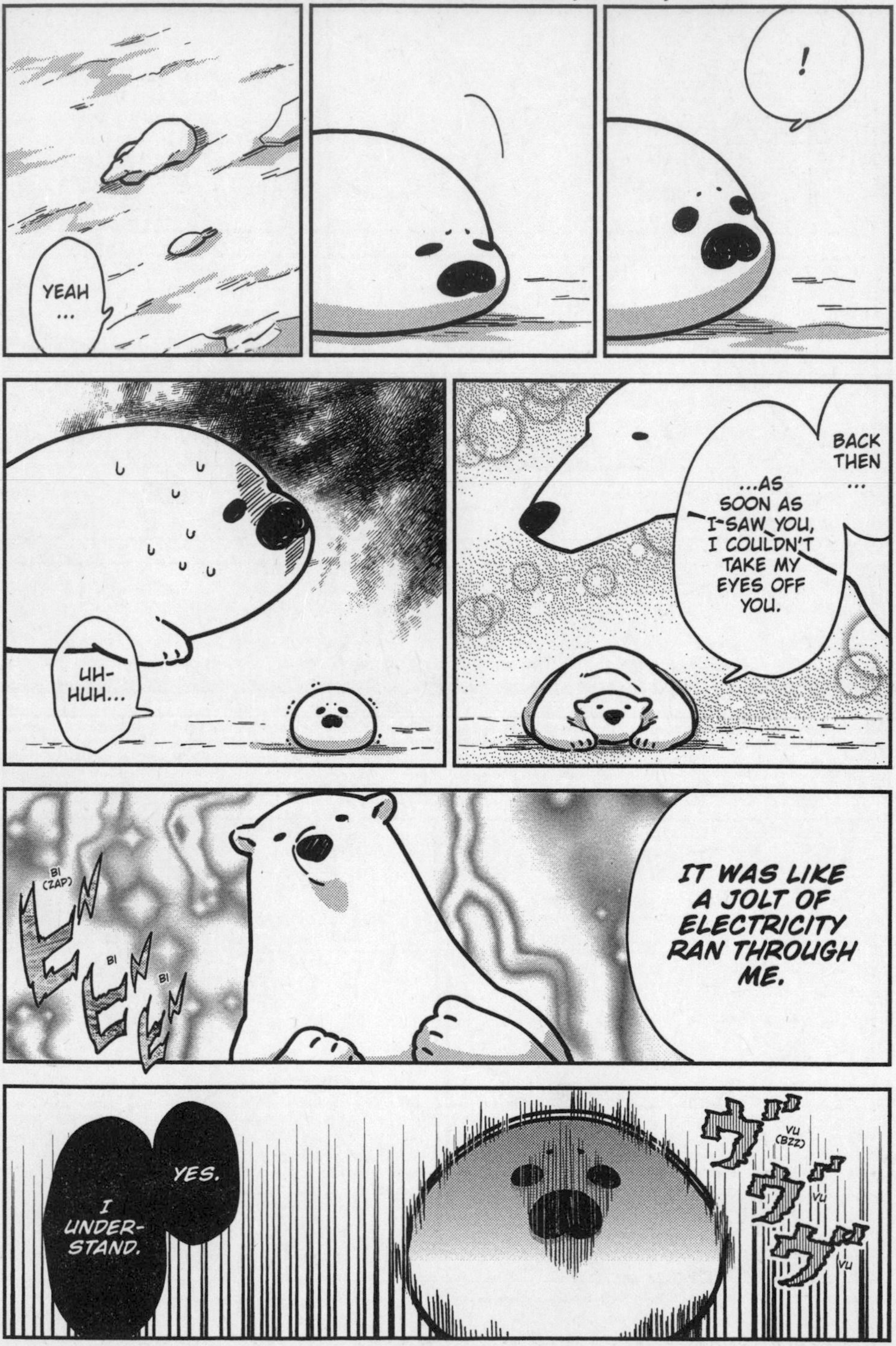

!
YEAH ...
BACK THEN ...
...AS SOON AS I SAW YOU, I COULDN'T TAKE MY EYES OFF YOU.
UH-HUH...
IT WAS LIKE A JOLT OF ELECTRICITY RAN THROUGH ME.
BI (ZAP)
BI
BI
VU (BZZ)
VU
VU
YES.
I UNDER-STAND.

THE SAME FEELING

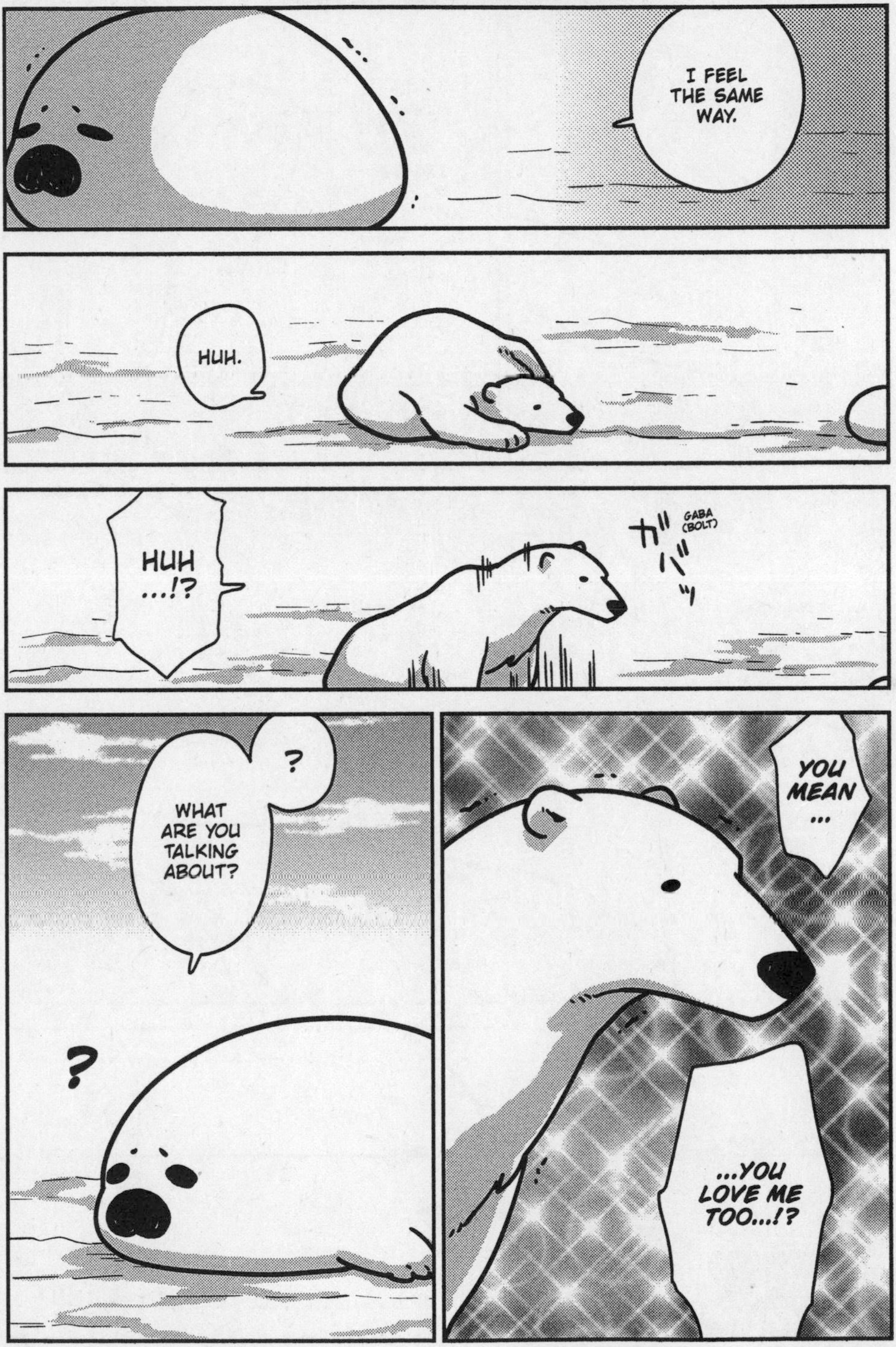

I FEEL THE SAME WAY.
HUH.
ガバッ
GABA (BOLT)
HUH ...!?
YOU MEAN ...
...YOU LOVE ME TOO...!?
?
WHAT ARE YOU TALKING ABOUT?
?

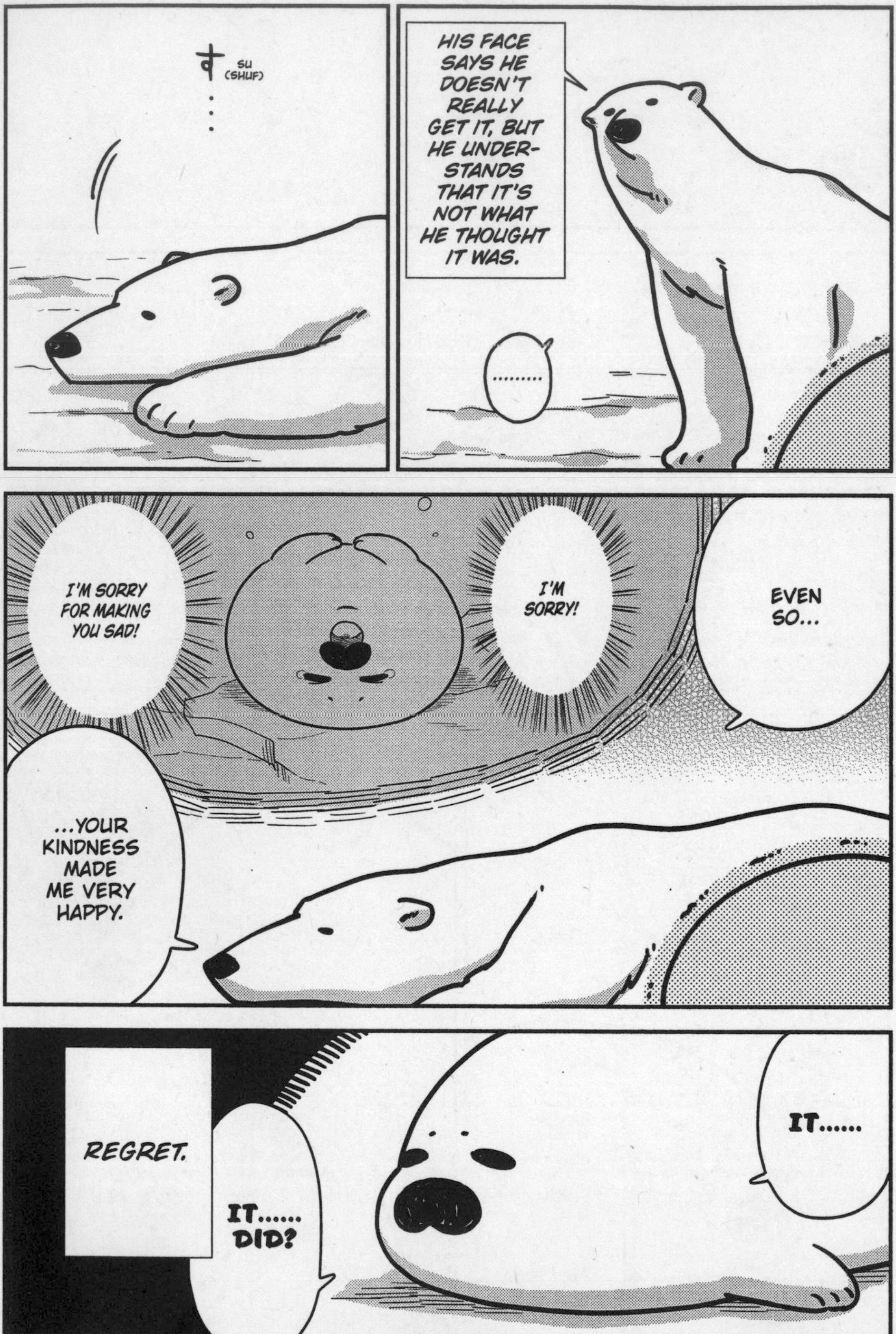
HIS FACE SAYS HE DOESN'T REALLY GET IT, BUT HE UNDERSTANDS THAT IT'S NOT WHAT HE THOUGHT IT WAS.
....
す SU (SHUF)
EVEN SO...
I'M SORRY!
I'M SORRY FOR MAKING YOU SAD!
...YOUR KINDNESS MADE ME VERY HAPPY.
IT......
IT...... DID?
REGRET.

I JUST WANT TO PROTECT YOU

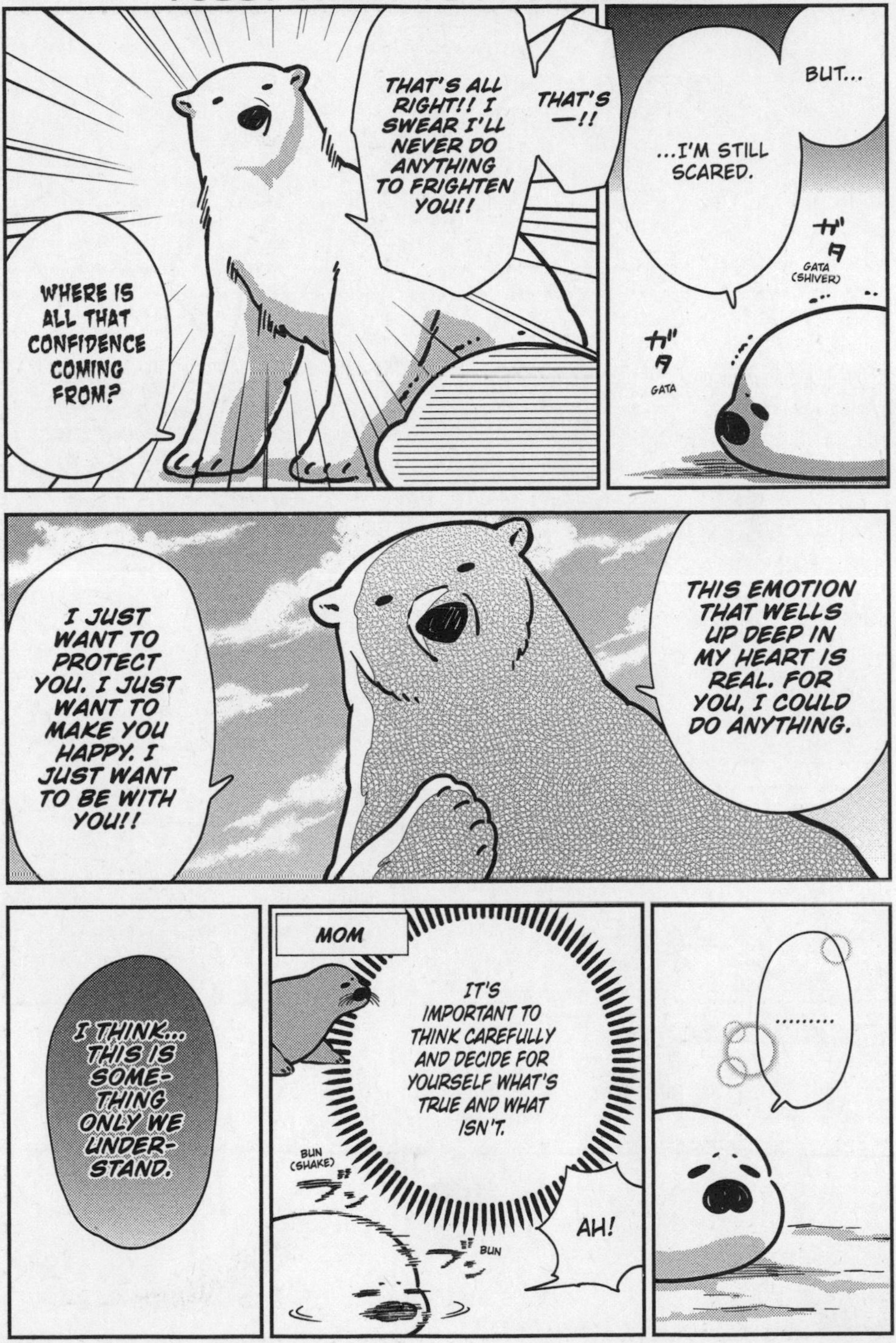

BUT...
...I'M STILL SCARED.
GATA (SHIVER)
GATA
THAT'S—!!
THAT'S ALL RIGHT!! I SWEAR I'LL NEVER DO ANYTHING TO FRIGHTEN YOU!!
WHERE IS ALL THAT CONFIDENCE COMING FROM?
THIS EMOTION THAT WELLS UP DEEP IN MY HEART IS REAL. FOR YOU, I COULD DO ANYTHING.
I JUST WANT TO PROTECT YOU. I JUST WANT TO MAKE YOU HAPPY. I JUST WANT TO BE WITH YOU!!
....
MOM
IT'S IMPORTANT TO THINK CAREFULLY AND DECIDE FOR YOURSELF WHAT'S TRUE AND WHAT ISN'T.
AH!
BUN
BUN (SHAKE)
I THINK... THIS IS SOME-THING ONLY WE UNDER-STAND.

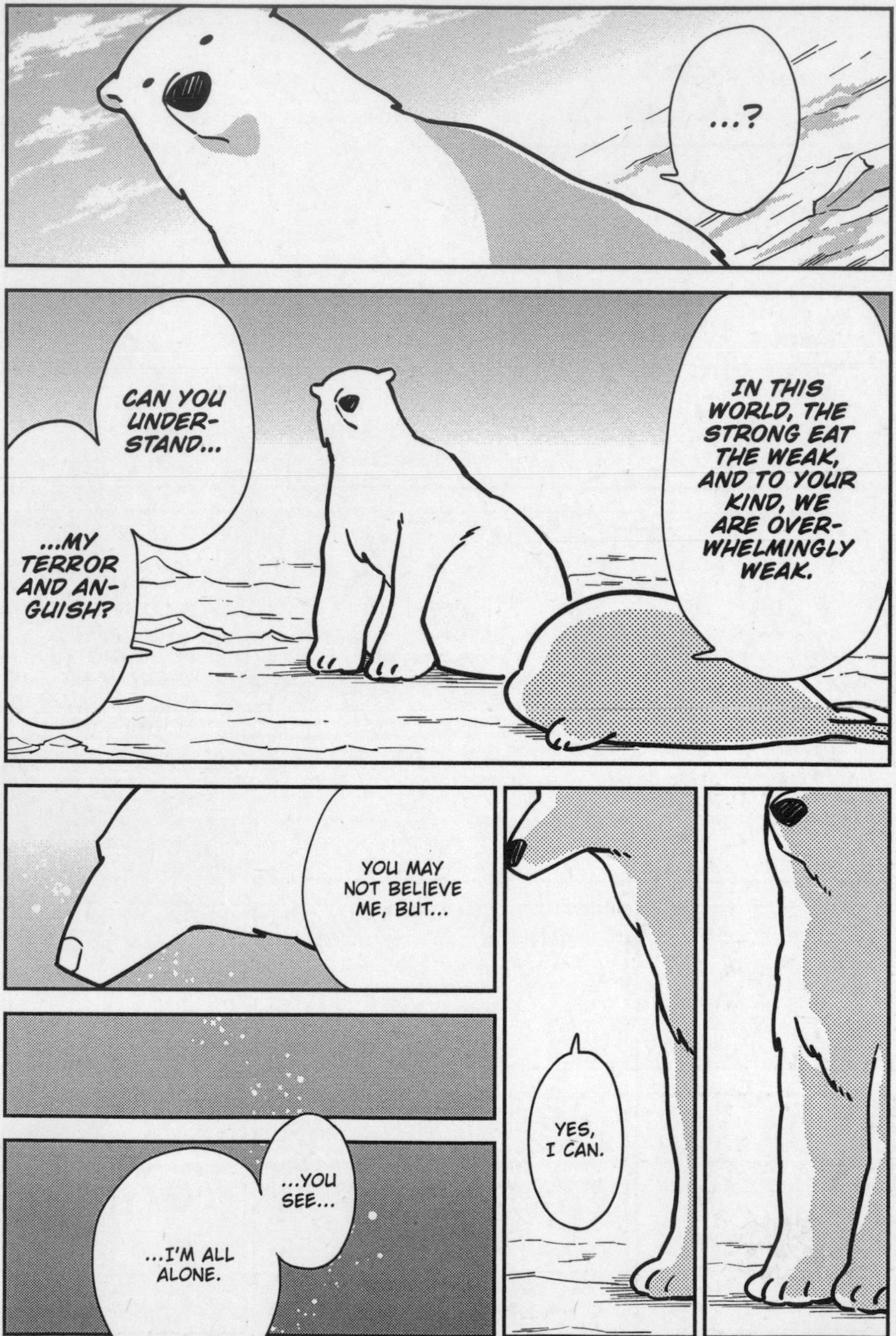
...?
IN THIS WORLD, THE STRONG EAT THE WEAK, AND TO YOUR KIND, WE ARE OVER-WHELMINGLY WEAK.
CAN YOU UNDER-STAND...
...MY TERROR AND AN-GUISH?
YES, I CAN.
YOU MAY NOT BELIEVE ME, BUT...
...YOU SEE...
...I'M ALL ALONE.

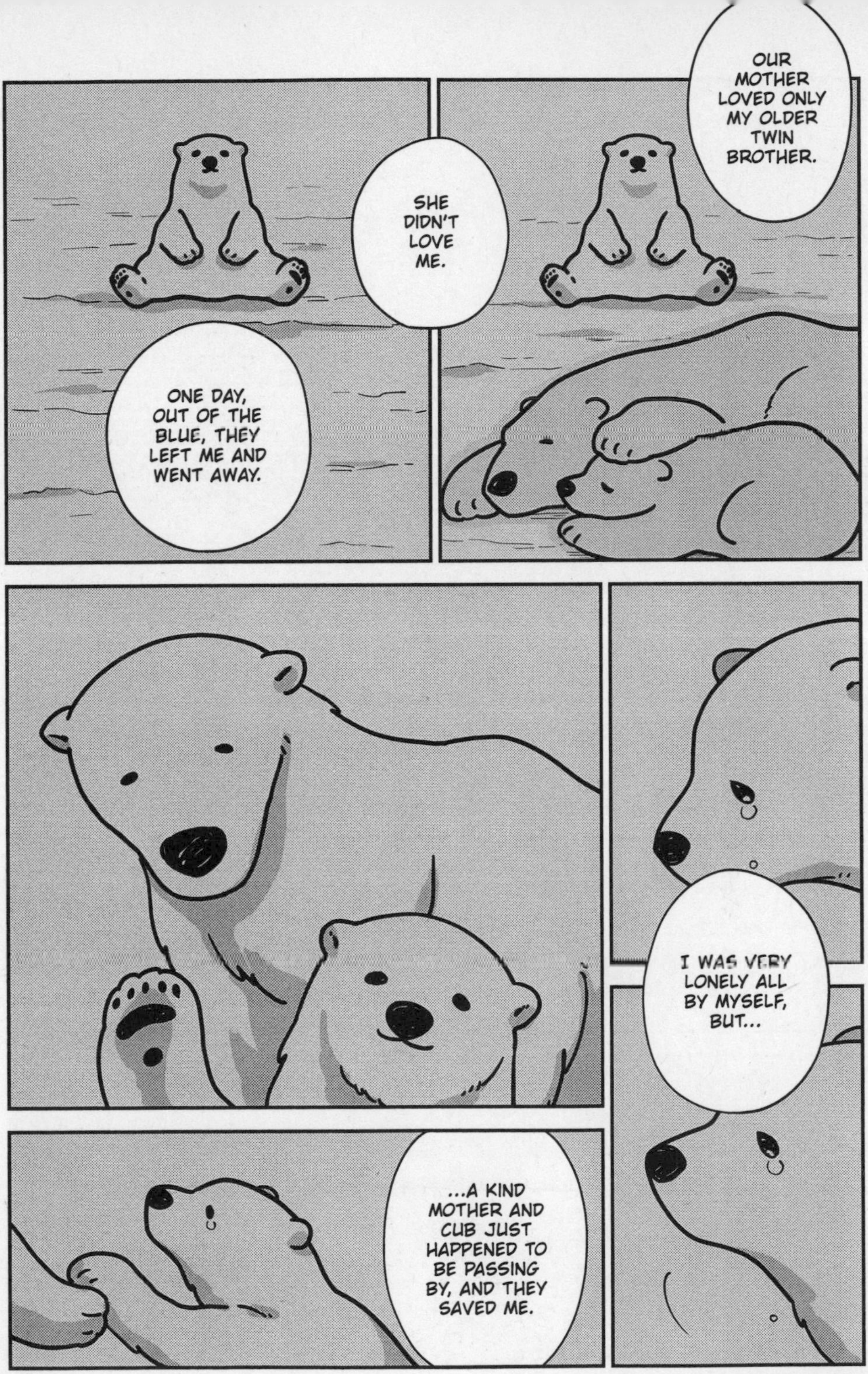
OUR MOTHER LOVED ONLY MY OLDER TWIN BROTHER.
SHE DIDN'T LOVE ME.
ONE DAY, OUT OF THE BLUE, THEY LEFT ME AND WENT AWAY.
I WAS VERY LONELY ALL BY MYSELF, BUT...
...A KIND MOTHER AND CUB JUST HAPPENED TO BE PASSING BY, AND THEY SAVED ME.

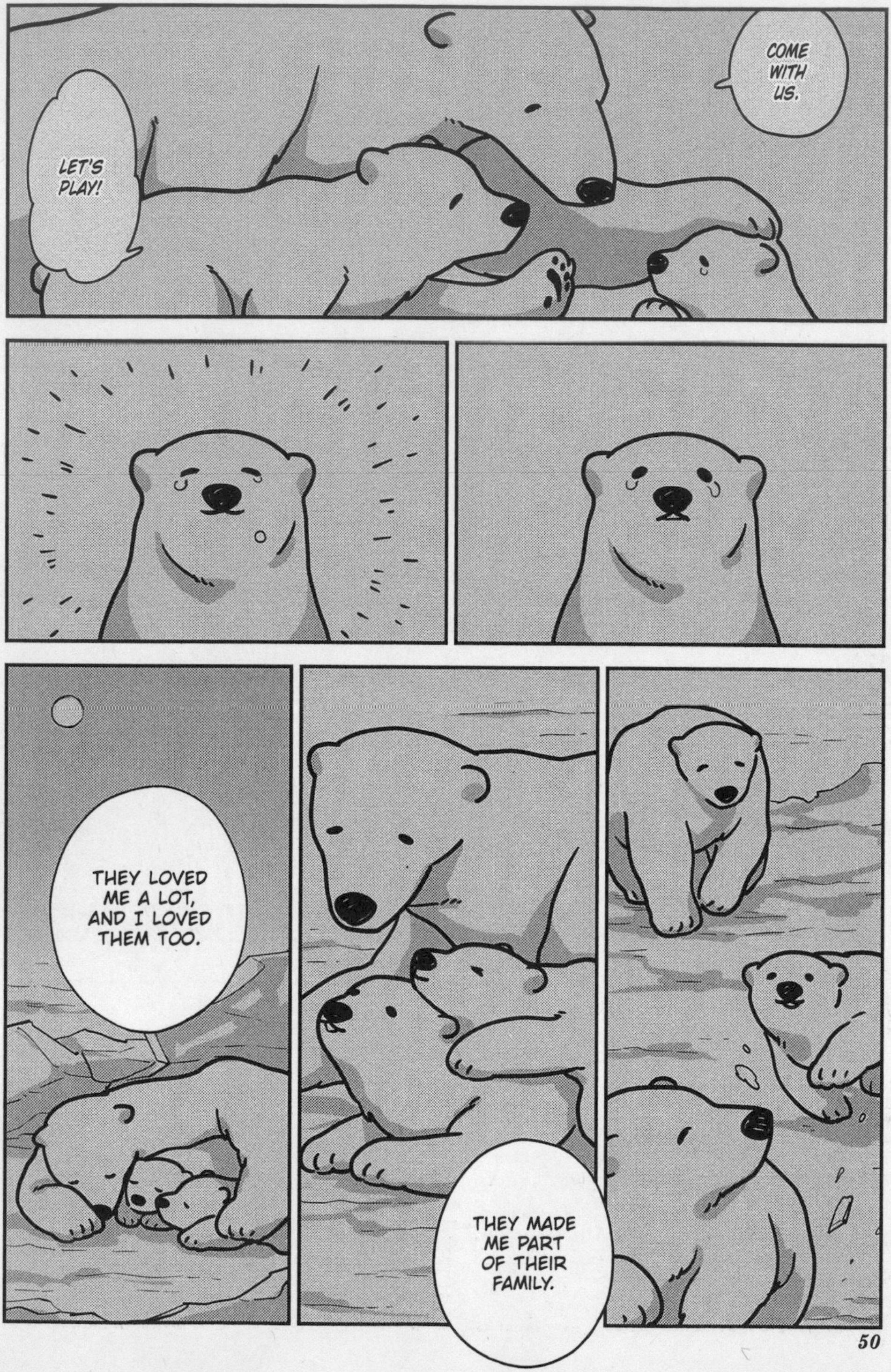
COME WITH US.
LET'S PLAY!
THEY MADE ME PART OF THEIR FAMILY.
THEY LOVED ME A LOT, AND I LOVED THEM TOO.

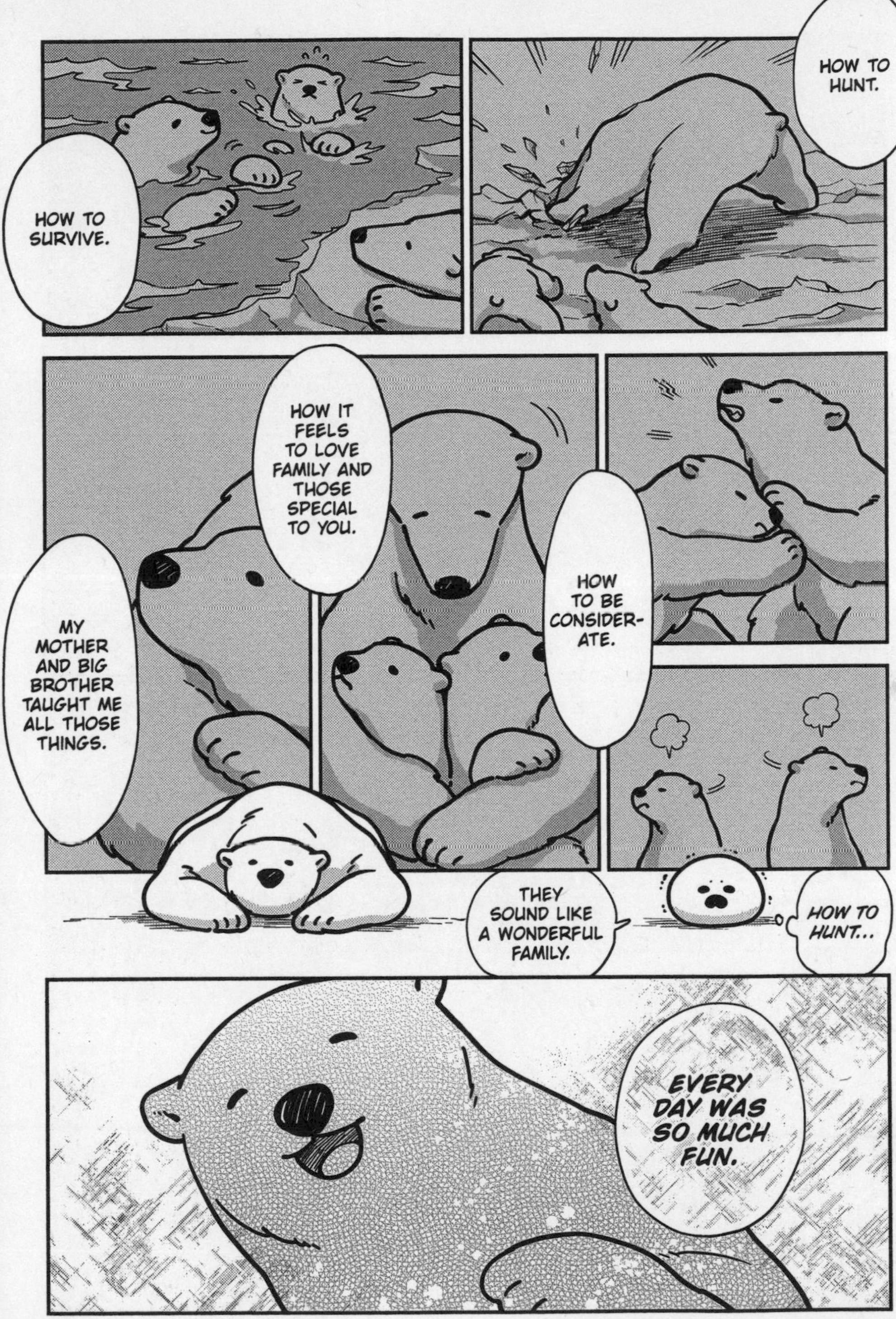
HOW TO HUNT.
HOW TO SURVIVE.
HOW TO BE CONSIDER-ATE.
HOW IT FEELS TO LOVE FAMILY AND THOSE SPECIAL TO YOU.
MY MOTHER AND BIG BROTHER TAUGHT ME ALL THOSE THINGS.
HOW TO HUNT...
THEY SOUND LIKE A WONDERFUL FAMILY.
EVERY DAY WAS SO MUCH FUN.

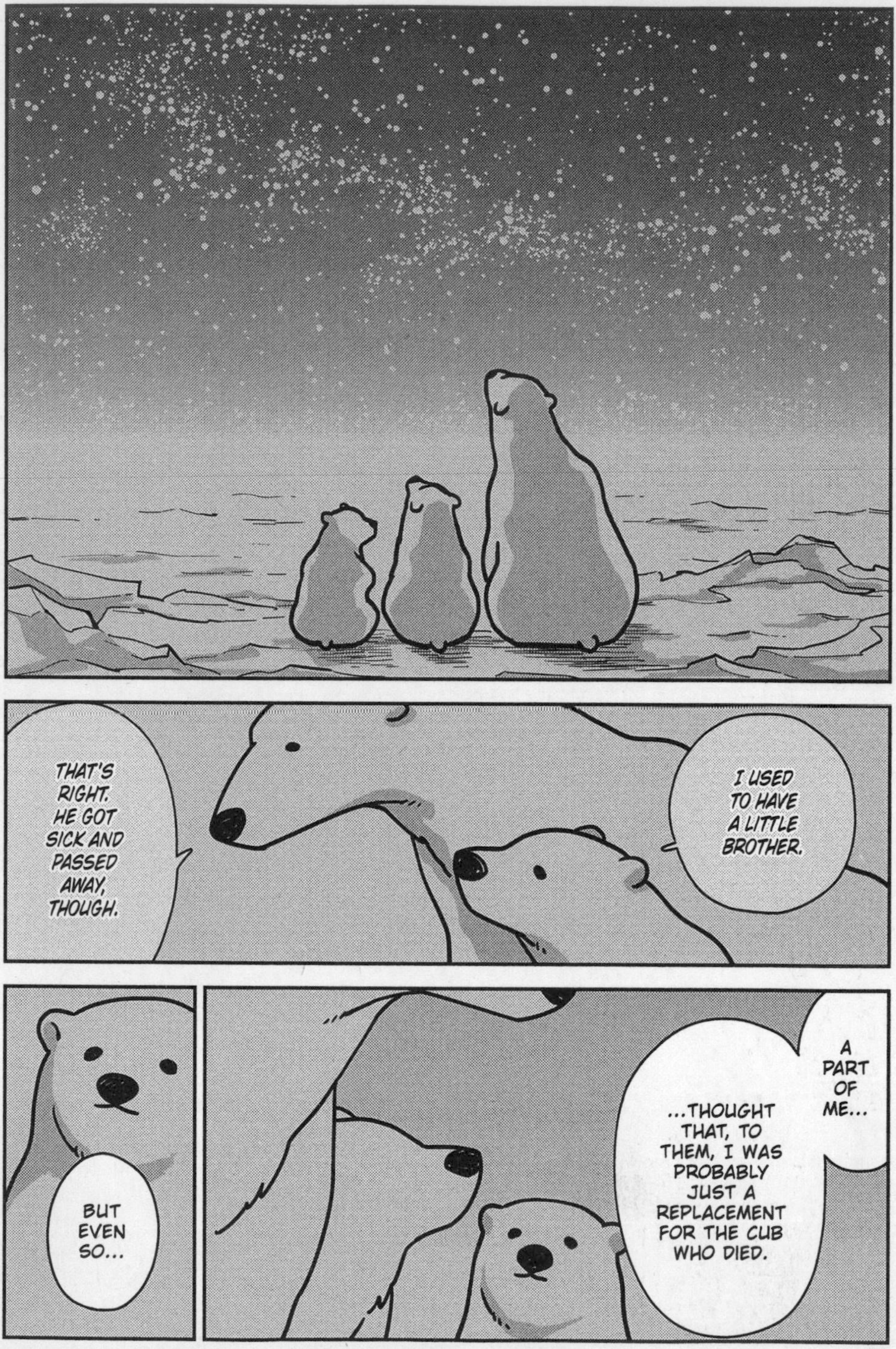
I USED TO HAVE A LITTLE BROTHER.
THAT'S RIGHT. HE GOT SICK AND PASSED AWAY, THOUGH.
A PART OF ME...
...THOUGHT THAT, TO THEM, I WAS PROBABLY JUST A REPLACEMENT FOR THE CUB WHO DIED.
BUT EVEN SO...

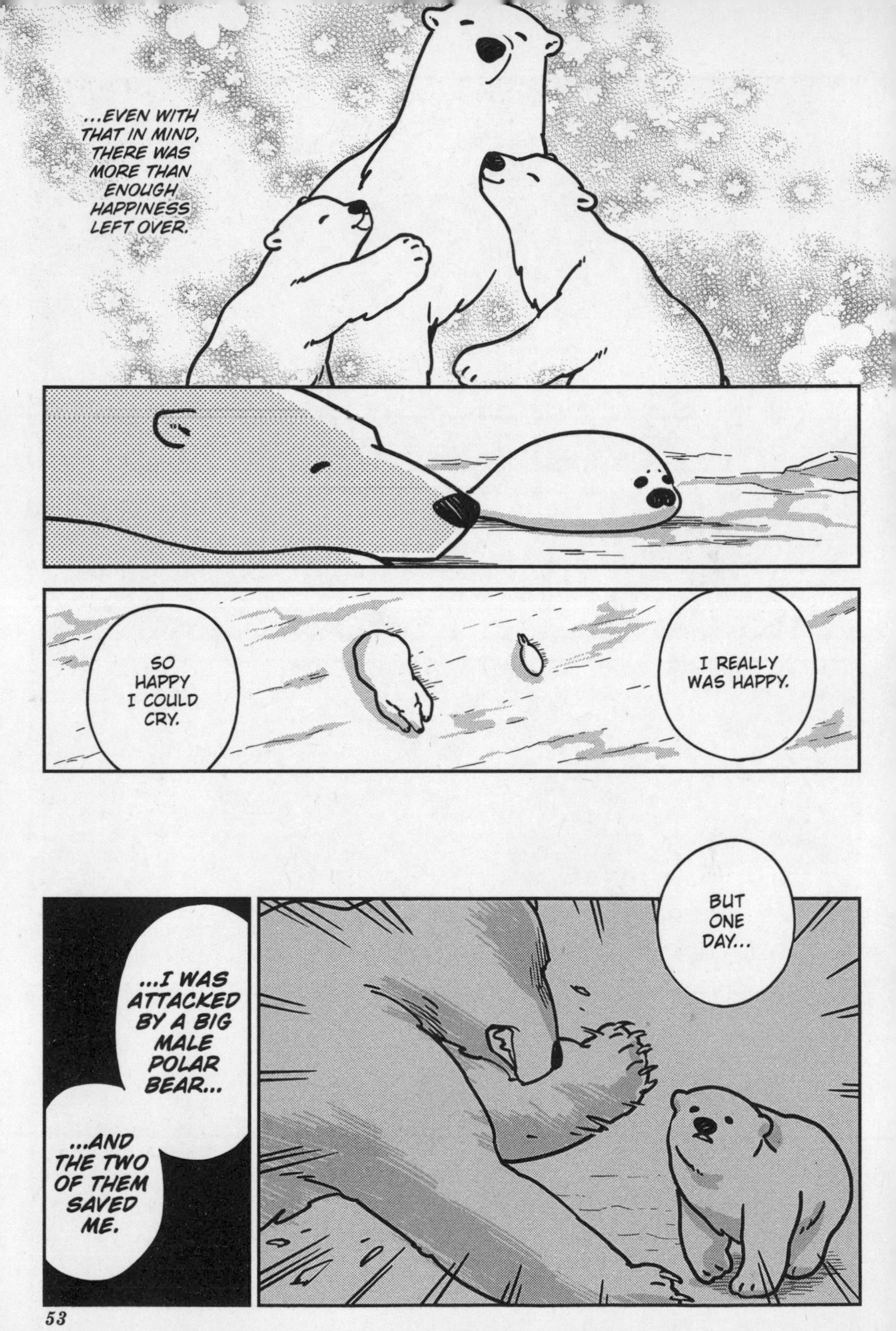
...EVEN WITH THAT IN MIND, THERE WAS MORE THAN ENOUGH HAPPINESS LEFT OVER.
I REALLY WAS HAPPY.
SO HAPPY I COULD CRY.
BUT ONE DAY...
...I WAS ATTACKED BY A BIG MALE POLAR BEAR...
...AND THE TWO OF THEM SAVED ME.

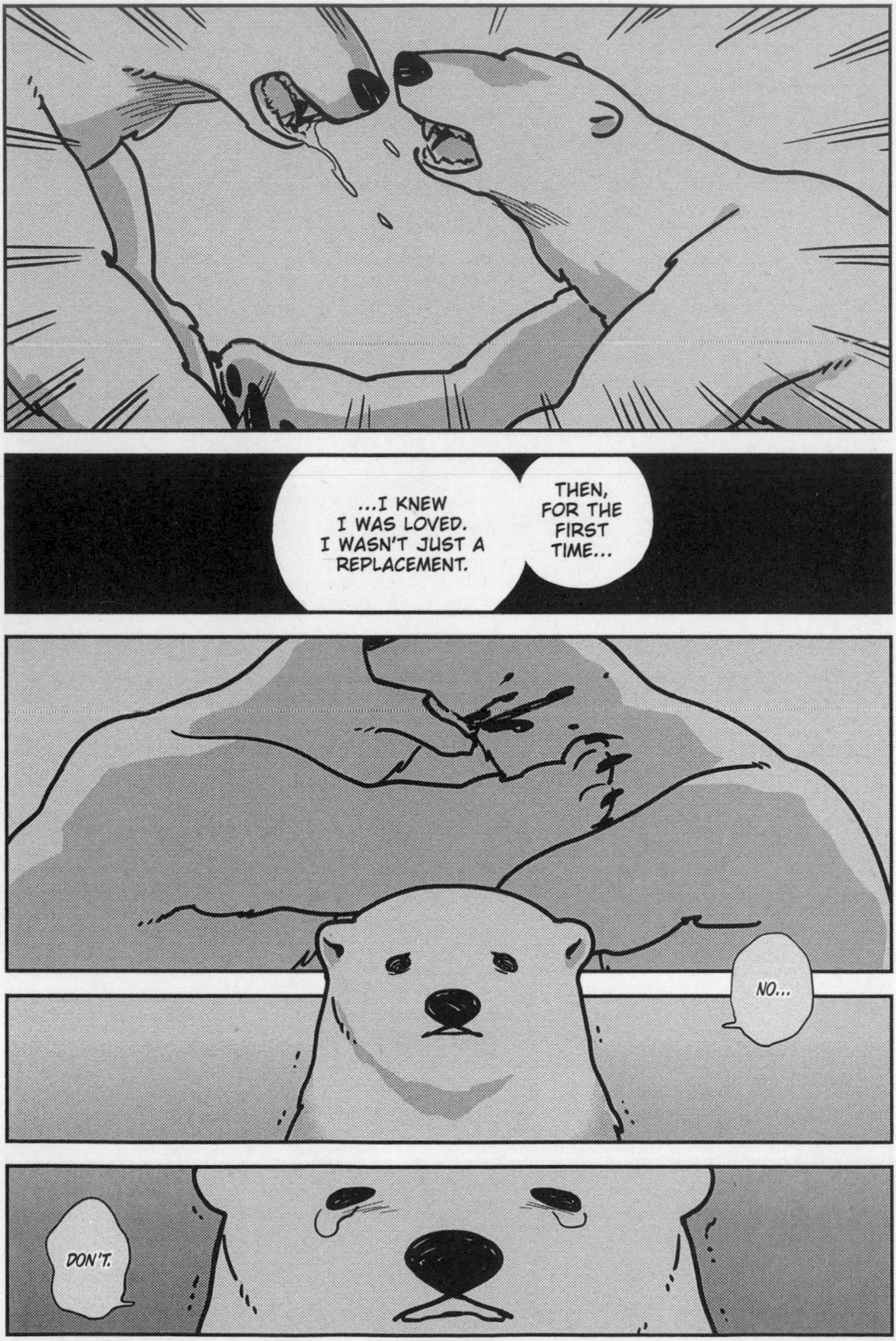
THEN, FOR THE FIRST TIME...
...I KNEW I WAS LOVED. I WASN'T JUST A REPLACEMENT.
NO...
DON'T.

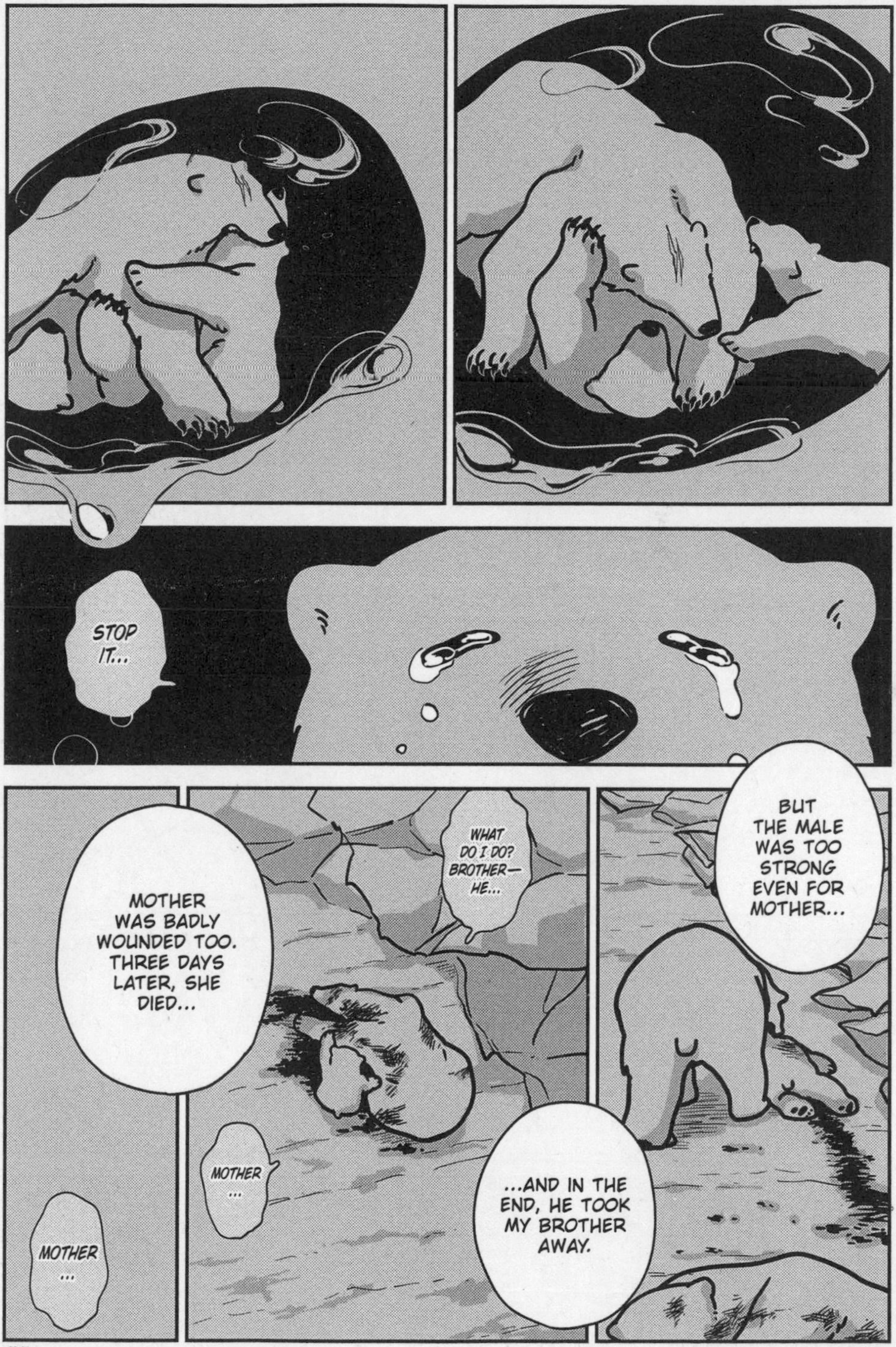
STOP IT...
BUT THE MALE WAS TOO STRONG EVEN FOR MOTHER...
...AND IN THE END, HE TOOK MY BROTHER AWAY.
WHAT DO I DO? BROTHER— HE...
MOTHER WAS BADLY WOUNDED TOO. THREE DAYS LATER, SHE DIED...
MOTHER ...
MOTHER ...

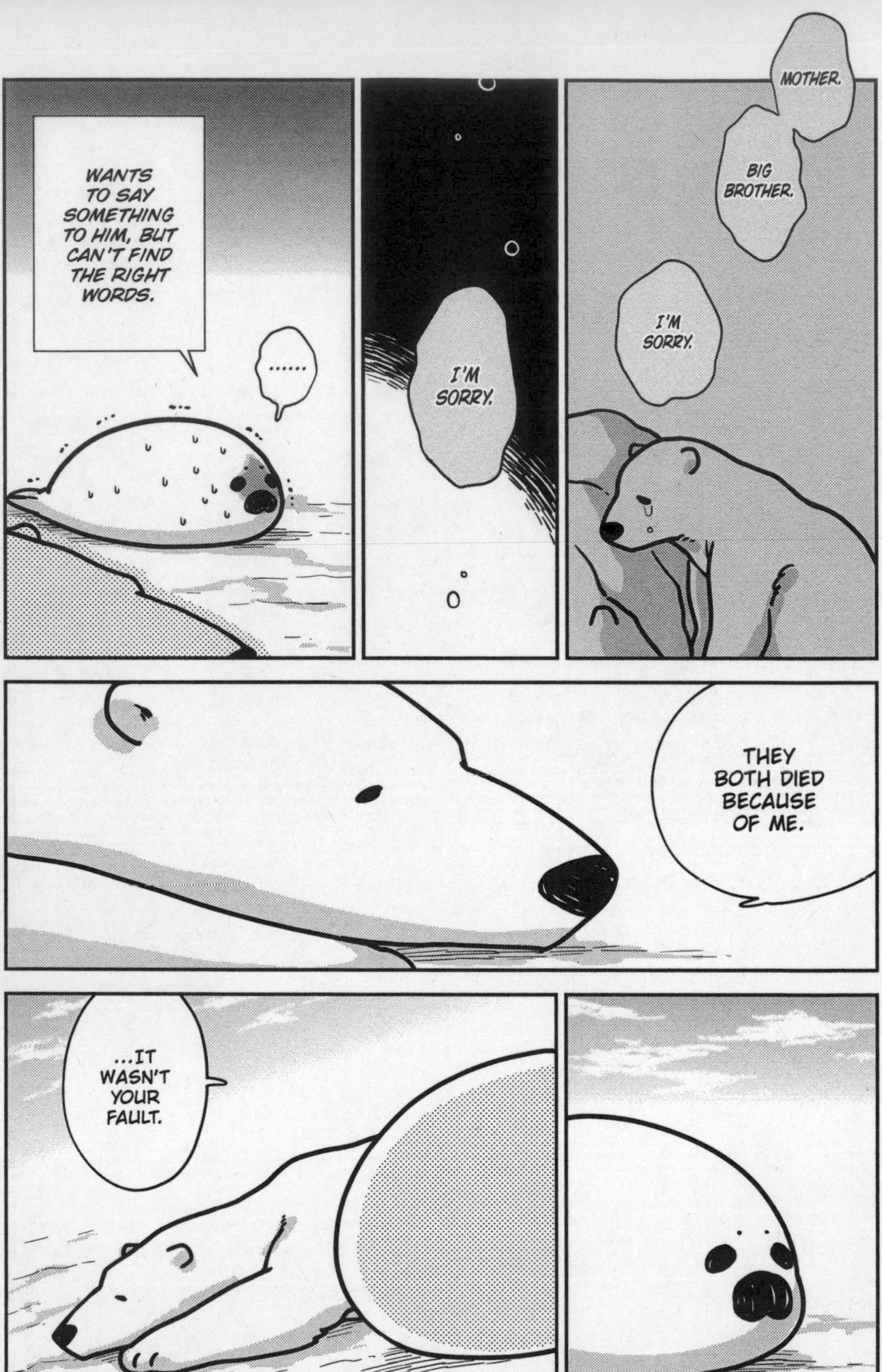
MOTHER.
BIG BROTHER.
I'M SORRY.
I'M SORRY.
WANTS TO SAY SOMETHING TO HIM, BUT CAN'T FIND THE RIGHT WORDS.
......
THEY BOTH DIED BECAUSE OF ME.
...IT WASN'T YOUR FAULT.

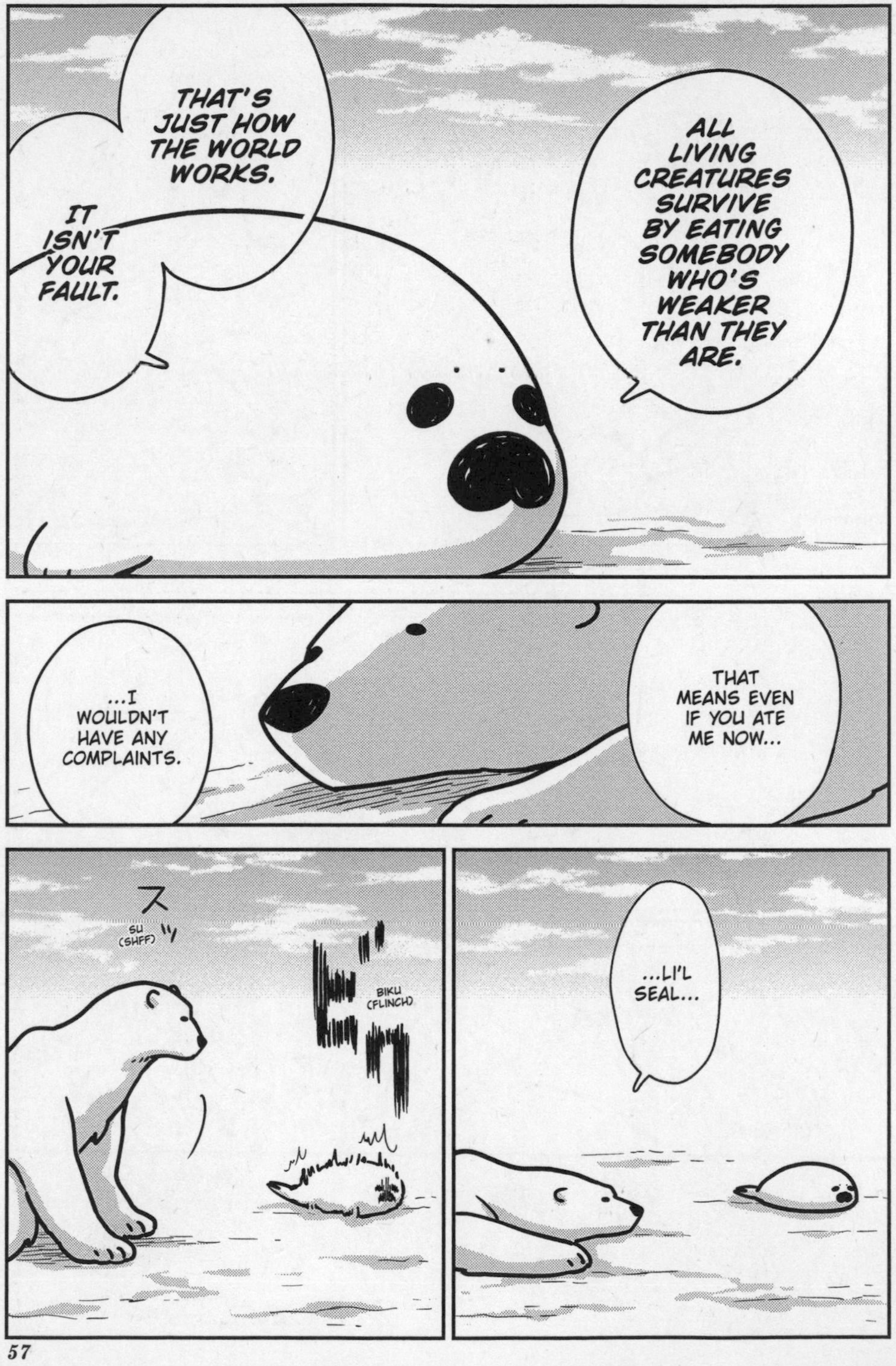
ALL LIVING CREATURES SURVIVE BY EATING SOMEBODY WHO'S WEAKER THAN THEY ARE.
THAT'S JUST HOW THE WORLD WORKS.
IT ISN'T YOUR FAULT.
THAT MEANS EVEN IF YOU ATE ME NOW...
...I WOULDN'T HAVE ANY COMPLAINTS.
...LI'L SEAL...
BIKU (FLINCH)
ス
SU (SHFF)

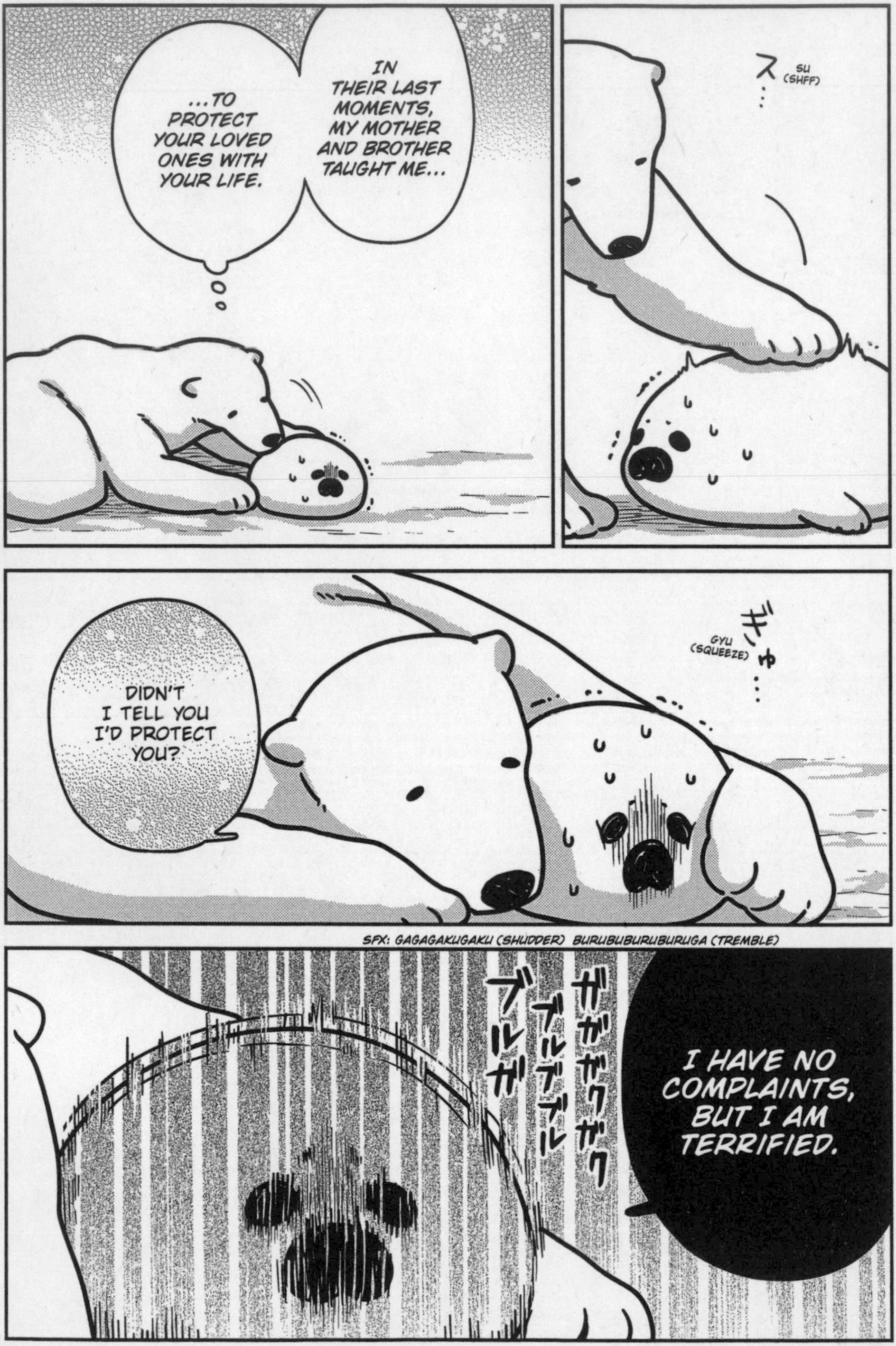
ス…
SU (SHFF)
IN THEIR LAST MOMENTS, MY MOTHER AND BROTHER TAUGHT ME...
...TO PROTECT YOUR LOVED ONES WITH YOUR LIFE.
ぎゅ…
GYU (SQUEEZE)
DIDN'T I TELL YOU I'D PROTECT YOU?
SFX: GAGAGAKUGAKU (SHUDDER) BURUBURUBURUGA (TREMBLE)
I HAVE NO COMPLAINTS, BUT I AM TERRIFIED.

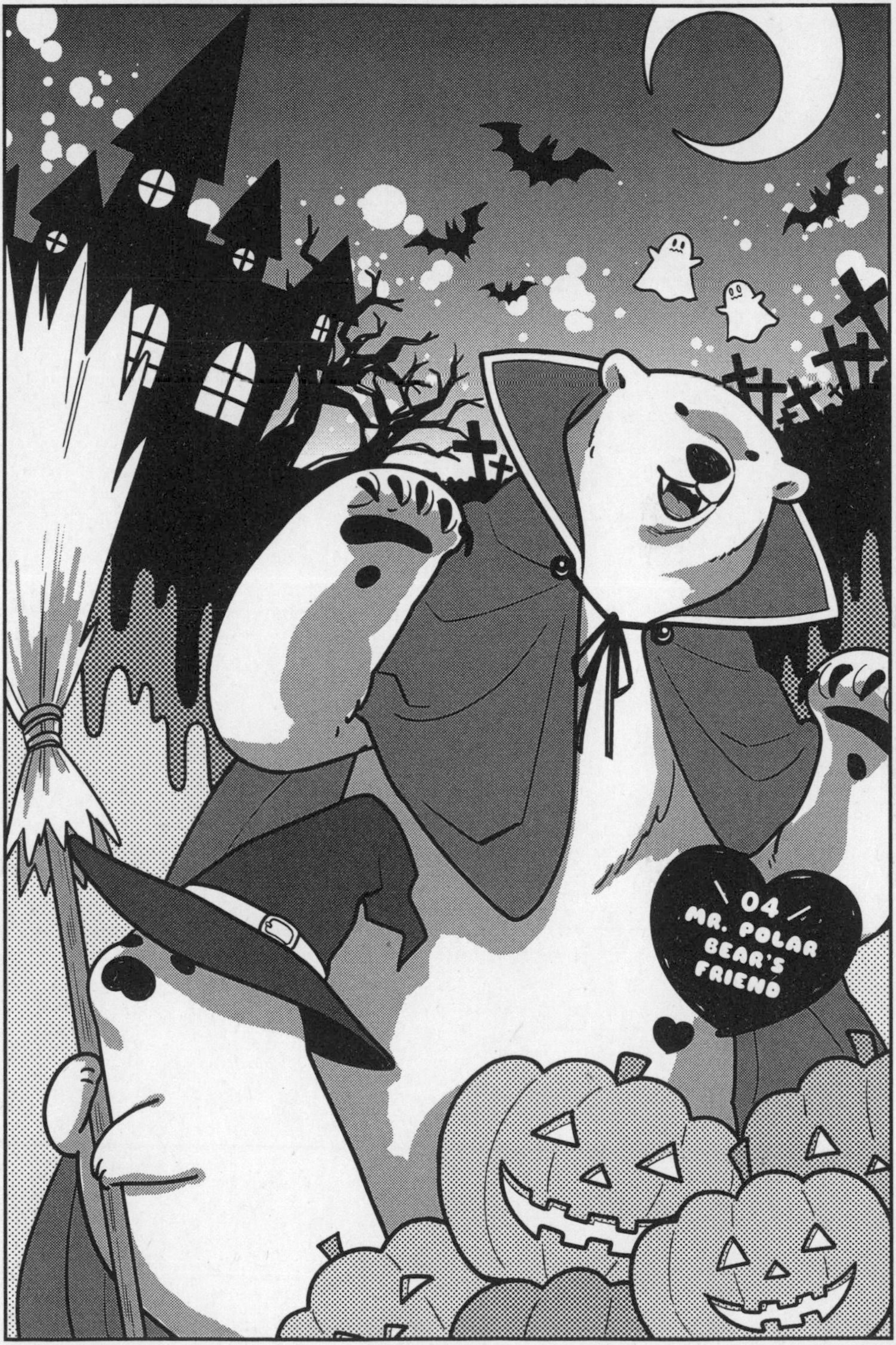
04
MR. POLAR BEAR'S FRIEND

AN UNWANTED TALENT

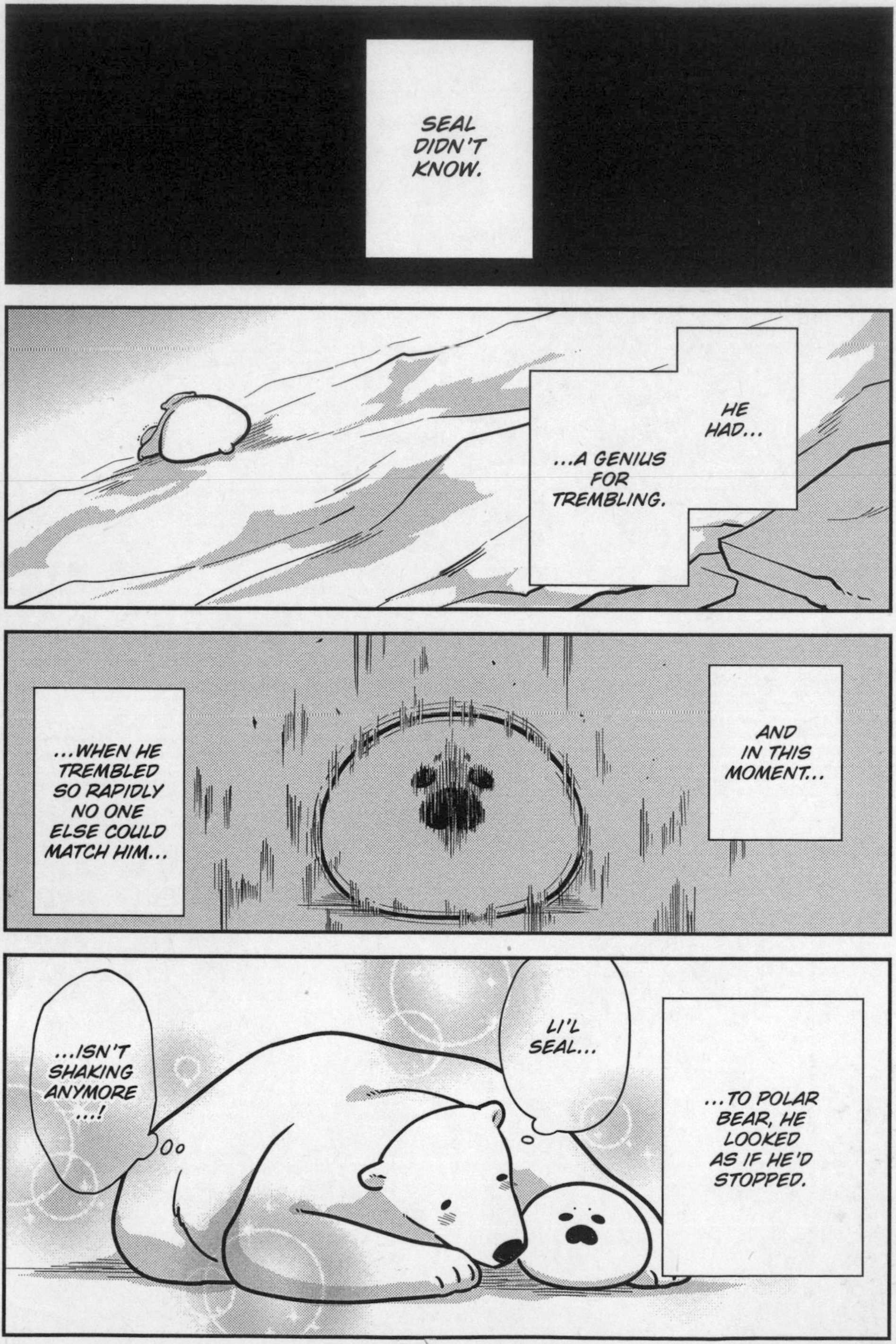
SEAL DIDN'T KNOW.
HE HAD...
...A GENIUS FOR TREMBLING.
AND IN THIS MOMENT...
...WHEN HE TREMBLED SO RAPIDLY NO ONE ELSE COULD MATCH HIM...
...TO POLAR BEAR, HE LOOKED AS IF HE'D STOPPED.
LI'L SEAL...
...ISN'T SHAKING ANYMORE ...!

MY FRIEND

IT'S OVER.
THIS TIME, I'M FINISHED FOR SURE.
HEH HEH.
DO (BADUMP)
....
WH— WHAT IS IT?
DO
DO
HEH HEH...
YOU LOOK YUMMY...
WELL, MY FRIEND TOLD ME SOMETHING, LONG AGO...
...AND I JUST THOUGHT, "SHE WAS RIGHT."
YOUR FRIEND?
YES. I SAY "FRIEND," BUT SHE WAS FAR MORE MATURE THAN I WAS.
A REAL LADY.

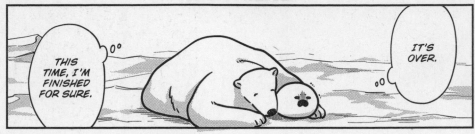

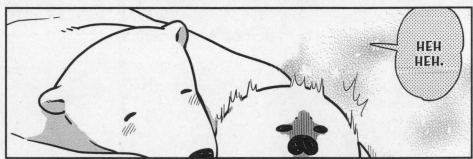

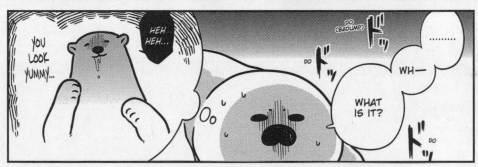

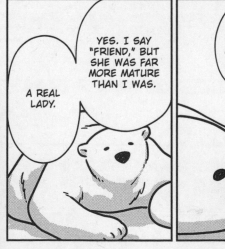

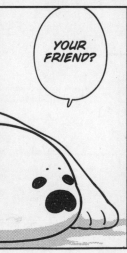

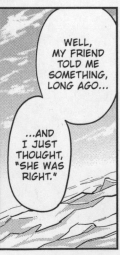

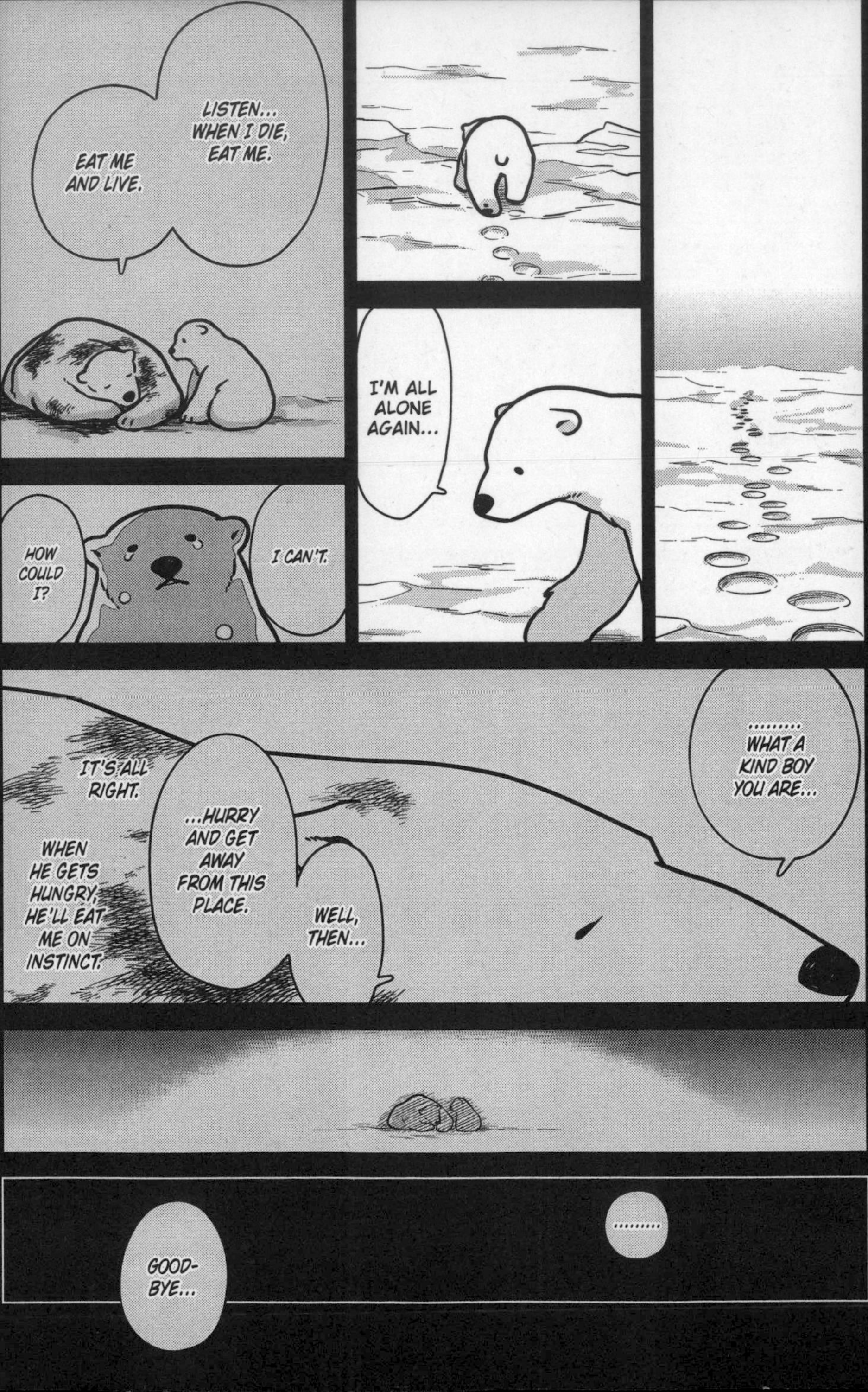
I'M ALL ALONE AGAIN...
LISTEN... WHEN I DIE, EAT ME.
EAT ME AND LIVE.
I CAN'T.
HOW COULD I?
.... WHAT A KIND BOY YOU ARE...
WELL, THEN...
...HURRY AND GET AWAY FROM THIS PLACE.
IT'S ALL RIGHT.
WHEN HE GETS HUNGRY, HE'LL EAT ME ON INSTINCT.
....
GOOD-BYE...

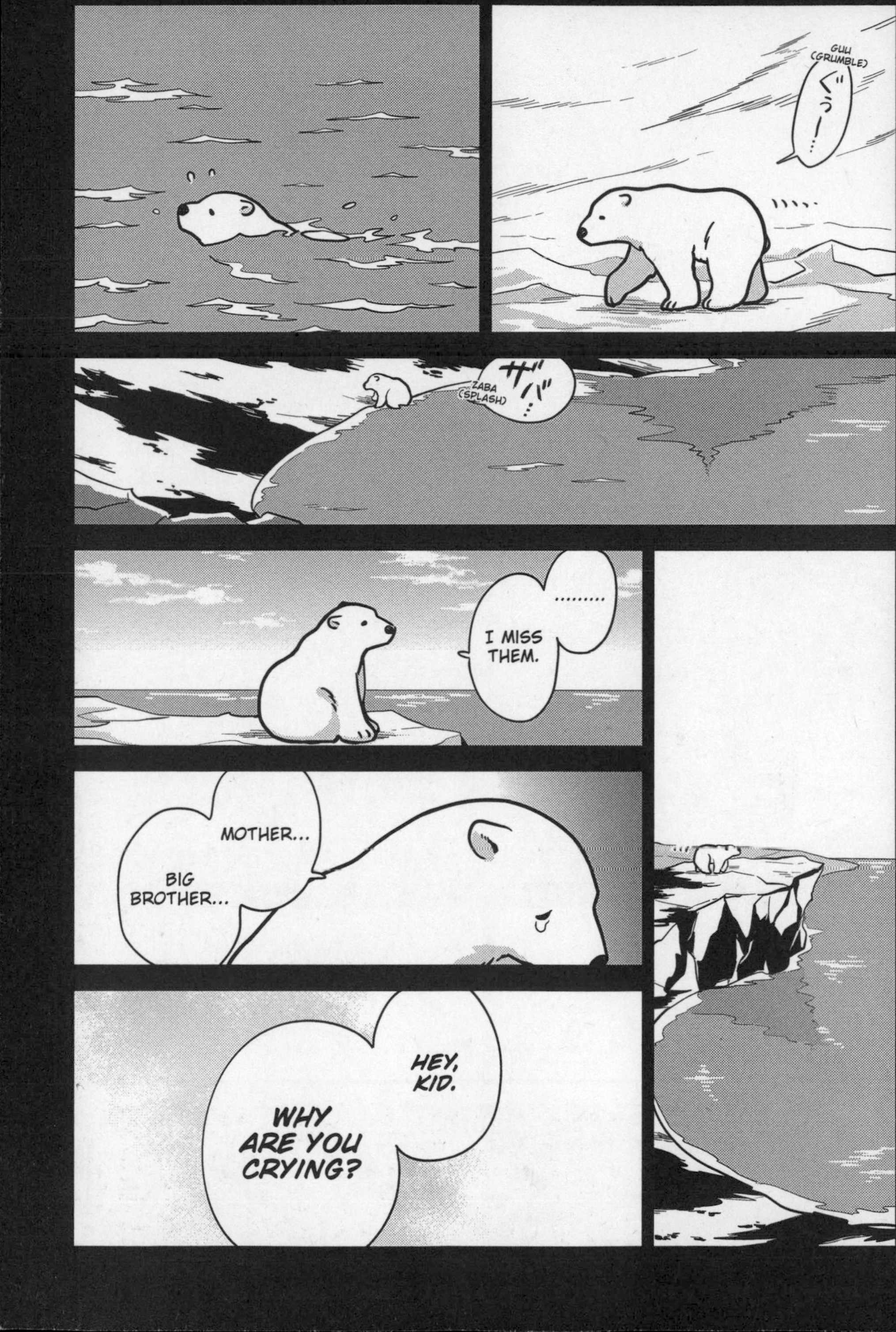
GUU (GRUMBLE)
ぐうー…
ZABA (SPLASH)
ザバ…
....
I MISS THEM.
MOTHER...
BIG BROTHER...
HEY, KID.
WHY ARE YOU CRYING?

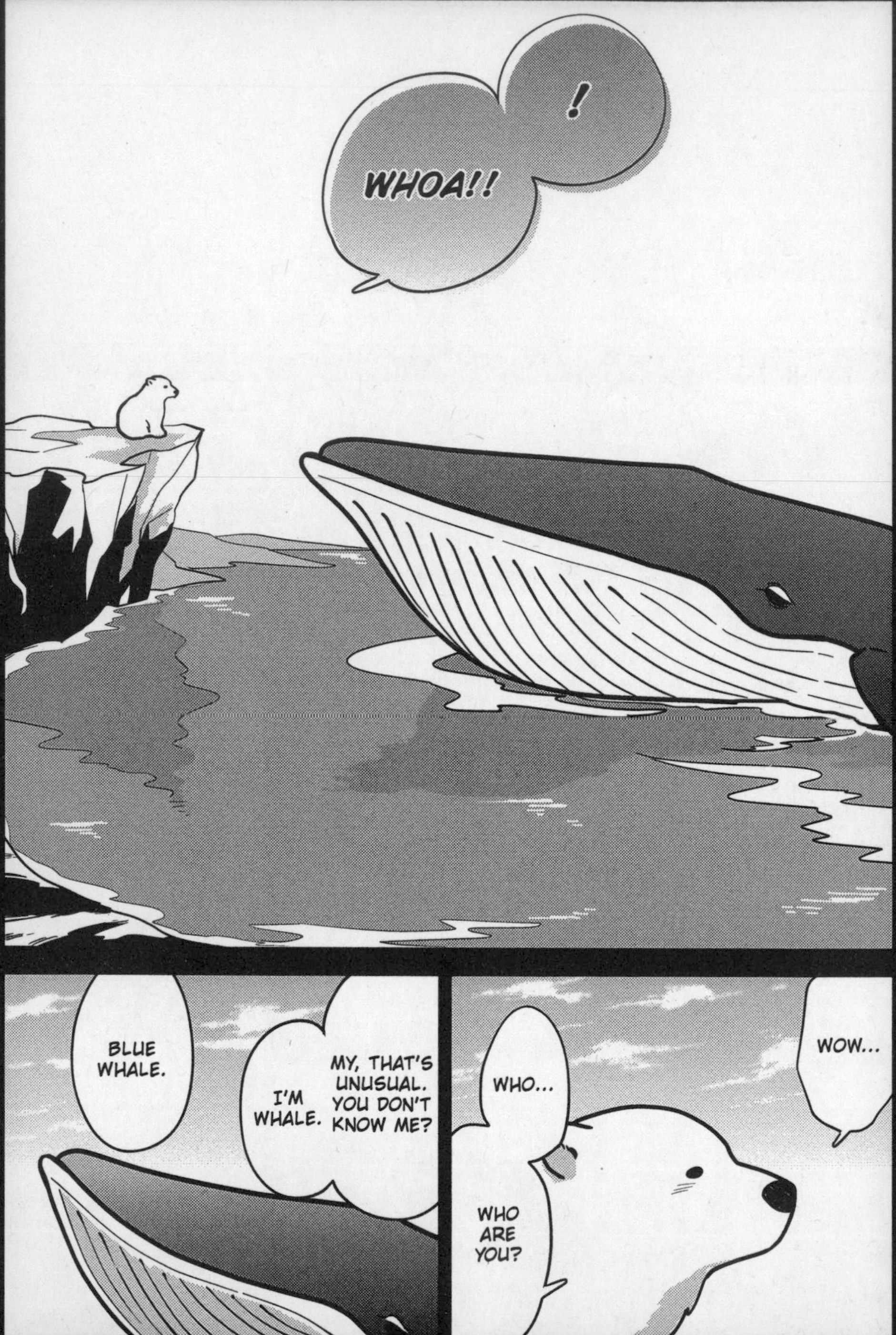
!
WHOA!!
WOW...
WHO...
WHO ARE YOU?
MY, THAT'S UNUSUAL. YOU DON'T KNOW ME?
I'M WHALE.
BLUE WHALE.

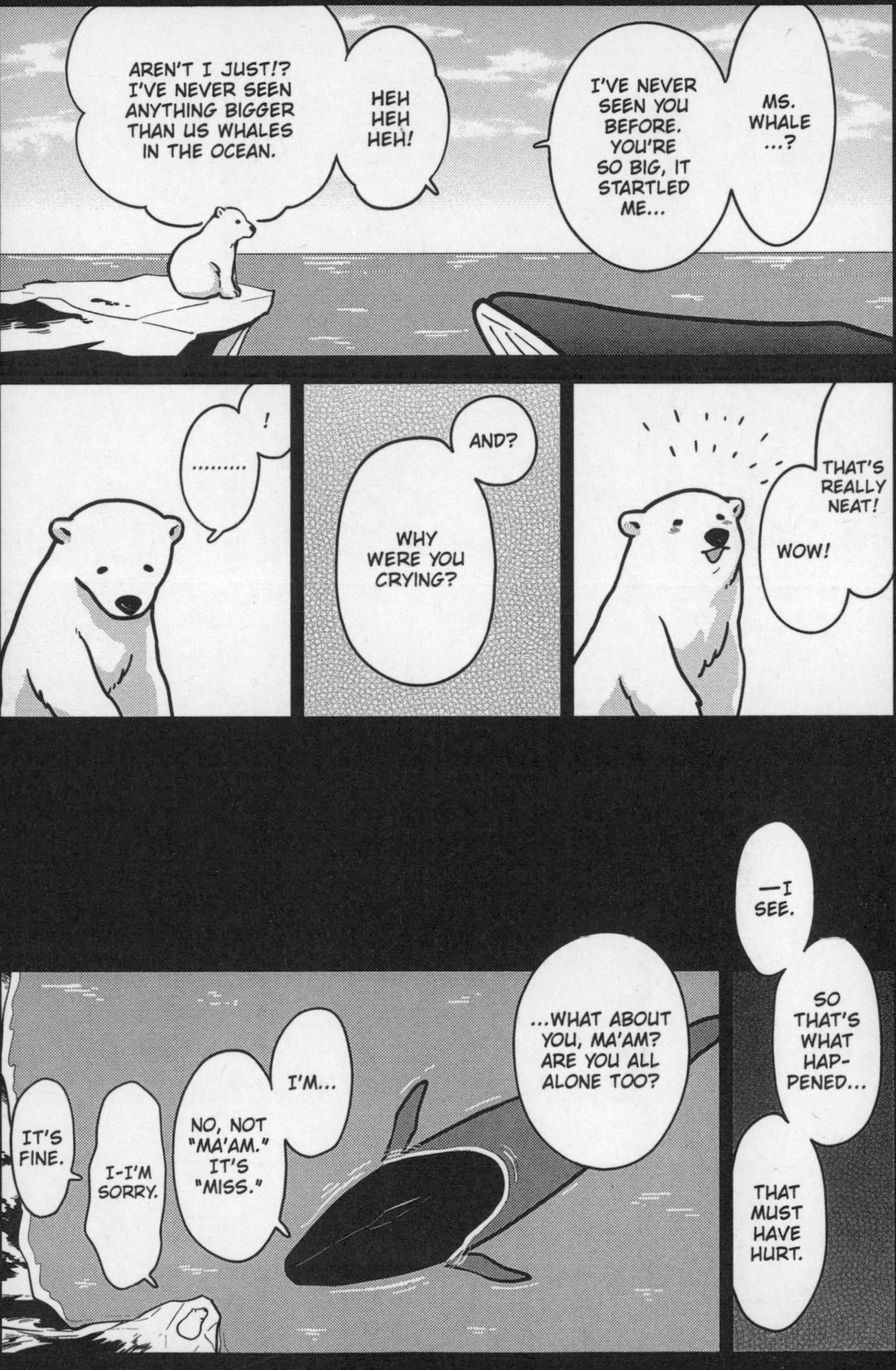
MS. WHALE ...?
I'VE NEVER SEEN YOU BEFORE. YOU'RE SO BIG, IT STARTLED ME...
HEH HEH HEH!
AREN'T I JUST!? I'VE NEVER SEEN ANYTHING BIGGER THAN US WHALES IN THE OCEAN.
THAT'S REALLY NEAT!
WOW!
AND?
WHY WERE YOU CRYING?
!
....
—I SEE.
SO THAT'S WHAT HAP-PENED...
THAT MUST HAVE HURT.
...WHAT ABOUT YOU, MA'AM? ARE YOU ALL ALONE TOO?
I'M...
NO, NOT "MA'AM." IT'S "MISS."
I-I'M SORRY.
IT'S FINE.

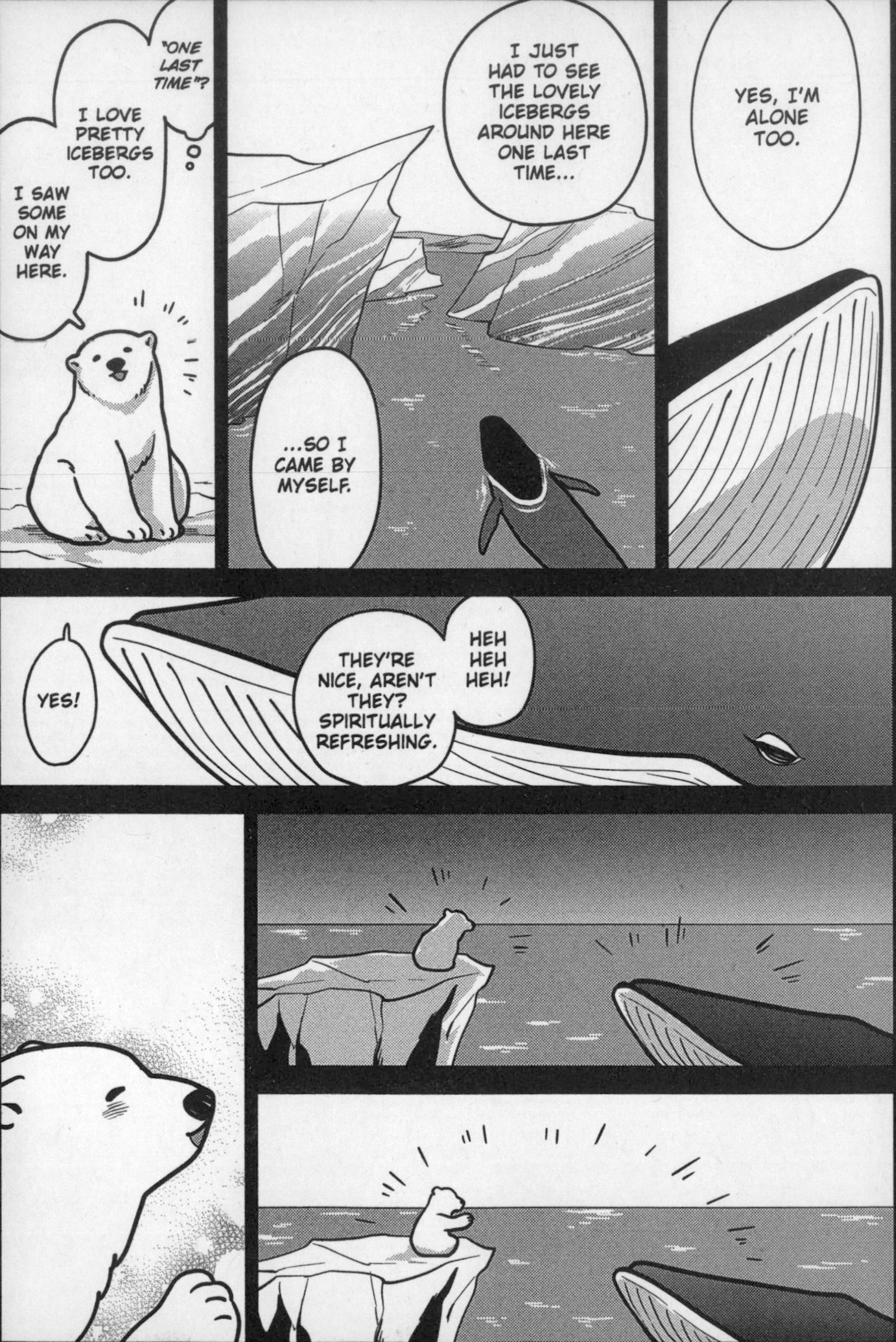
YES, I'M ALONE TOO.
I JUST HAD TO SEE THE LOVELY ICEBERGS AROUND HERE ONE LAST TIME...
...SO I CAME BY MYSELF.
"ONE LAST TIME"?
I LOVE PRETTY ICEBERGS TOO.
I SAW SOME ON MY WAY HERE.
HEH HEH HEH!
THEY'RE NICE, AREN'T THEY? SPIRITUALLY REFRESHING.
YES!

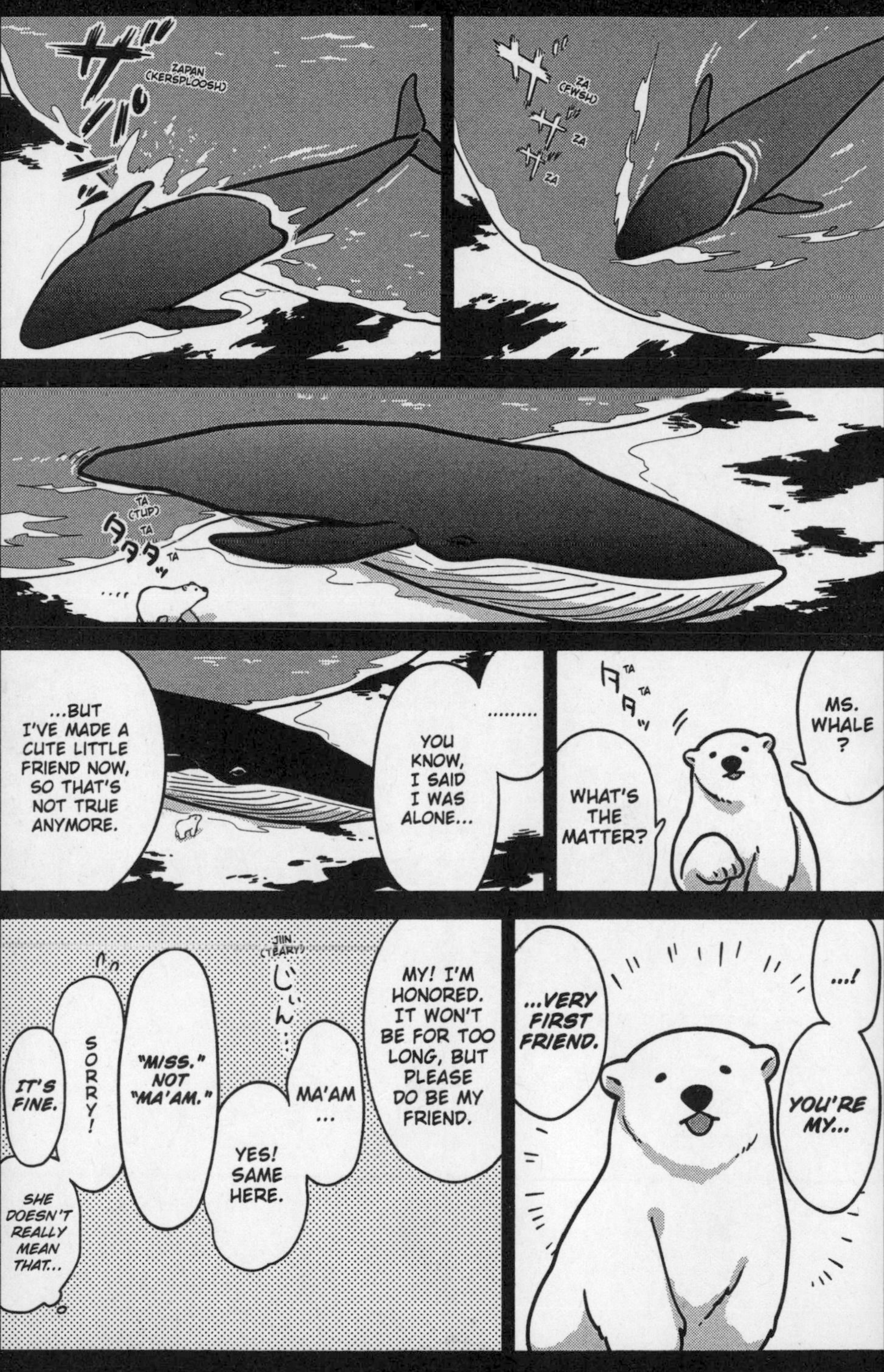
ZA (FWSH)
ZA
ZA
ZAPAN (KERSPLOOSH)
TA (TUP)
TA
TA
MS. WHALE ?
TA
TA
WHAT'S THE MATTER?
....
YOU KNOW, I SAID I WAS ALONE...
...BUT I'VE MADE A CUTE LITTLE FRIEND NOW, SO THAT'S NOT TRUE ANYMORE.
...!
YOU'RE MY...
...VERY FIRST FRIEND.
MY! I'M HONORED. IT WON'T BE FOR TOO LONG, BUT PLEASE DO BE MY FRIEND.
JIIN (TEARY)
YES! SAME HERE.
MA'AM ...
"MISS." NOT "MA'AM."
SORRY!
IT'S FINE.
SHE DOESN'T REALLY MEAN THAT...

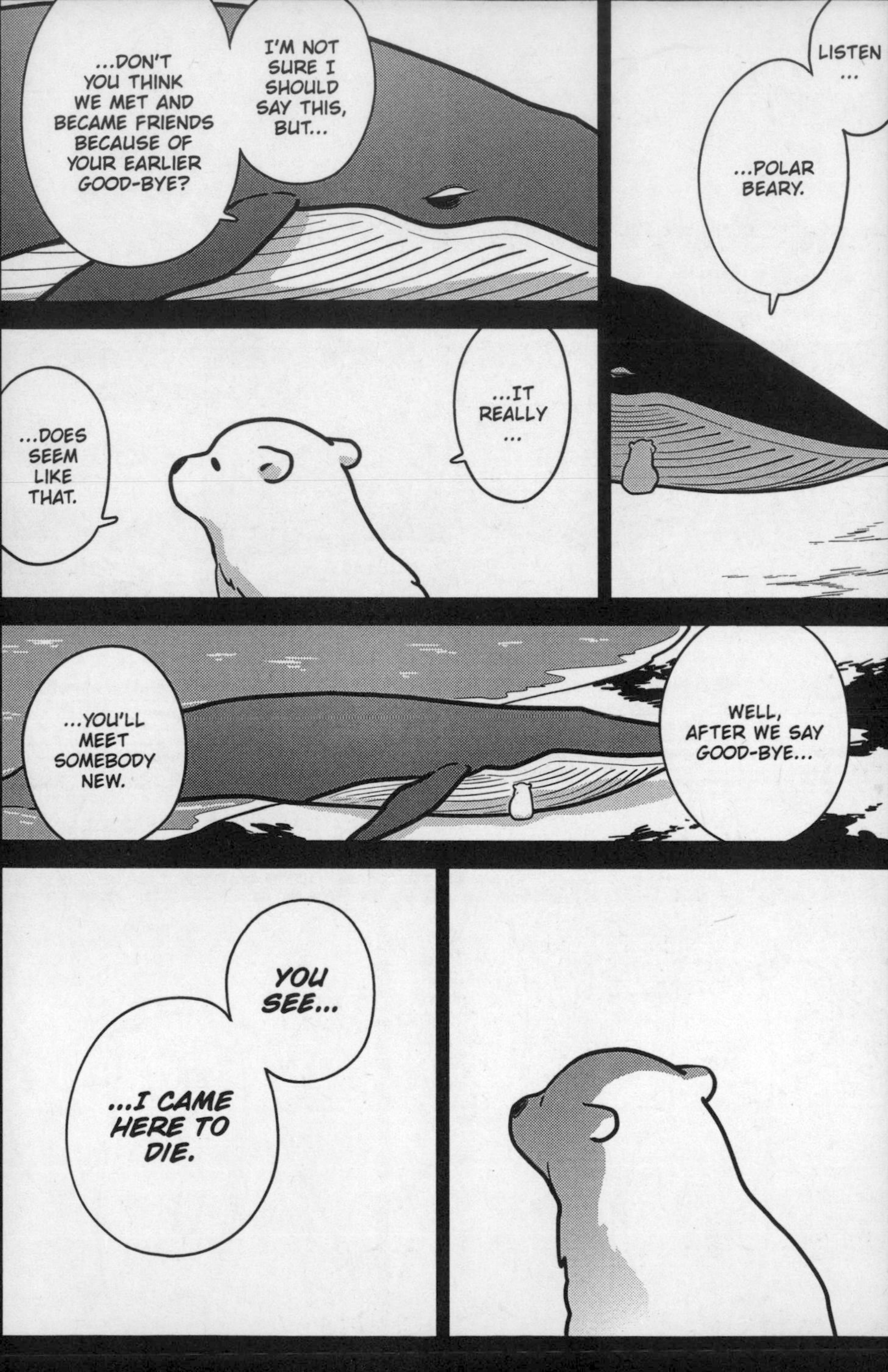
LISTEN ...
...POLAR BEARY.
I'M NOT SURE I SHOULD SAY THIS, BUT...
...DON'T YOU THINK WE MET AND BECAME FRIENDS BECAUSE OF YOUR EARLIER GOOD-BYE?
...IT REALLY ...
...DOES SEEM LIKE THAT.
WELL, AFTER WE SAY GOOD-BYE...
...YOU'LL MEET SOMEBODY NEW.
YOU SEE...
...I CAME HERE TO DIE.

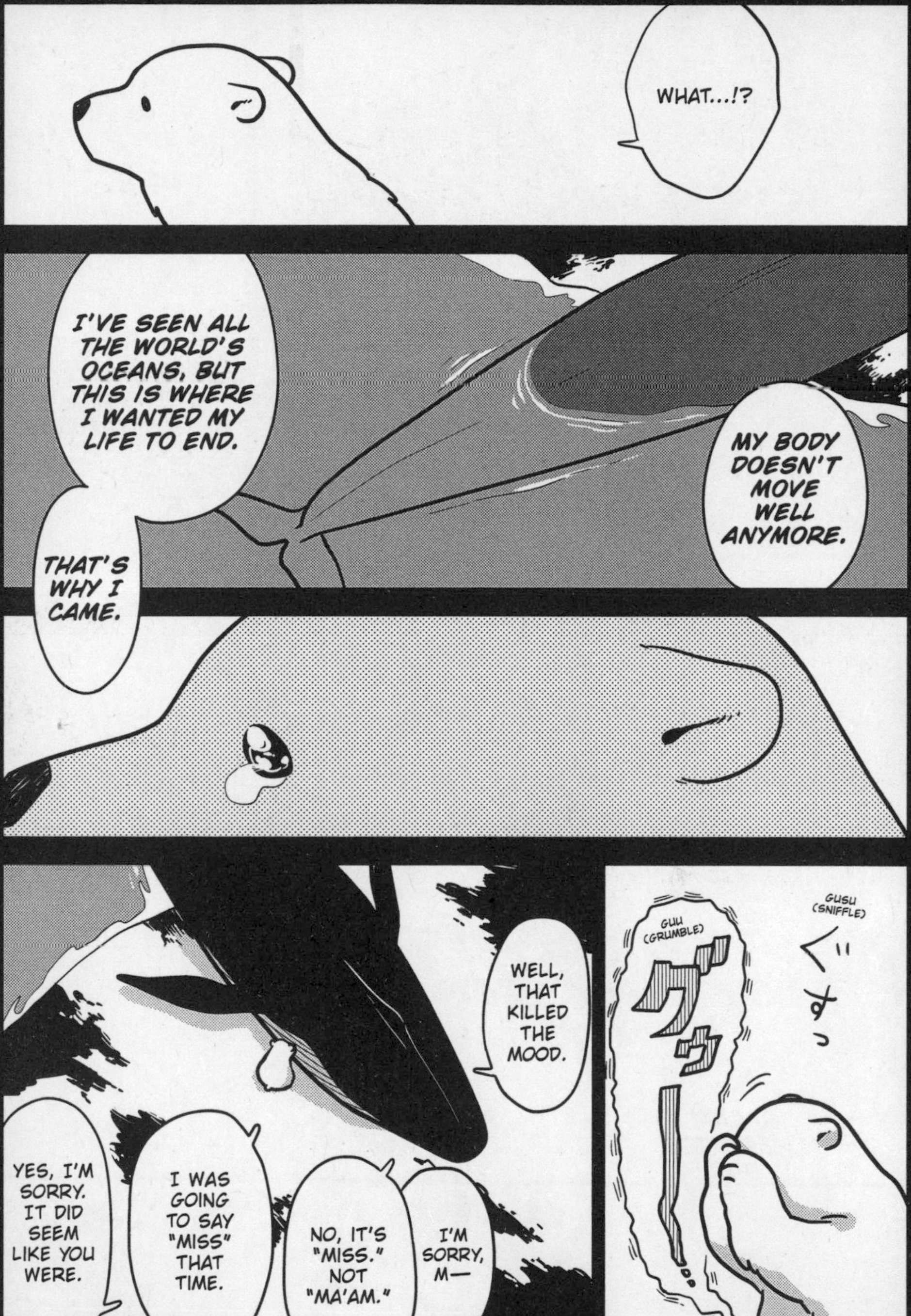
WHAT...!?
MY BODY DOESN'T MOVE WELL ANYMORE.
I'VE SEEN ALL THE WORLD'S OCEANS, BUT THIS IS WHERE I WANTED MY LIFE TO END.
THAT'S WHY I CAME.
GUSU (SNIFFLE)
ぐすっ
GUU (GRUMBLE)
ヴゥー…
WELL, THAT KILLED THE MOOD.
I'M SORRY, M—
NO, IT'S "MISS." NOT "MA'AM."
I WAS GOING TO SAY "MISS" THAT TIME.
YES, I'M SORRY. IT DID SEEM LIKE YOU WERE.

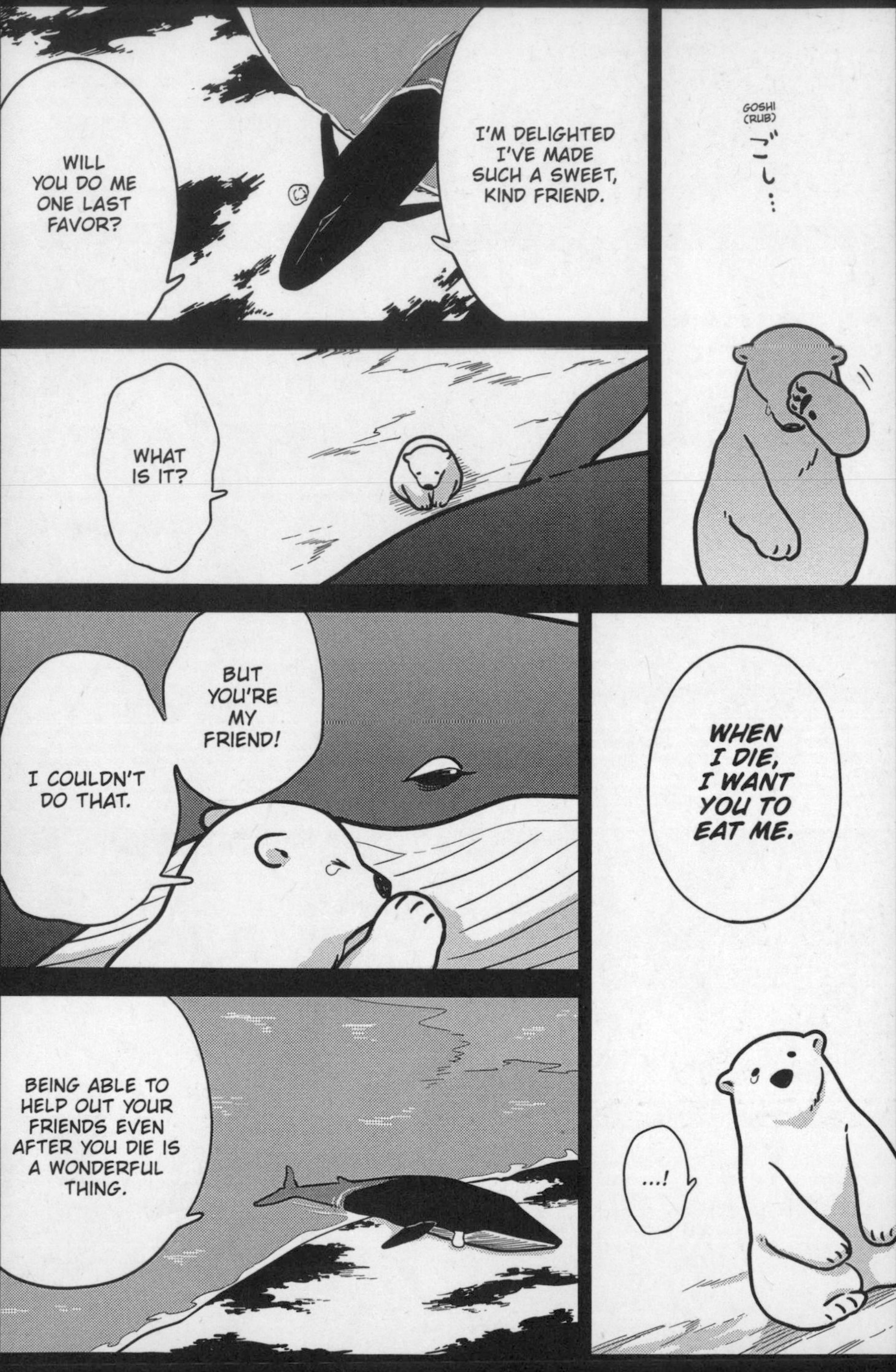
GOSHI (RUB)
ごし…
I'M DELIGHTED I'VE MADE SUCH A SWEET, KIND FRIEND.
WILL YOU DO ME ONE LAST FAVOR?
WHAT IS IT?
WHEN I DIE, I WANT YOU TO EAT ME.
...!
I COULDN'T DO THAT.
BUT YOU'RE MY FRIEND!
BEING ABLE TO HELP OUT YOUR FRIENDS EVEN AFTER YOU DIE IS A WONDERFUL THING.

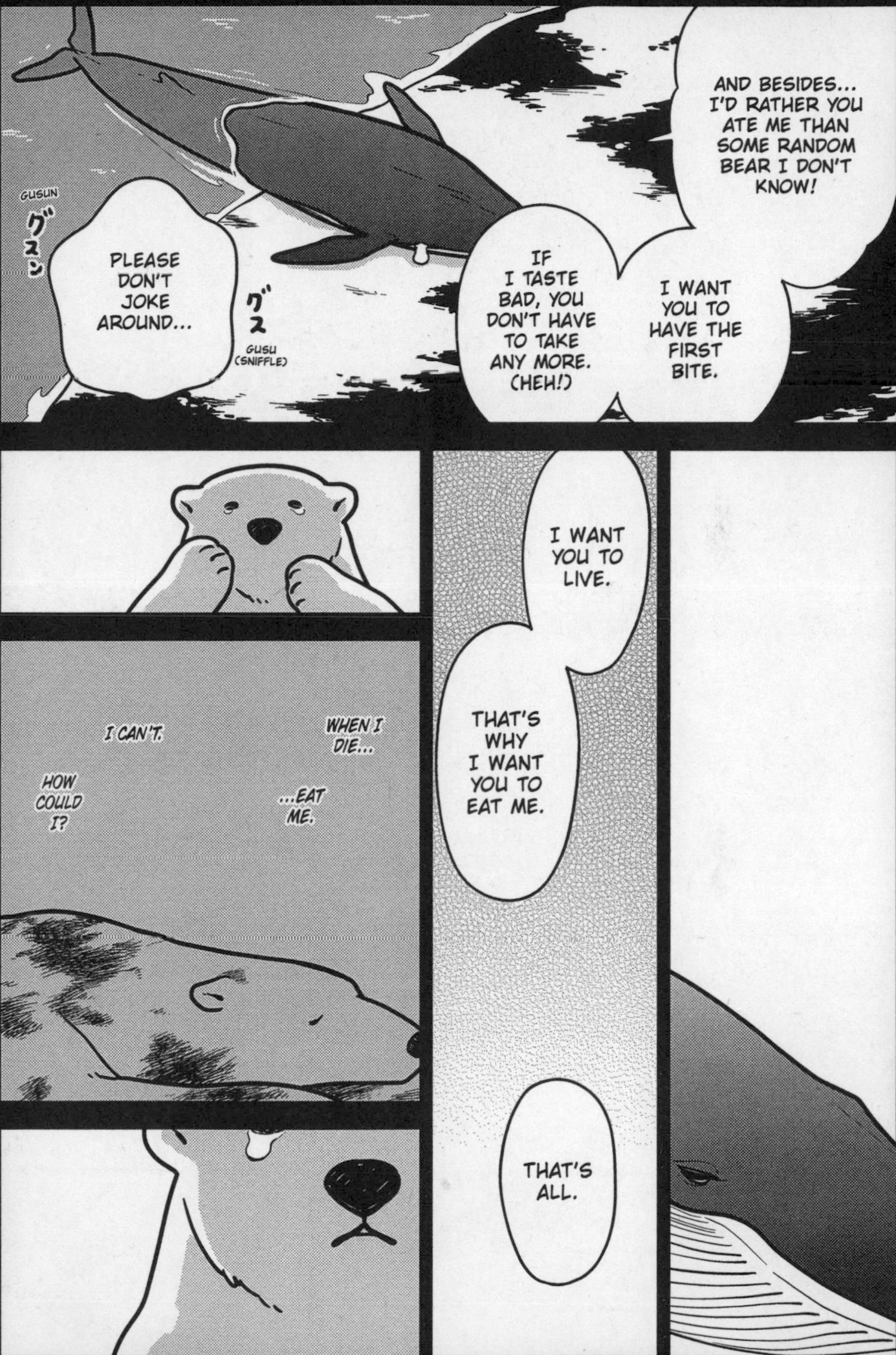
AND BESIDES... I'D RATHER YOU ATE ME THAN SOME RANDOM BEAR I DON'T KNOW!
I WANT YOU TO HAVE THE FIRST BITE.
IF I TASTE BAD, YOU DON'T HAVE TO TAKE ANY MORE. (HEH!)
グス
GUSU (SNIFFLE)
PLEASE DON'T JOKE AROUND...
グスン
GUSUN
I WANT YOU TO LIVE.
THAT'S WHY I WANT YOU TO EAT ME.
THAT'S ALL.
WHEN I DIE...
...EAT ME.
I CAN'T.
HOW COULD I?

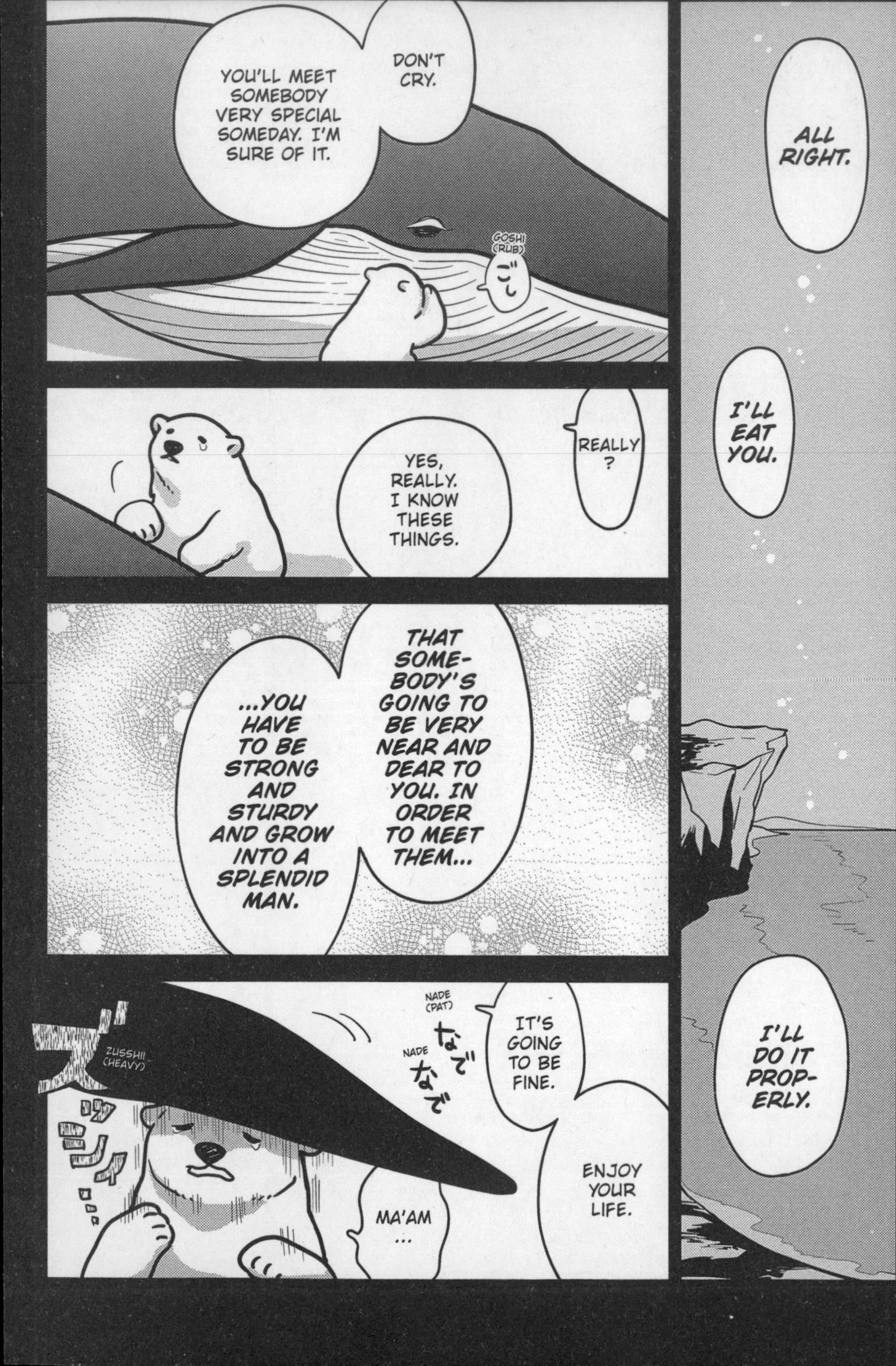
ALL RIGHT.
I'LL EAT YOU.
I'LL DO IT PROPERLY.
DON'T CRY.
YOU'LL MEET SOMEBODY VERY SPECIAL SOMEDAY. I'M SURE OF IT.
GOSHI (RUB)
ごし
REALLY?
YES, REALLY. I KNOW THESE THINGS.
THAT SOMEBODY'S GOING TO BE VERY NEAR AND DEAR TO YOU. IN ORDER TO MEET THEM...
...YOU HAVE TO BE STRONG AND STURDY AND GROW INTO A SPLENDID MAN.
IT'S GOING TO BE FINE.
ENJOY YOUR LIFE.
NADE (PAT)
なで
NADE
なで
ZUSSHII (HEAVY)
MA'AM...

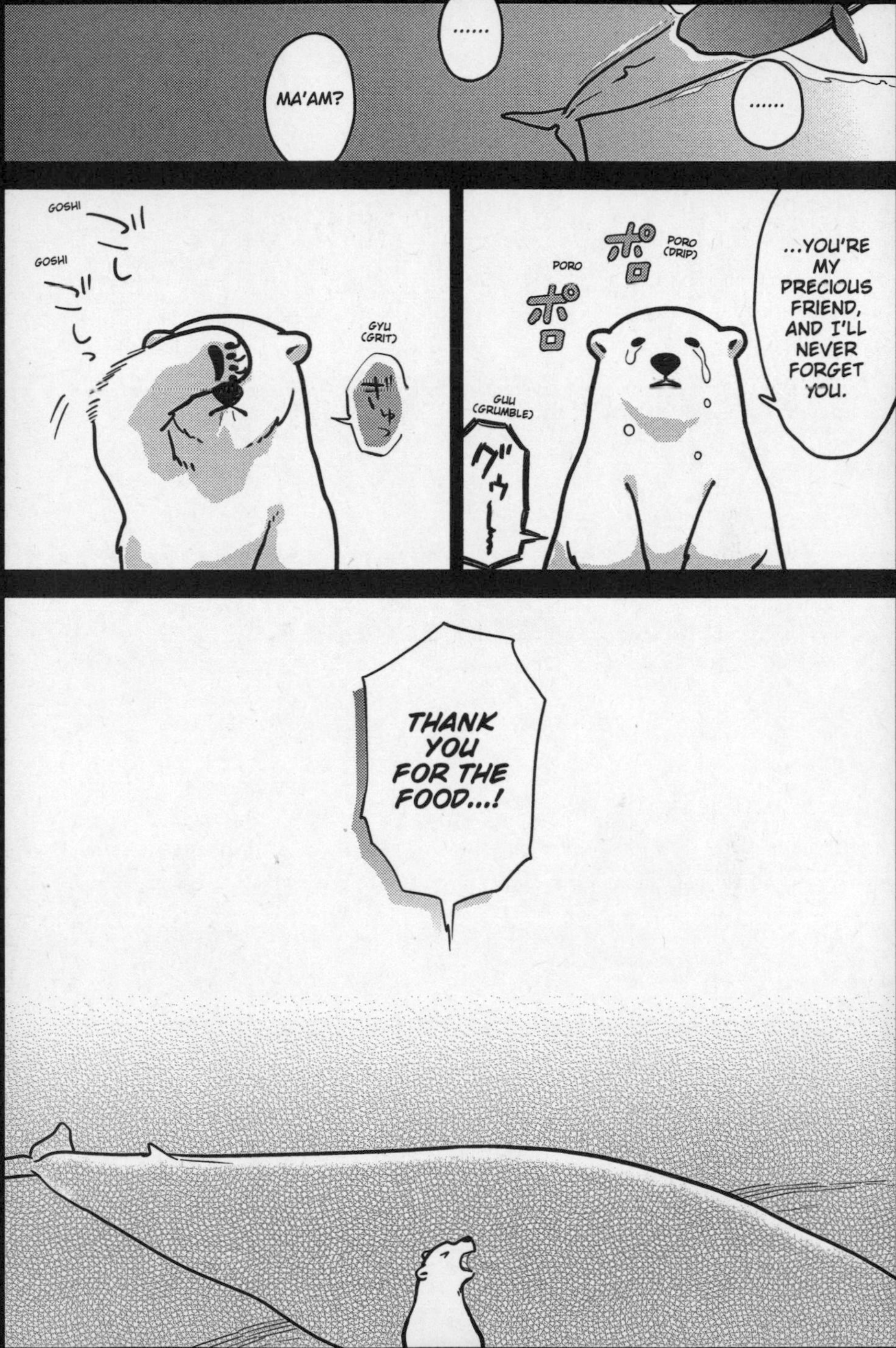
......
......
MA'AM?
...YOU'RE MY PRECIOUS FRIEND, AND I'LL NEVER FORGET YOU.
PORO (DRIP)
PORO
GUU (GRUMBLE)
GYU (GRIT)
GOSHI
GOSHI
THANK YOU FOR THE FOOD...!

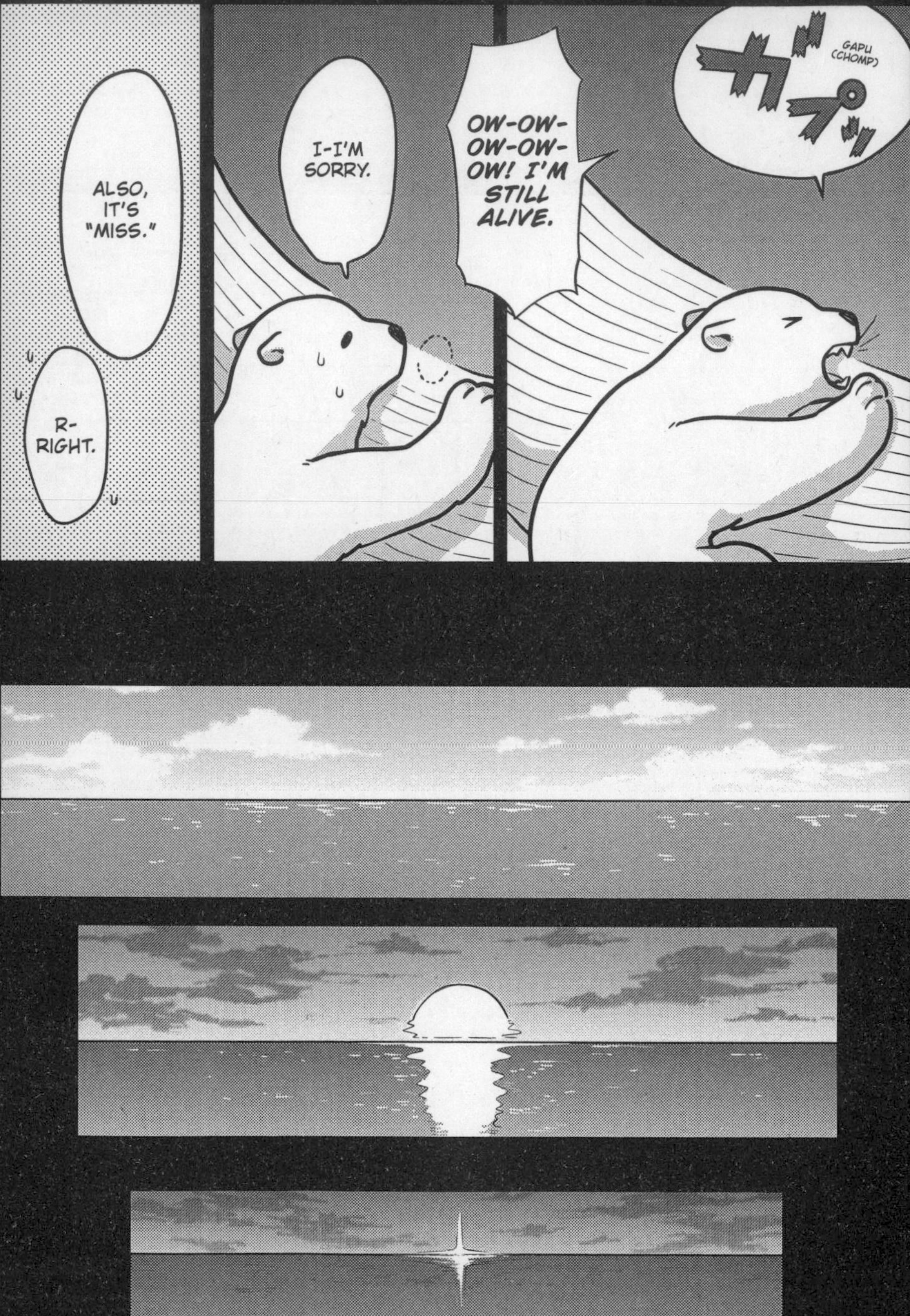
ガプッ
GAPU (CHOMP)
OW-OW-OW-OW-OW! I'M STILL ALIVE.
I-I'M SORRY.
ALSO, IT'S "MISS."
R-RIGHT.

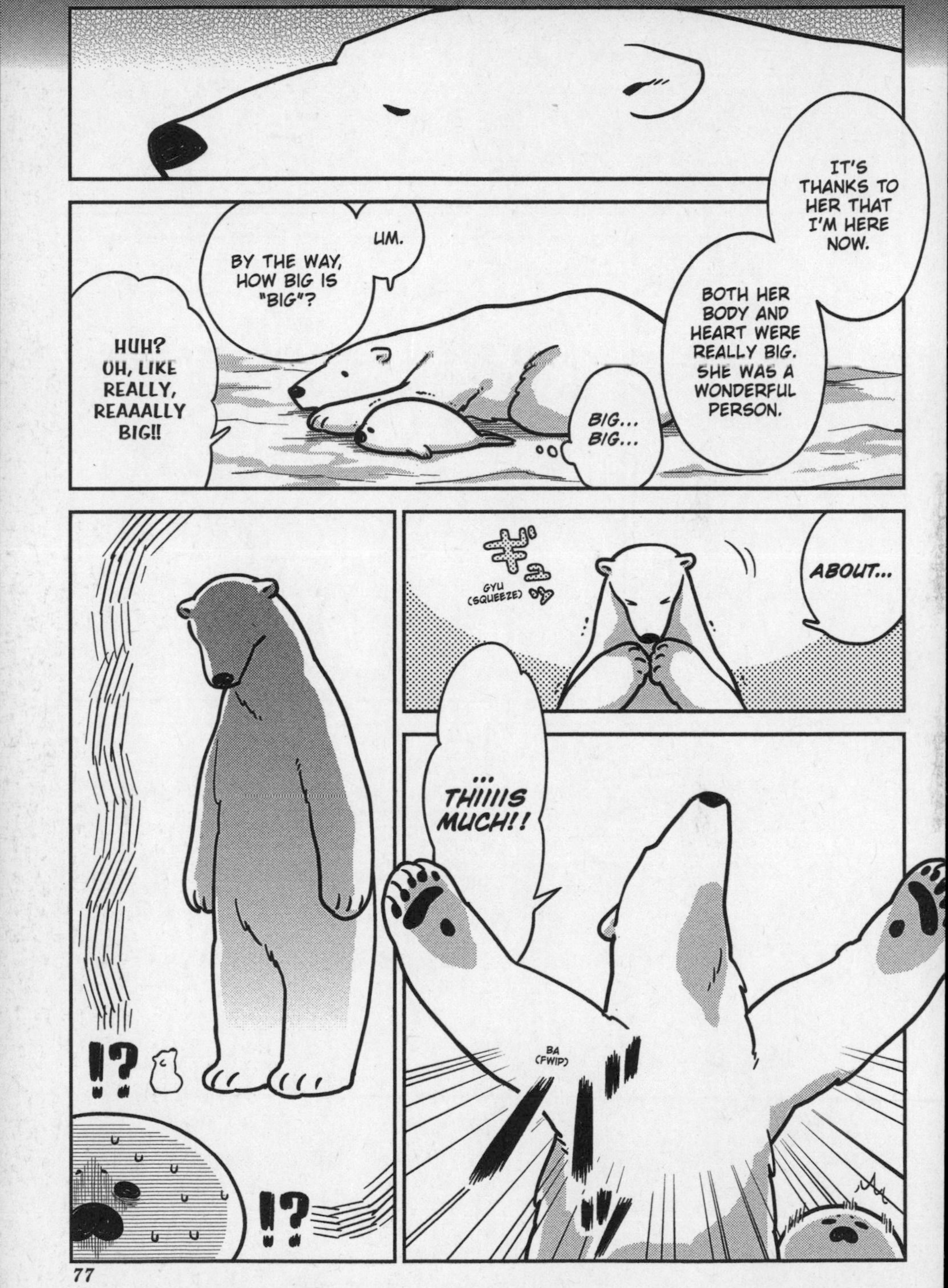
IT'S THANKS TO HER THAT I'M HERE NOW.
BOTH HER BODY AND HEART WERE REALLY BIG. SHE WAS A WONDERFUL PERSON.
BIG... BIG...
UM.
BY THE WAY, HOW BIG IS "BIG"?
HUH? OH, LIKE REALLY, REAAALLY BIG!!
ABOUT...
GYU (SQUEEZE)
...THIIIIS MUCH!!
BA (FWIP)
!?
!?

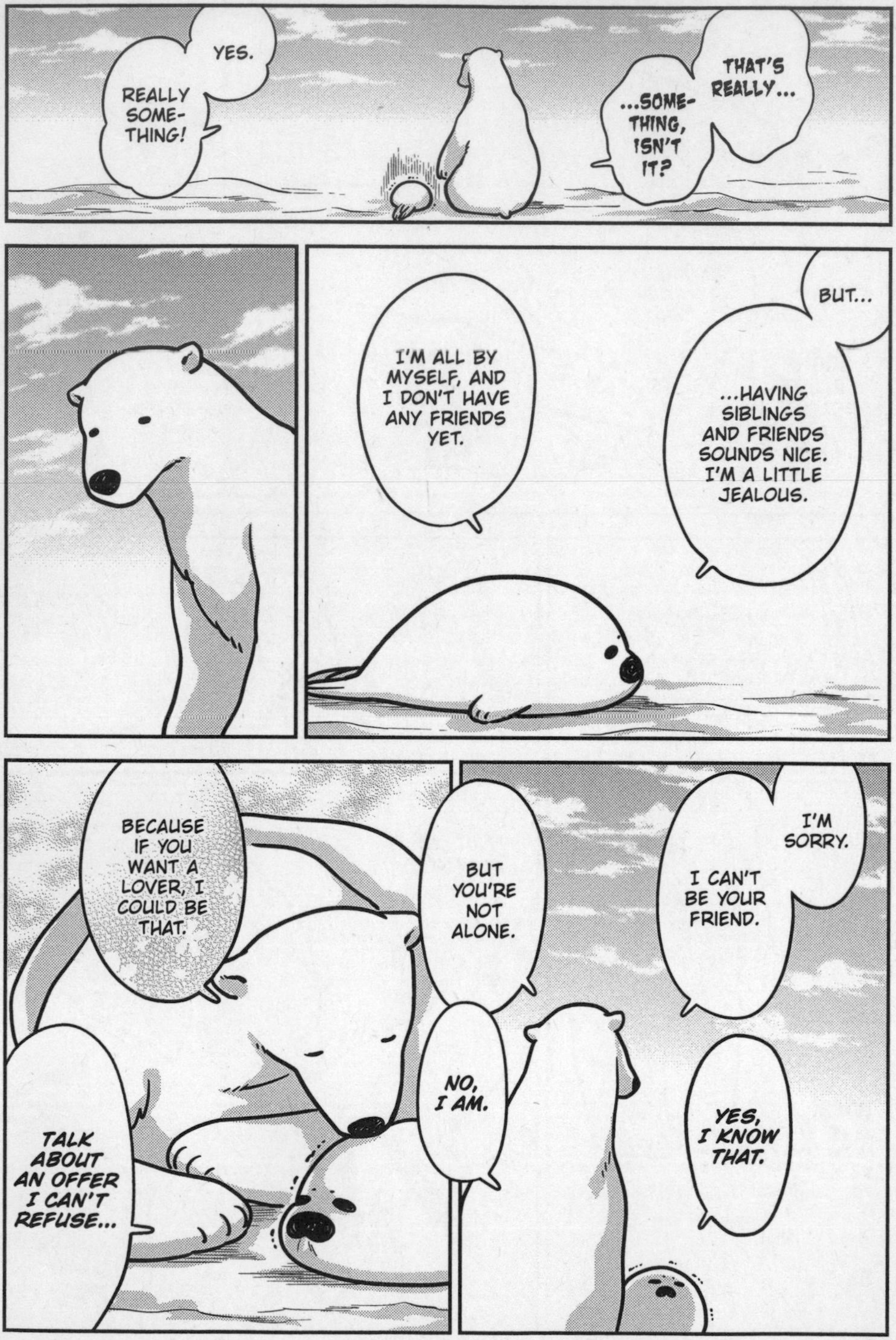
THAT'S REALLY...
...SOME-THING, ISN'T IT?
YES.
REALLY SOME-THING!
BUT...
...HAVING SIBLINGS AND FRIENDS SOUNDS NICE. I'M A LITTLE JEALOUS.
I'M ALL BY MYSELF, AND I DON'T HAVE ANY FRIENDS YET.
I'M SORRY.
I CAN'T BE YOUR FRIEND.
BUT YOU'RE NOT ALONE.
NO, I AM.
YES, I KNOW THAT.
BECAUSE IF YOU WANT A LOVER, I COULD BE THAT.
TALK ABOUT AN OFFER I CAN'T REFUSE...

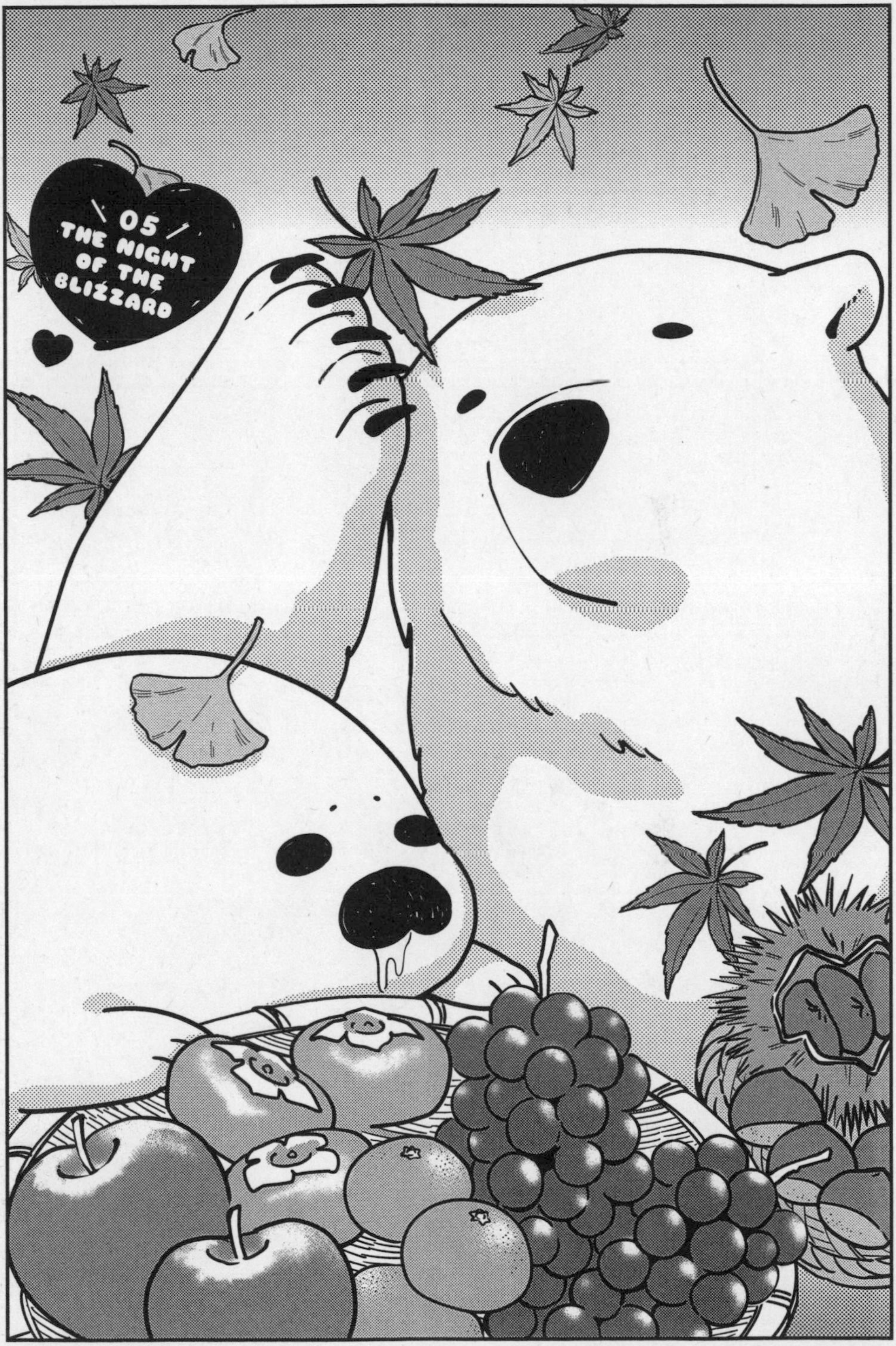
05
THE NIGHT OF THE BLIZZARD

IF YOU DON'T SAY IT, THEY WON'T GET IT

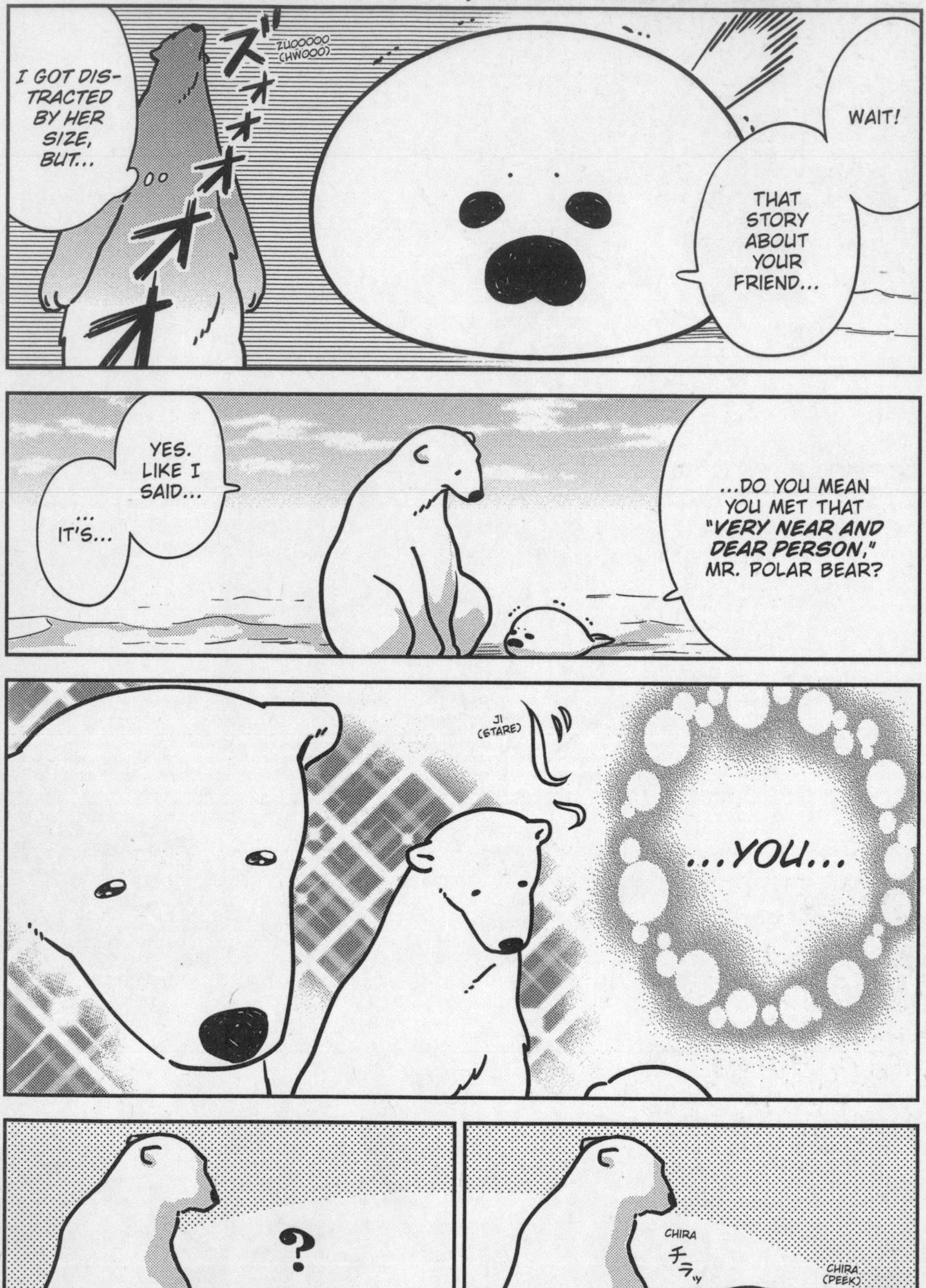
WAIT!
THAT STORY ABOUT YOUR FRIEND...
ZUOOOOO (HWOOO)
I GOT DISTRACTED BY HER SIZE, BUT...
...DO YOU MEAN YOU MET THAT "VERY NEAR AND DEAR PERSON," MR. POLAR BEAR?
YES. LIKE I SAID...
... IT'S...
...YOU...
JI (STARE)
CHIRA (PEEK)
チラッ
CHIRA
チラッ
?

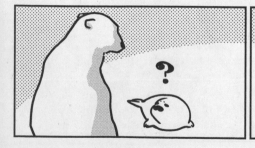

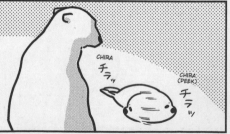

EVEN IF YOU SAY IT, THEY STILL WON'T GET IT

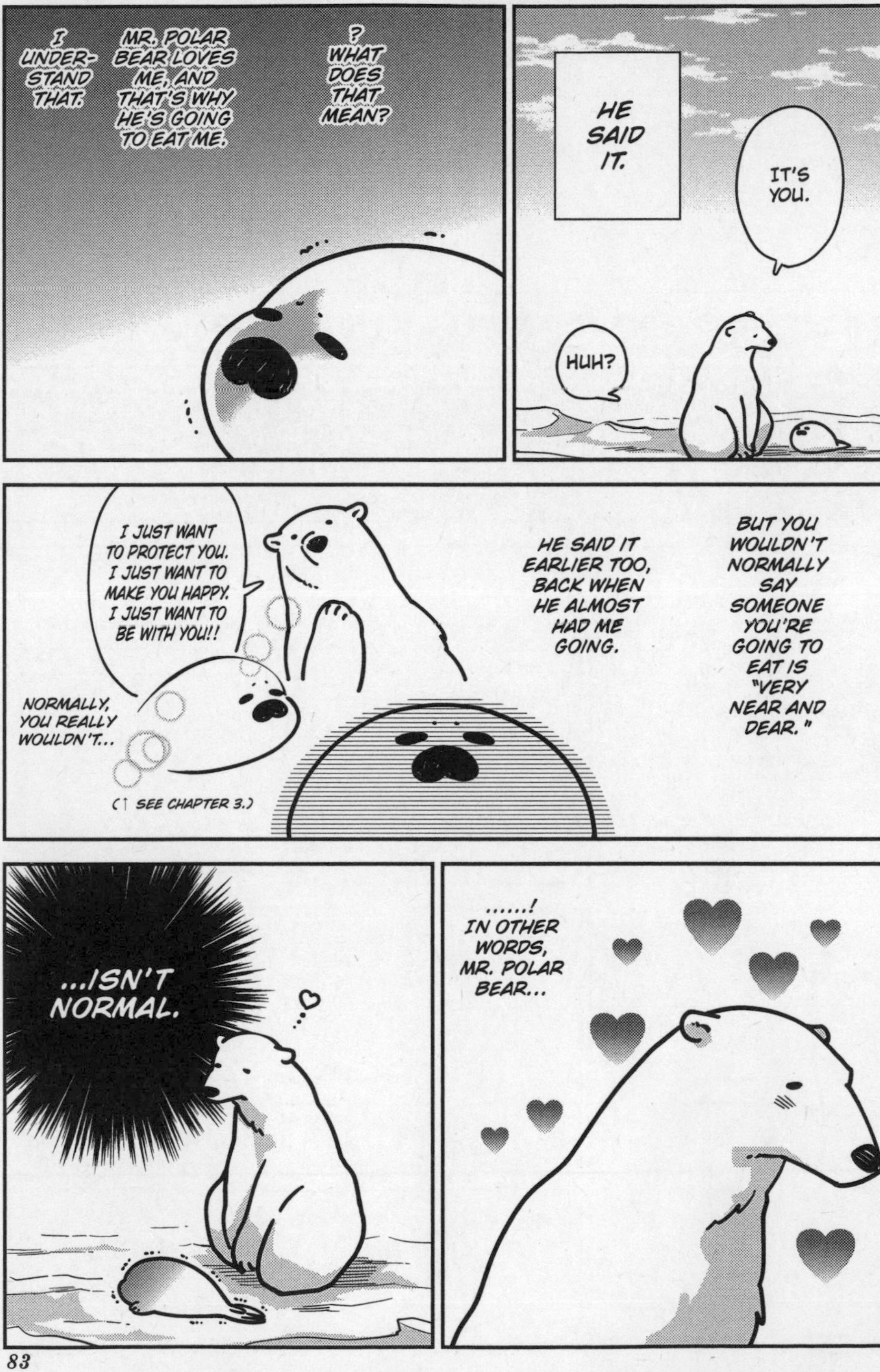
IT'S YOU.
HE SAID IT.
HUH?
? WHAT DOES THAT MEAN?
MR. POLAR BEAR LOVES ME, AND THAT'S WHY HE'S GOING TO EAT ME.
I UNDERSTAND THAT.
BUT YOU WOULDN'T NORMALLY SAY SOMEONE YOU'RE GOING TO EAT IS "VERY NEAR AND DEAR."
HE SAID IT EARLIER TOO, BACK WHEN HE ALMOST HAD ME GOING.
I JUST WANT TO PROTECT YOU. I JUST WANT TO MAKE YOU HAPPY. I JUST WANT TO BE WITH YOU!!
NORMALLY, YOU REALLY WOULDN'T...
(↑ SEE CHAPTER 3.)
......! IN OTHER WORDS, MR. POLAR BEAR...
...ISN'T NORMAL.

YOUR WISH IS...

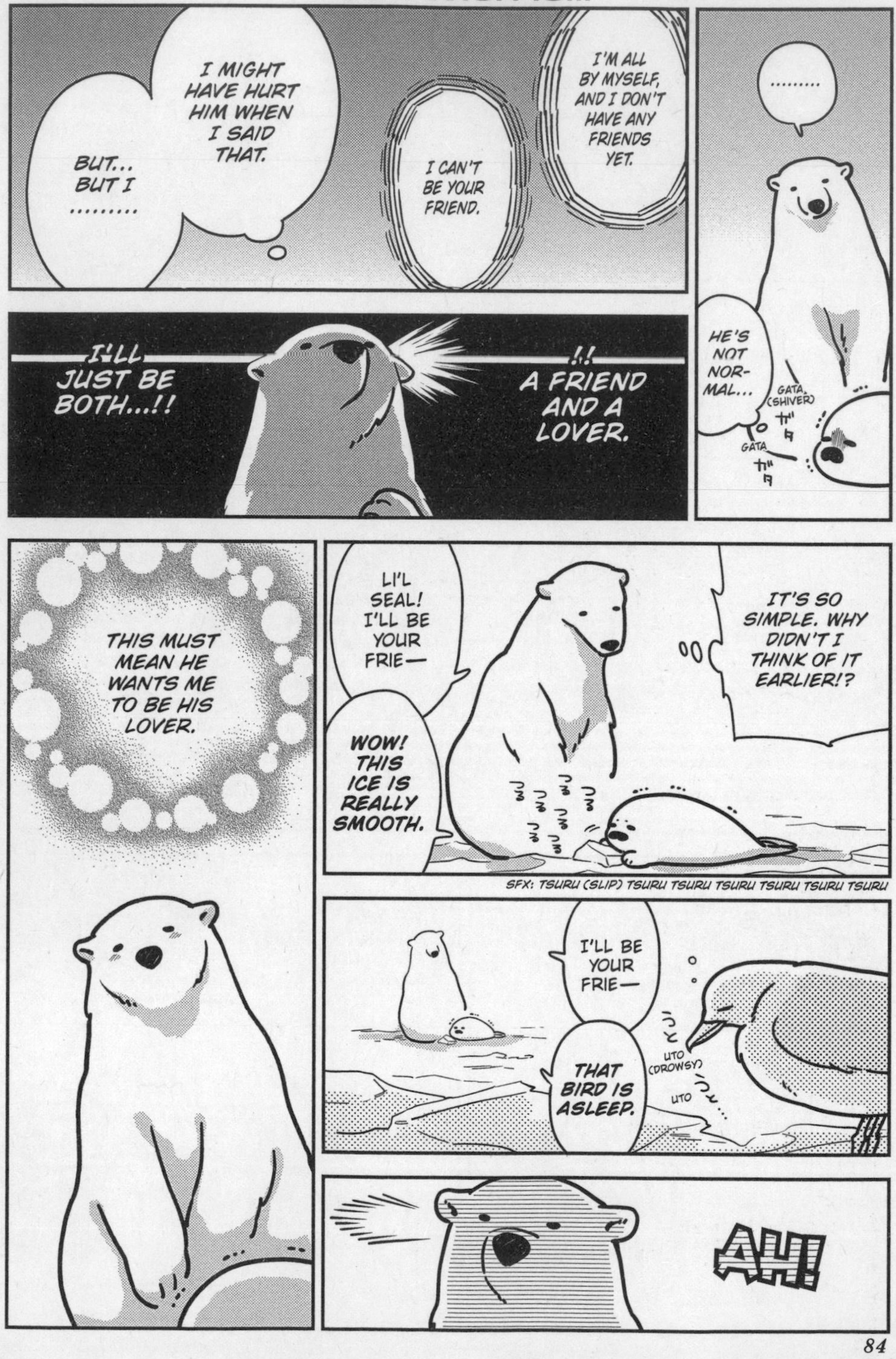

....
HE'S NOT NOR-MAL...
GATA (SHIVER)
GATA
I'M ALL BY MYSELF, AND I DON'T HAVE ANY FRIENDS YET.
I CAN'T BE YOUR FRIEND.
I MIGHT HAVE HURT HIM WHEN I SAID THAT.
BUT... BUT I ....
!!
A FRIEND AND A LOVER.
I'LL JUST BE BOTH...!!
IT'S SO SIMPLE. WHY DIDN'T I THINK OF IT EARLIER!?
LI'L SEAL! I'LL BE YOUR FRIE—
WOW! THIS ICE IS REALLY SMOOTH.
SFX: TSURU (SLIP) TSURU TSURU TSURU TSURU TSURU TSURU
I'LL BE YOUR FRIE—
THAT BIRD IS ASLEEP.
UTO (DROWSY)
UTO
AH!
THIS MUST MEAN HE WANTS ME TO BE HIS LOVER.

I WANT TO GO BACK TO MY MOM

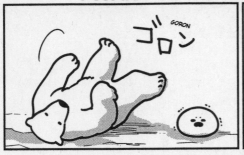

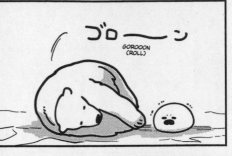

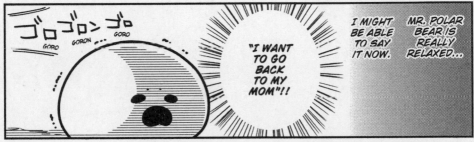

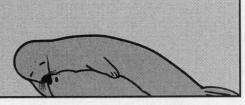

ゴローーン
GOROOON (ROLL)
ゴロン
GORON
MR. POLAR BEAR IS REALLY RELAXED...
I MIGHT BE ABLE TO SAY IT NOW.
"I WANT TO GO BACK TO MY MOM"!!
ゴロゴロンゴロ
GORO
GORON
GORO
I ALMOST GAVE UP ON SURVIVING ONCE... WELL, NO, LOTS OF TIMES...
BUT I DO WANT TO LIVE, AND I DO WANT TO SEE MOM AGAIN!!
ゴロン
GORON
UM...!!

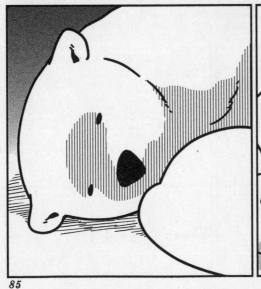

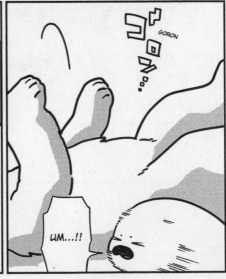

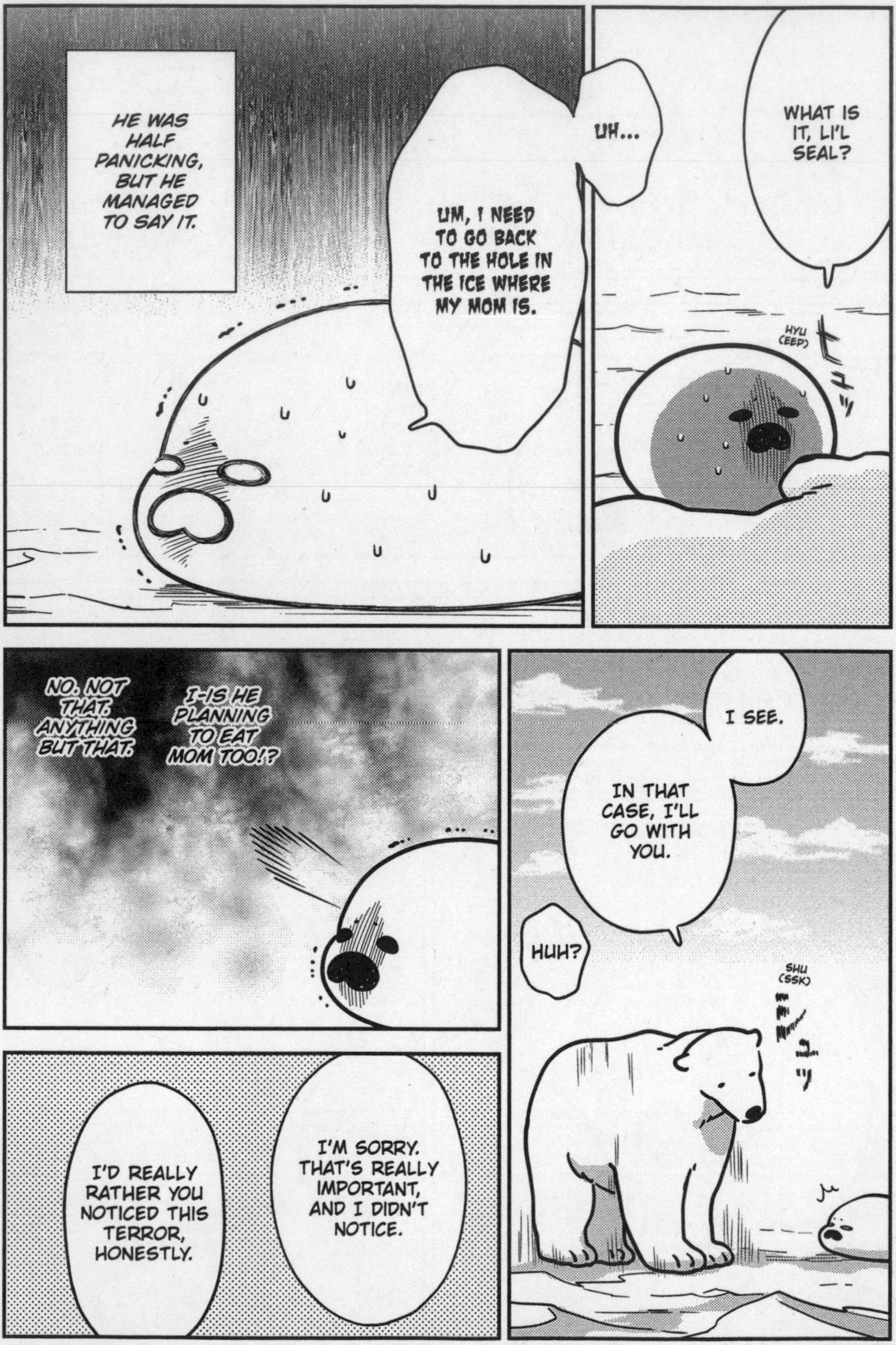
WHAT IS IT, LI'L SEAL?
HYU (EEP)
UH...
UM, I NEED TO GO BACK TO THE HOLE IN THE ICE WHERE MY MOM IS.
HE WAS HALF PANICKING, BUT HE MANAGED TO SAY IT.
I SEE.
IN THAT CASE, I'LL GO WITH YOU.
HUH?
SHU (SSK)
I-IS HE PLANNING TO EAT MOM TOO!?
NO. NOT THAT. ANYTHING BUT THAT.
I'M SORRY. THAT'S REALLY IMPORTANT, AND I DIDN'T NOTICE.
I'D REALLY RATHER YOU NOTICED THIS TERROR, HONESTLY.

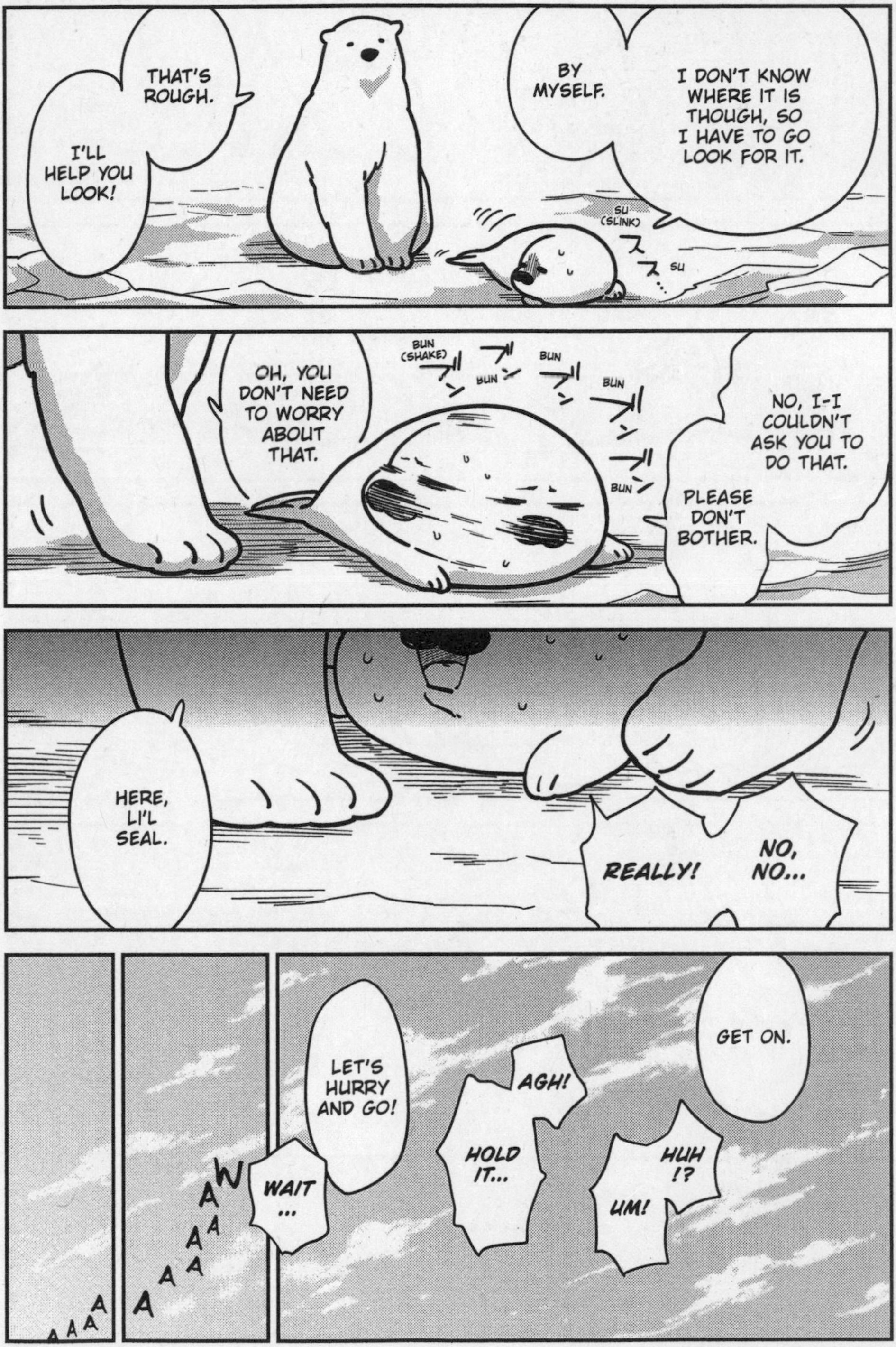
I DON'T KNOW WHERE IT IS THOUGH, SO I HAVE TO GO LOOK FOR IT.
BY MYSELF.
SU (SLINK)
SU
THAT'S ROUGH.
I'LL HELP YOU LOOK!
NO, I-I COULDN'T ASK YOU TO DO THAT.
PLEASE DON'T BOTHER.
BUN (SHAKE)
BUN
BUN
BUN
BUN
OH, YOU DON'T NEED TO WORRY ABOUT THAT.
NO, NO...
REALLY!
HERE, LI'L SEAL.
GET ON.
HUH !?
UM!
AGH!
HOLD IT...
LET'S HURRY AND GO!
WAIT ...
WAAAAAAA
AAAA

DREAM-WORLD

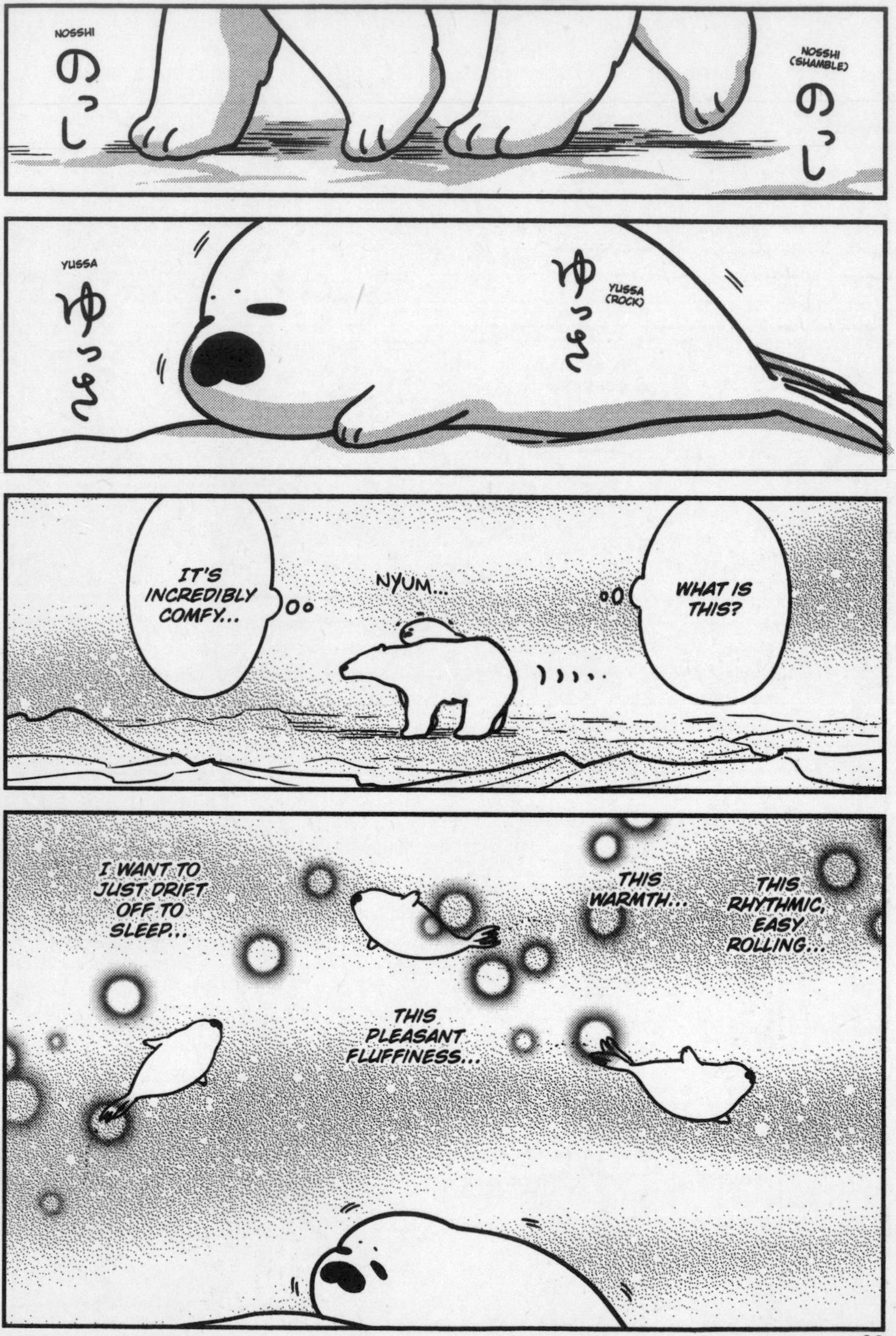
のっし
NOSSHI (SHAMBLE)
のっし
NOSSHI
ゆっさ
YUSSA (ROCK)
ゆっさ
YUSSA
WHAT IS THIS?
NYUM...
IT'S INCREDIBLY COMFY...
THIS RHYTHMIC, EASY ROLLING...
THIS WARMTH...
THIS PLEASANT FLUFFINESS...
I WANT TO JUST DRIFT OFF TO SLEEP...

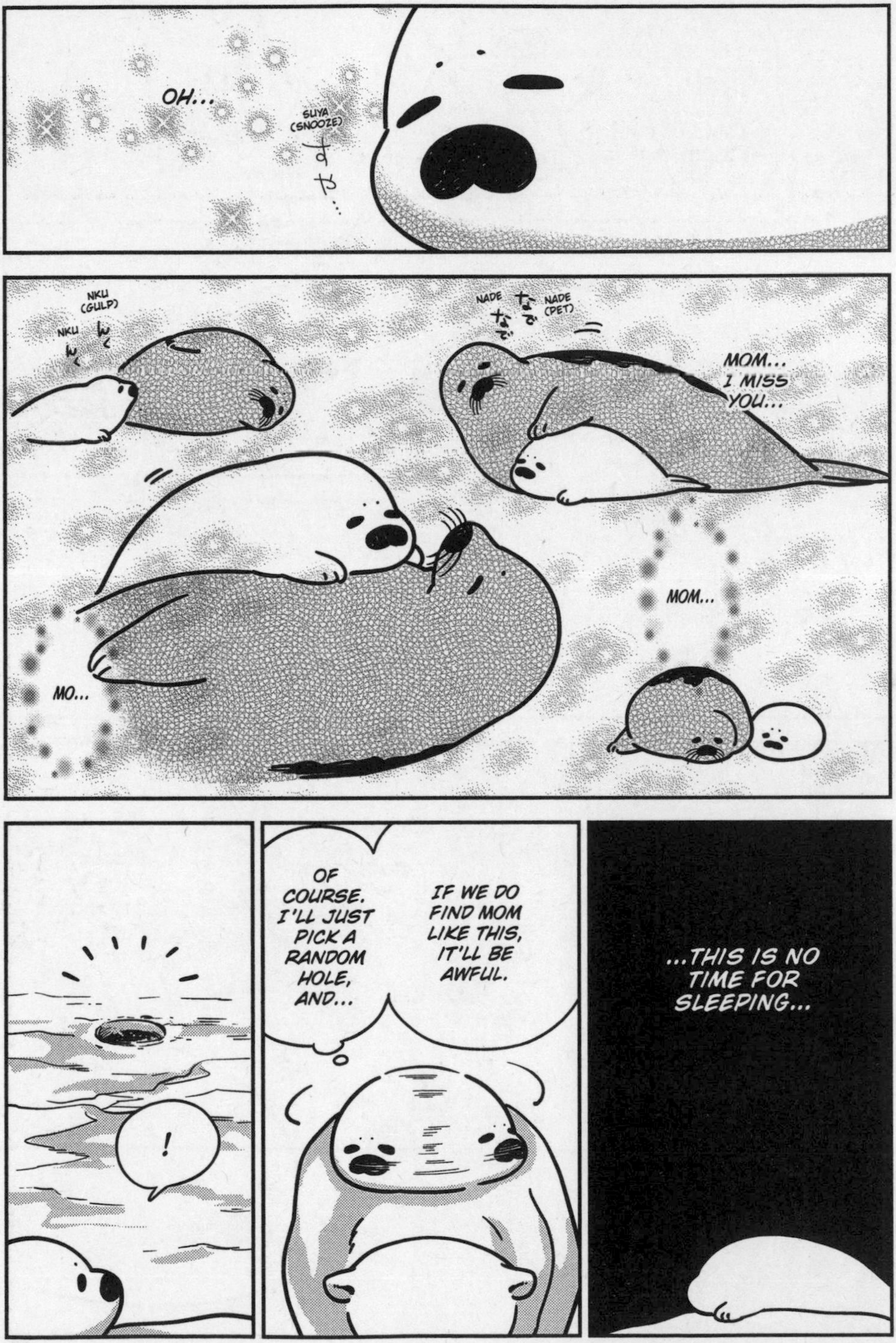
SUIYA (SNOOZE)
すや…
OH...
NADE
なで
NADE (PET)
なで
MOM... I MISS YOU...
NKU (GULP)
んく
NKU
んく
MOM...
MO...
...THIS IS NO TIME FOR SLEEPING...
IF WE DO FIND MOM LIKE THIS, IT'LL BE AWFUL.
OF COURSE. I'LL JUST PICK A RANDOM HOLE, AND...
!

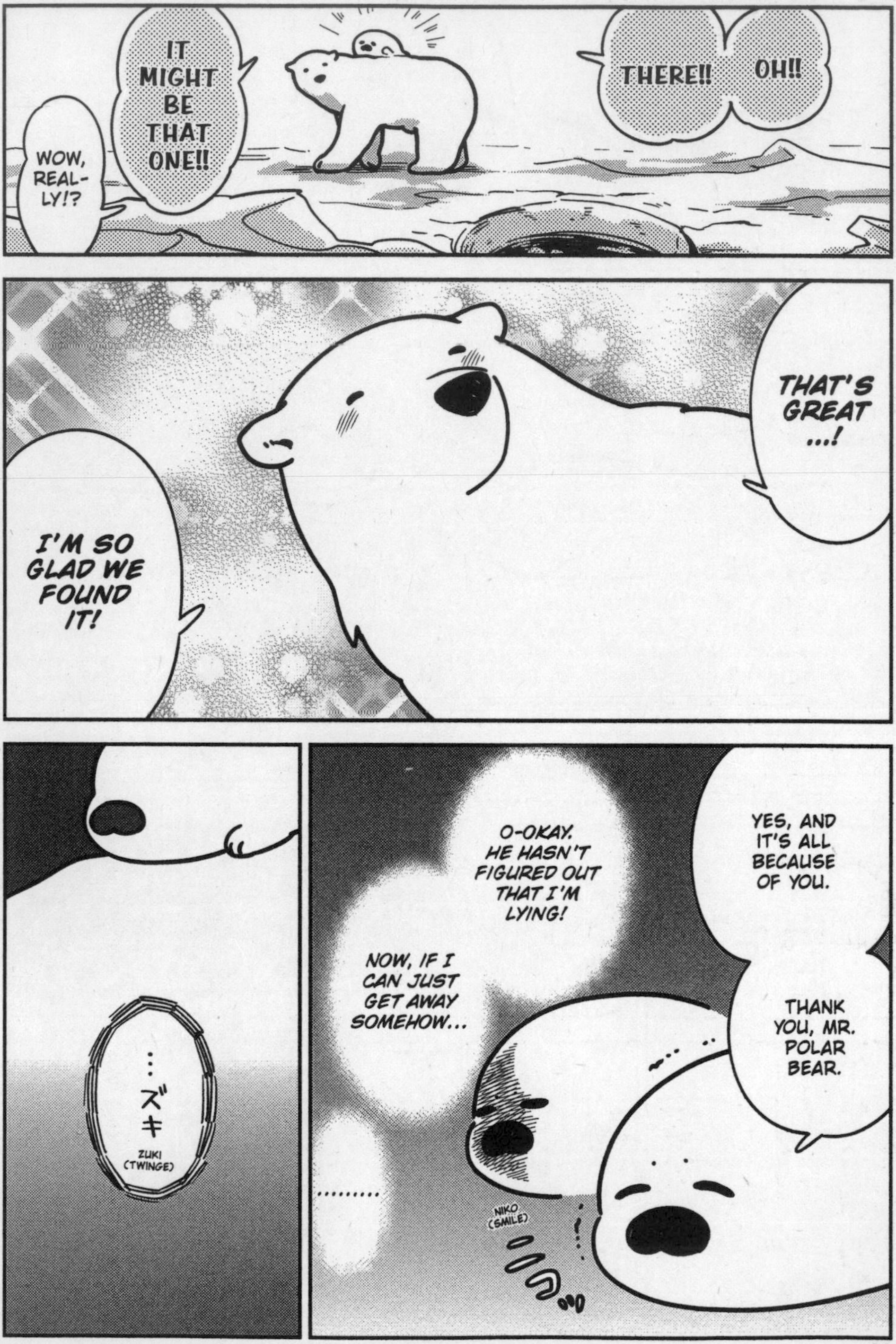
OH!!
THERE!!
IT MIGHT BE THAT ONE!!
WOW, REALLY!?
THAT'S GREAT ...!
I'M SO GLAD WE FOUND IT!
YES, AND IT'S ALL BECAUSE OF YOU.
O-OKAY. HE HASN'T FIGURED OUT THAT I'M LYING!
NOW, IF I CAN JUST GET AWAY SOMEHOW...
THANK YOU, MR. POLAR BEAR.
....
NIKO (SMILE)
...ズキ
ZUKI (TWINGE)

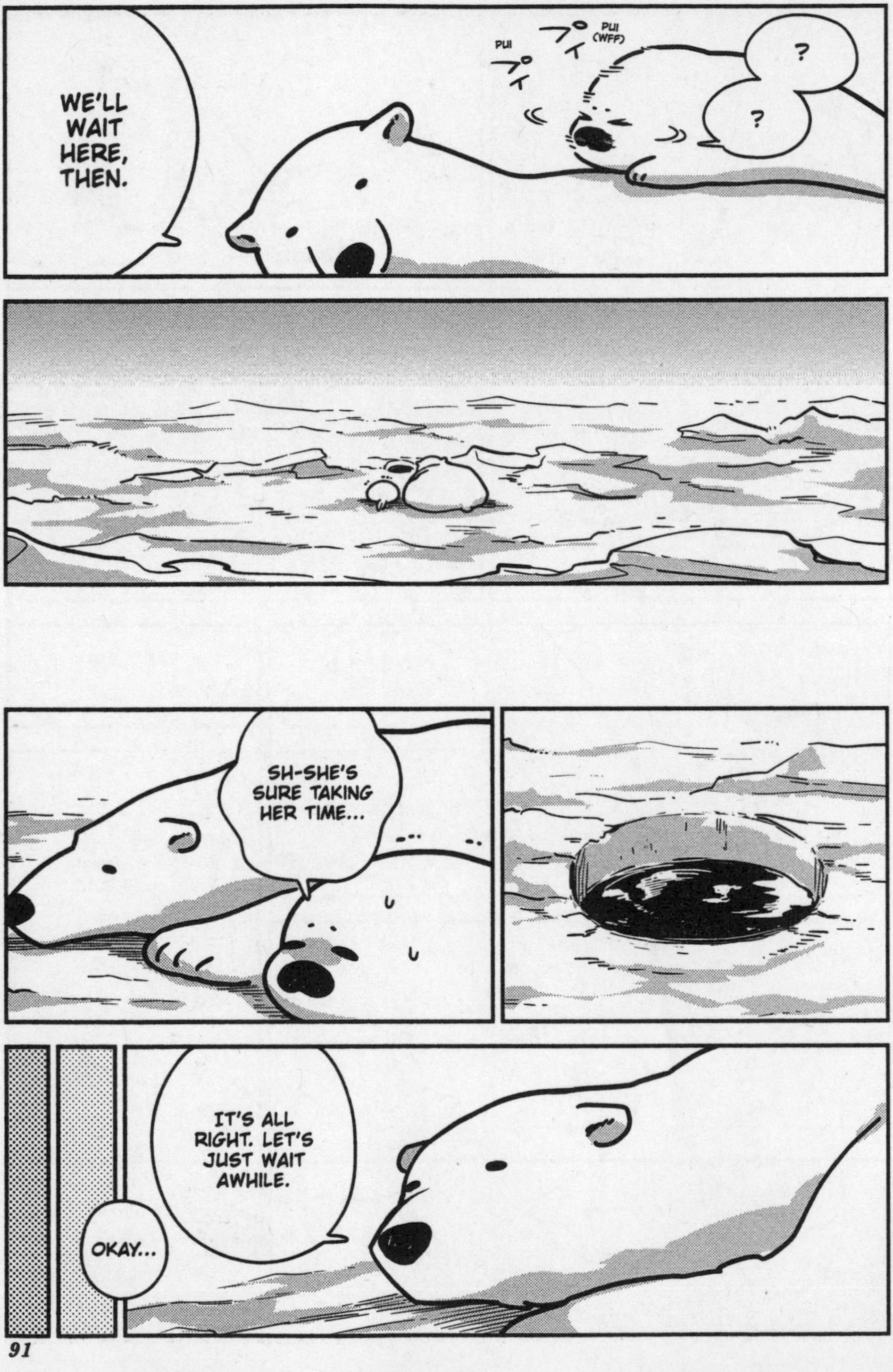
?
?
PUI (WFF)
PUI
WE'LL WAIT HERE, THEN.
SH-SHE'S SURE TAKING HER TIME...
IT'S ALL RIGHT. LET'S JUST WAIT AWHILE.
OKAY...

THE NIGHT OF THE BLIZZARD

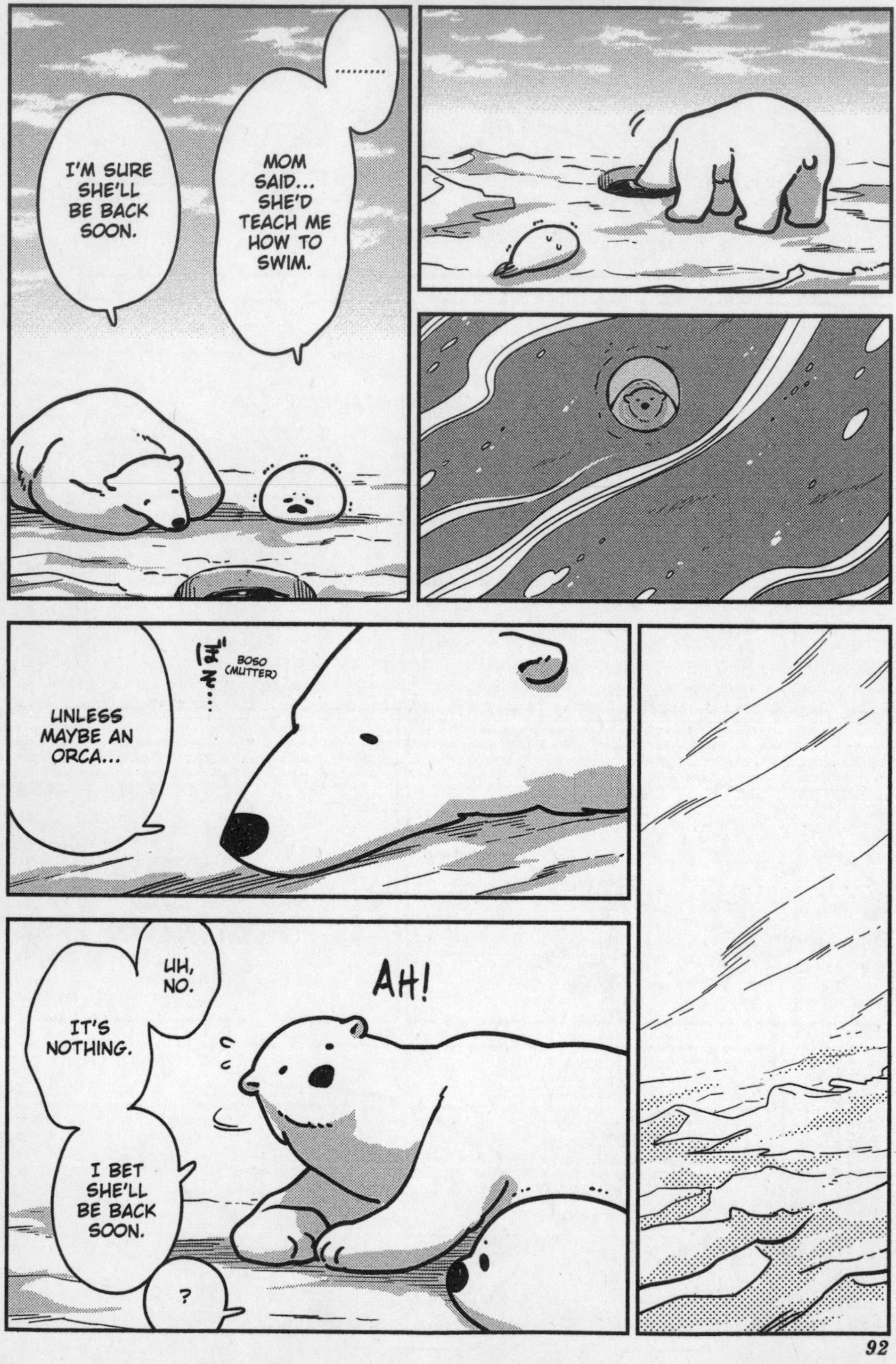

....
MOM SAID... SHE'D TEACH ME HOW TO SWIM.
I'M SURE SHE'LL BE BACK SOON.
ぼそ…
BOSO (MUTTER)
UNLESS MAYBE AN ORCA...
AH!
UH, NO.
IT'S NOTHING.
I BET SHE'LL BE BACK SOON.
?

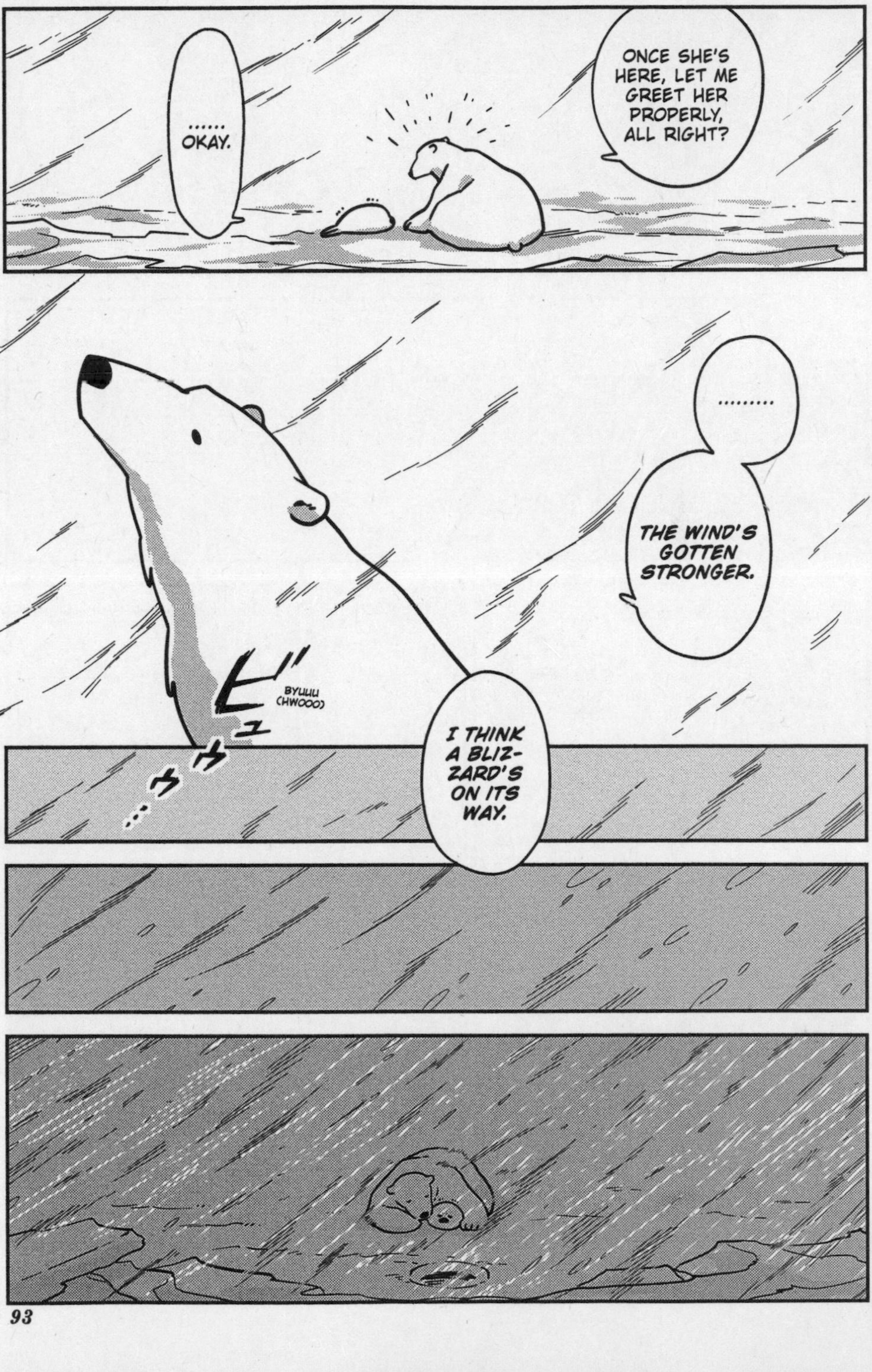
ONCE SHE'S HERE, LET ME GREET HER PROPERLY, ALL RIGHT?
...... OKAY.
....
THE WIND'S GOTTEN STRONGER.
I THINK A BLIZ-ZARD'S ON ITS WAY.
BYUUU (HWOOO)

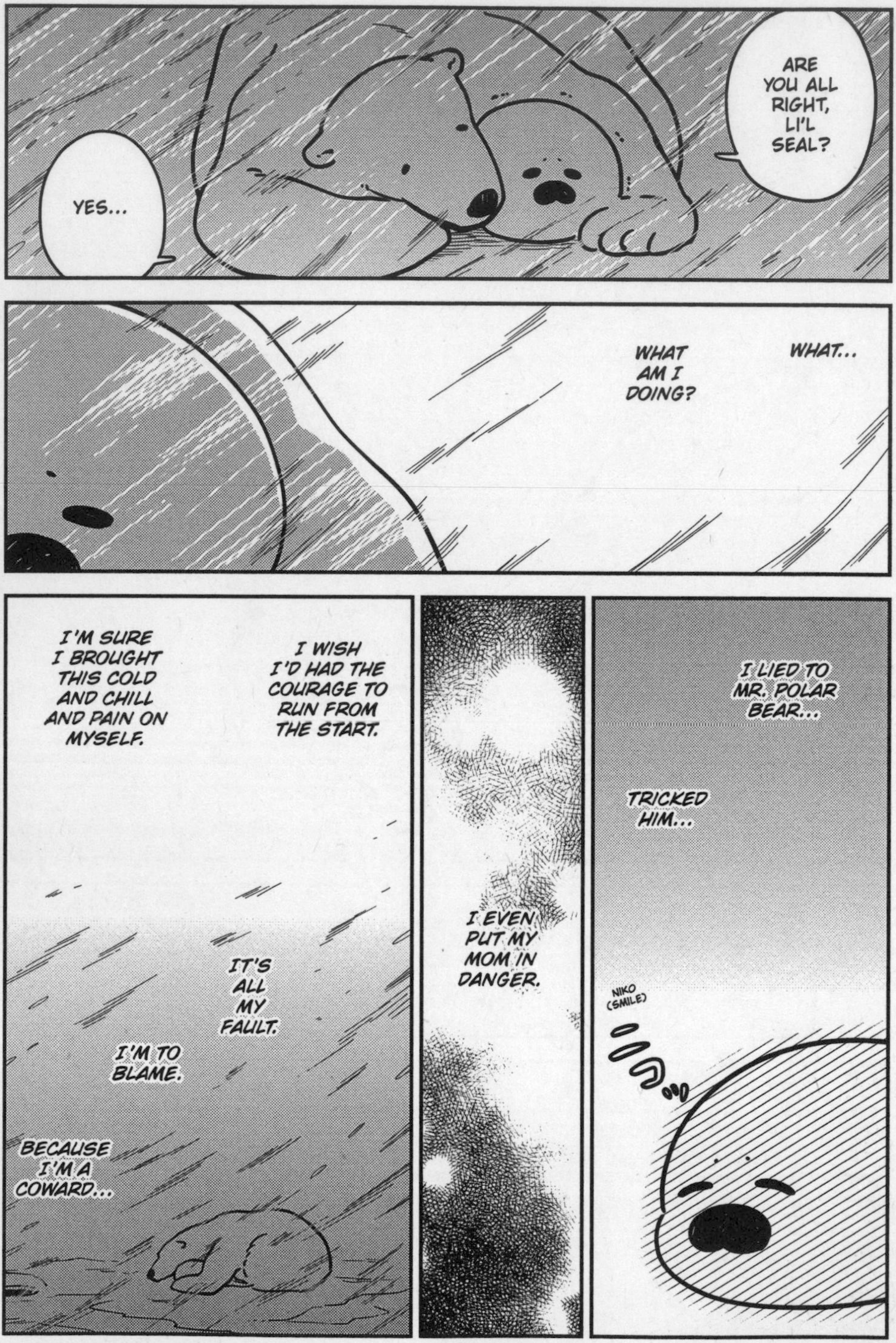
ARE YOU ALL RIGHT, LI'L SEAL?
YES...
WHAT...
WHAT AM I DOING?
I LIED TO MR. POLAR BEAR...
TRICKED HIM...
NIKO (SMILE)
I EVEN PUT MY MOM IN DANGER.
I WISH I'D HAD THE COURAGE TO RUN FROM THE START.
I'M SURE I BROUGHT THIS COLD AND CHILL AND PAIN ON MYSELF.
IT'S ALL MY FAULT.
I'M TO BLAME.
BECAUSE I'M A COWARD...

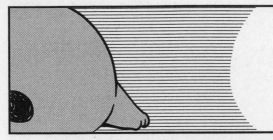

...I MIGHT BE ABLE TO BLEND INTO THE BLIZZARD AND GET AWAY NOW.

.... BUT...

LI'L SEAL!?

WAAAAAAH!

W—

GABA (SHUP)

GU (STRAIN)

ZA

ZA (SHUF)

GOOOOOO (FOOOM)

ZA

95

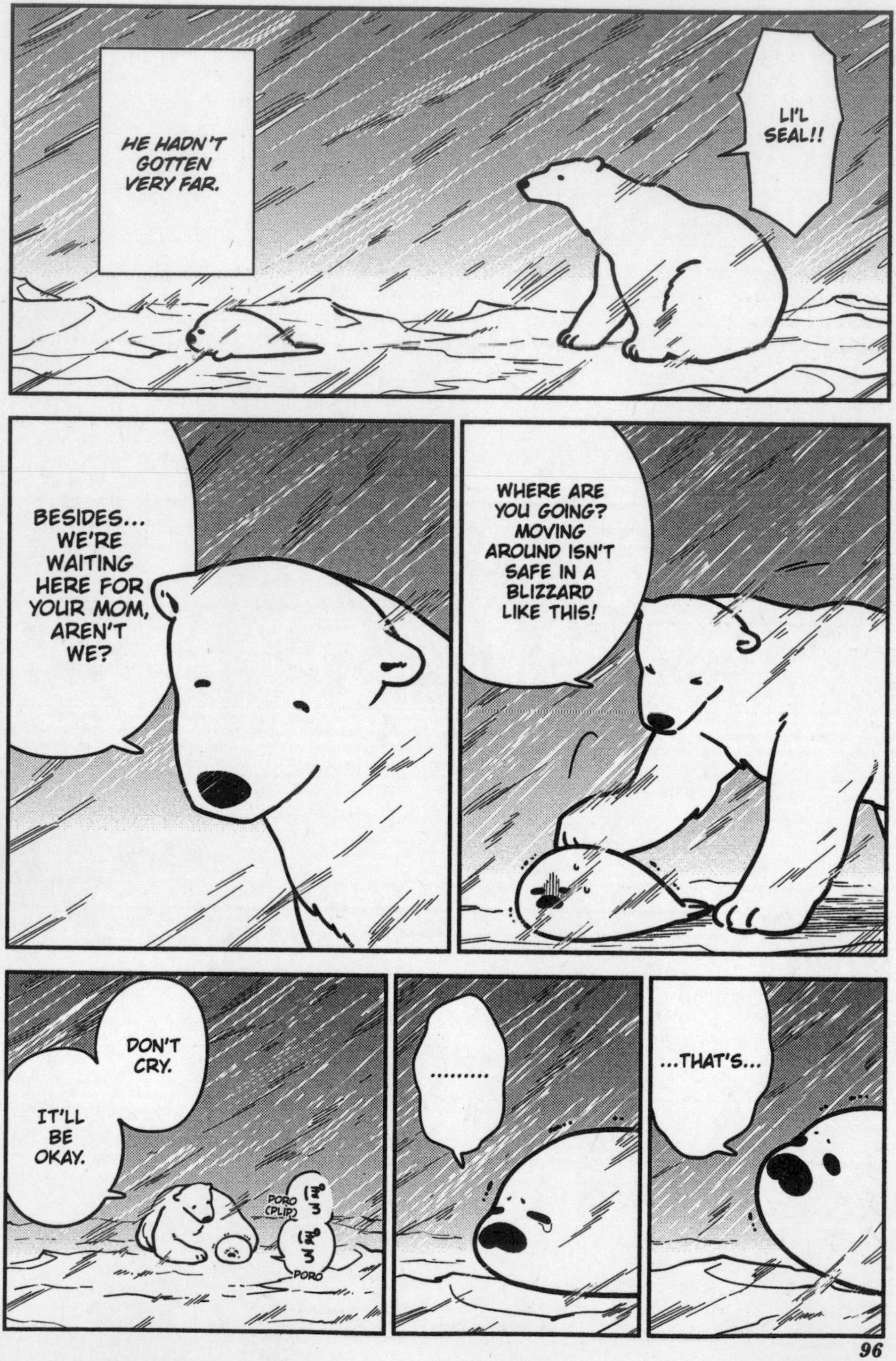
LI'L SEAL!!
HE HADN'T GOTTEN VERY FAR.
WHERE ARE YOU GOING? MOVING AROUND ISN'T SAFE IN A BLIZZARD LIKE THIS!
BESIDES... WE'RE WAITING HERE FOR YOUR MOM, AREN'T WE?
...THAT'S...
....
DON'T CRY.
IT'LL BE OKAY.
PORO (PLIP)
PORO

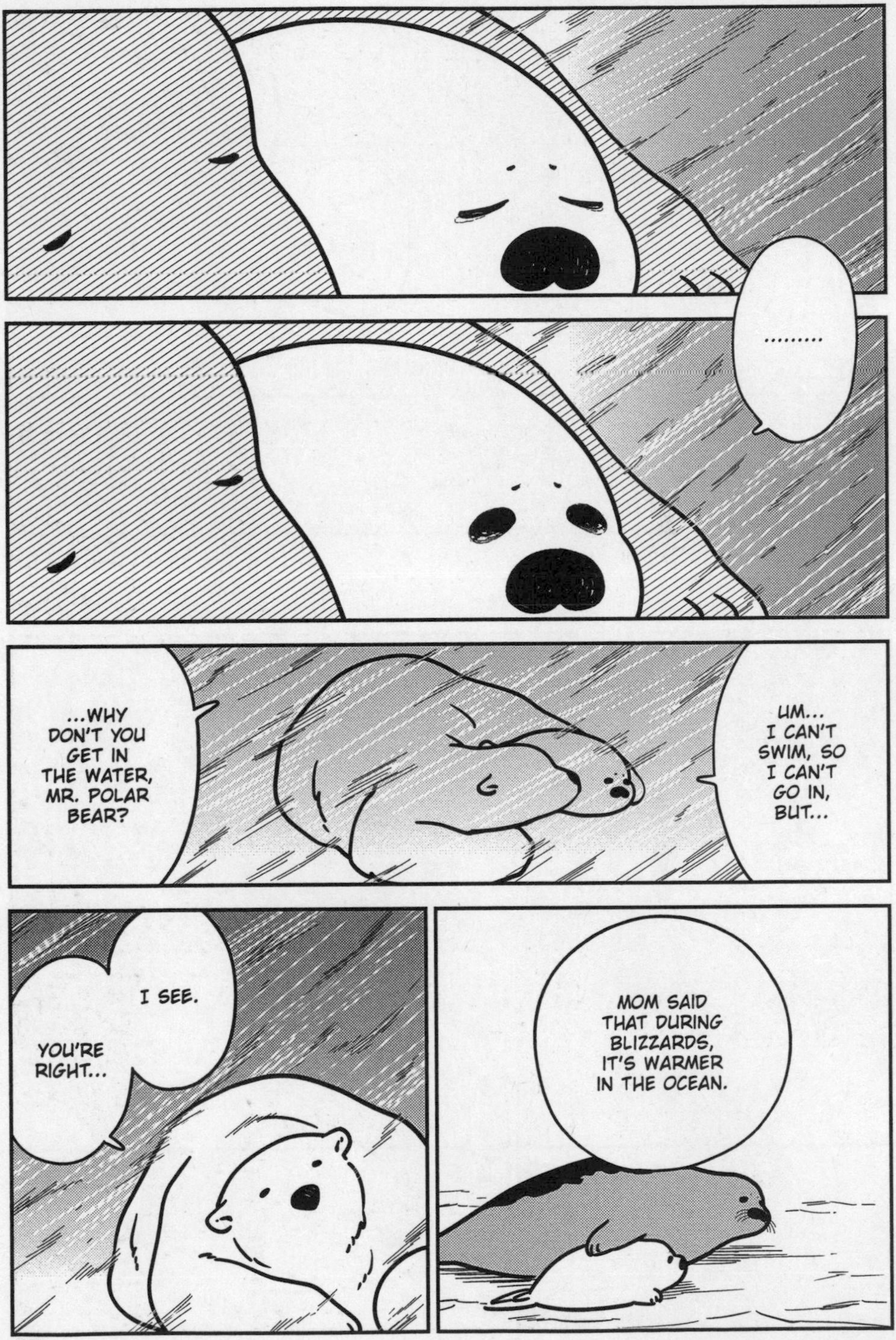
....
UM... I CAN'T SWIM, SO I CAN'T GO IN, BUT...
...WHY DON'T YOU GET IN THE WATER, MR. POLAR BEAR?
MOM SAID THAT DURING BLIZZARDS, IT'S WARMER IN THE OCEAN.
I SEE.
YOU'RE RIGHT...

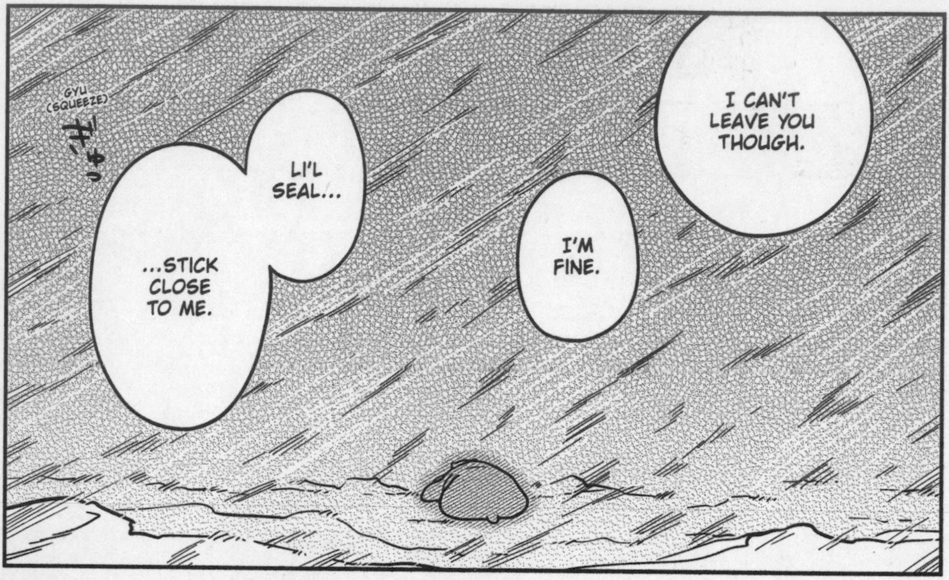
I CAN'T LEAVE YOU THOUGH.
I'M FINE.
LI'L SEAL...
...STICK CLOSE TO ME.
GYU (SQUEEZE)

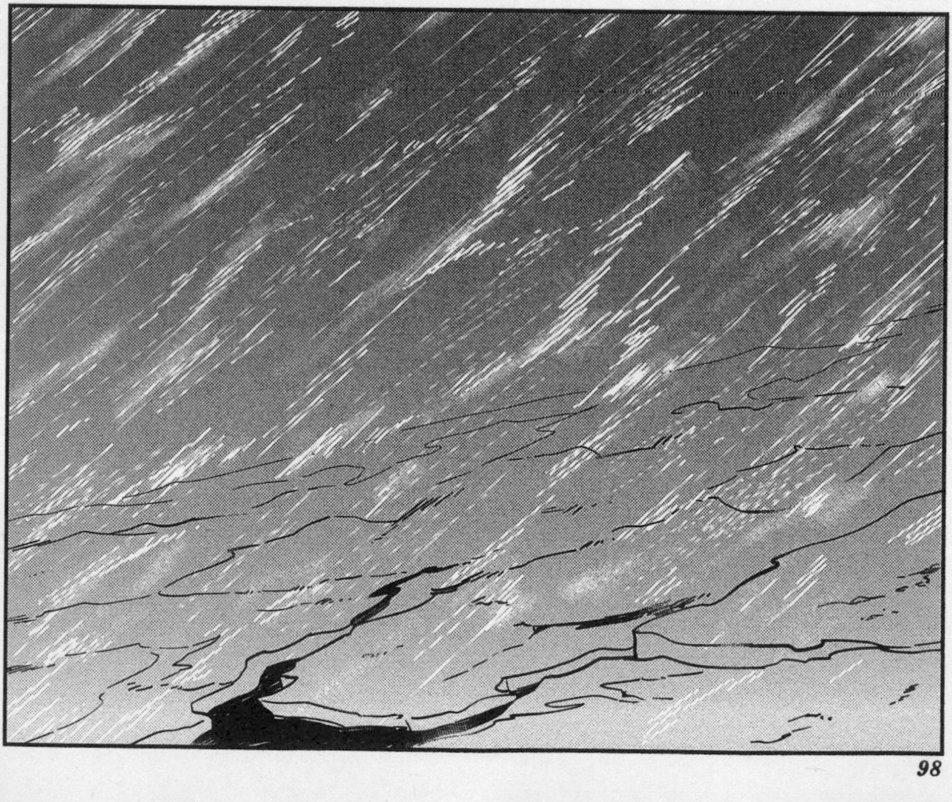

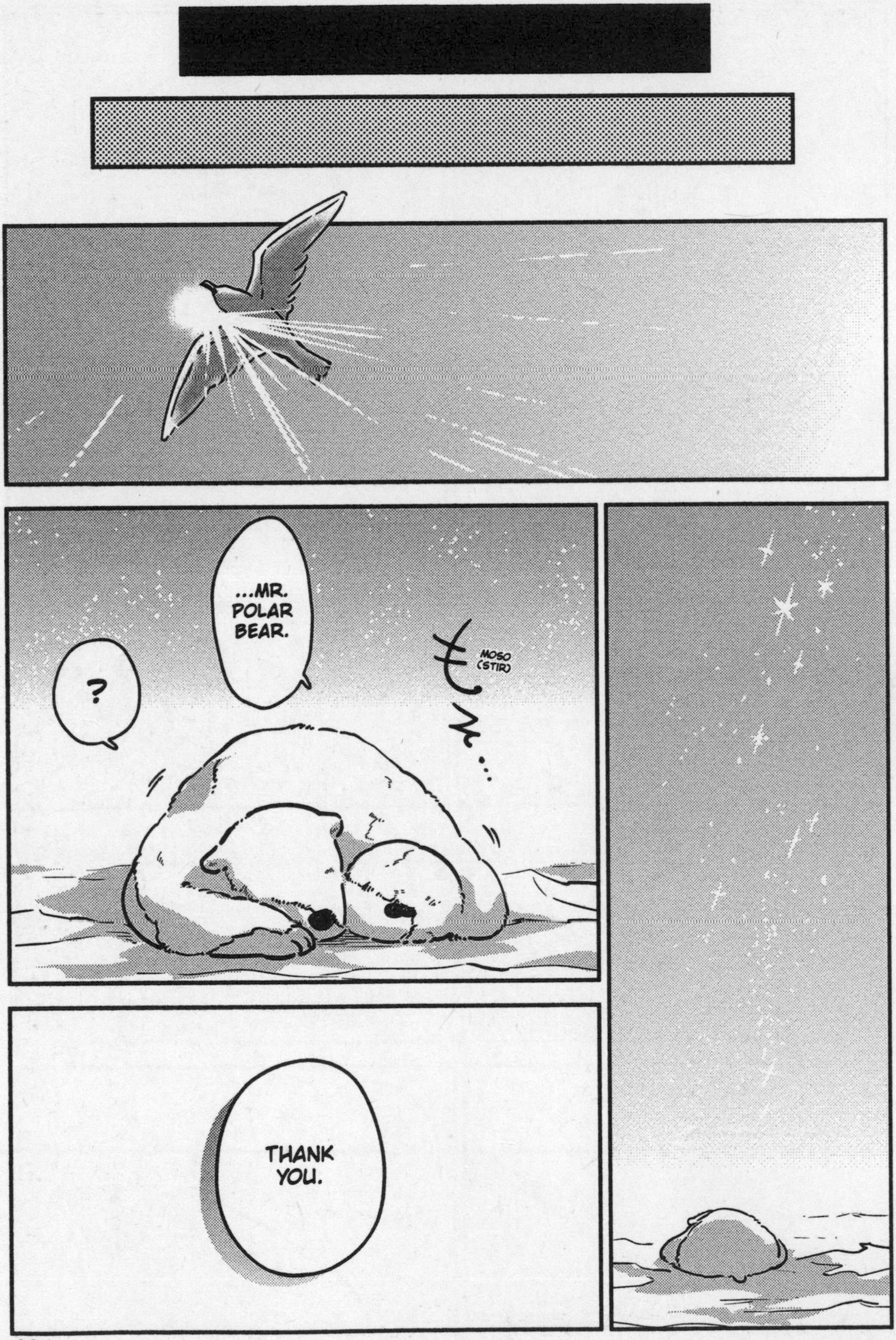
もぞ…
MOSO (STIR)
...MR. POLAR BEAR.
?
THANK YOU.

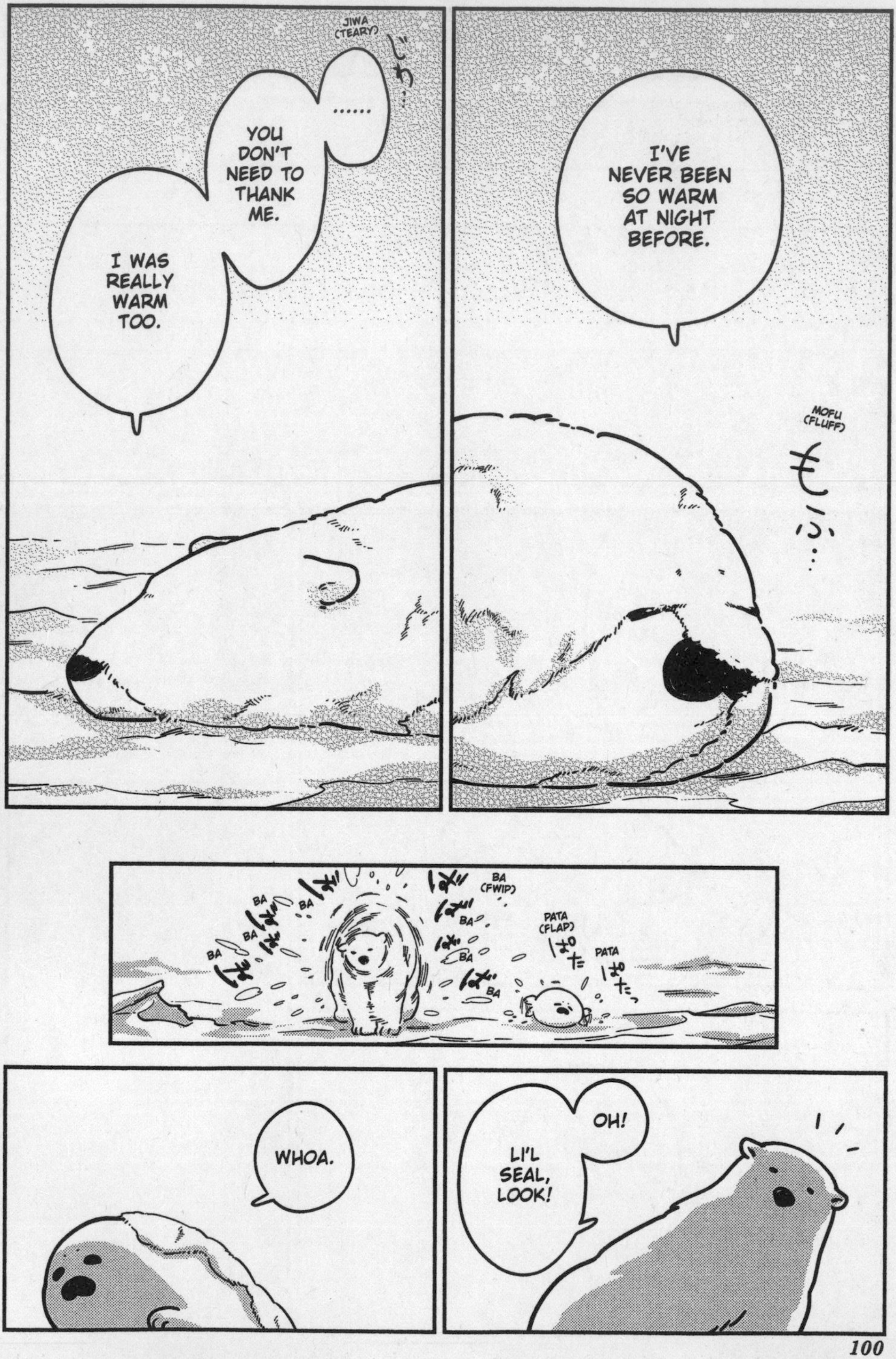
I'VE NEVER BEEN SO WARM AT NIGHT BEFORE.
MOFU (FLUFF)
もふ…
JIWA (TEARY)
じわ…
......
YOU DON'T NEED TO THANK ME.
I WAS REALLY WARM TOO.
BA (FWIP)
PATA (FLAP)
PATA
OH!
LI'L SEAL, LOOK!
WHOA.

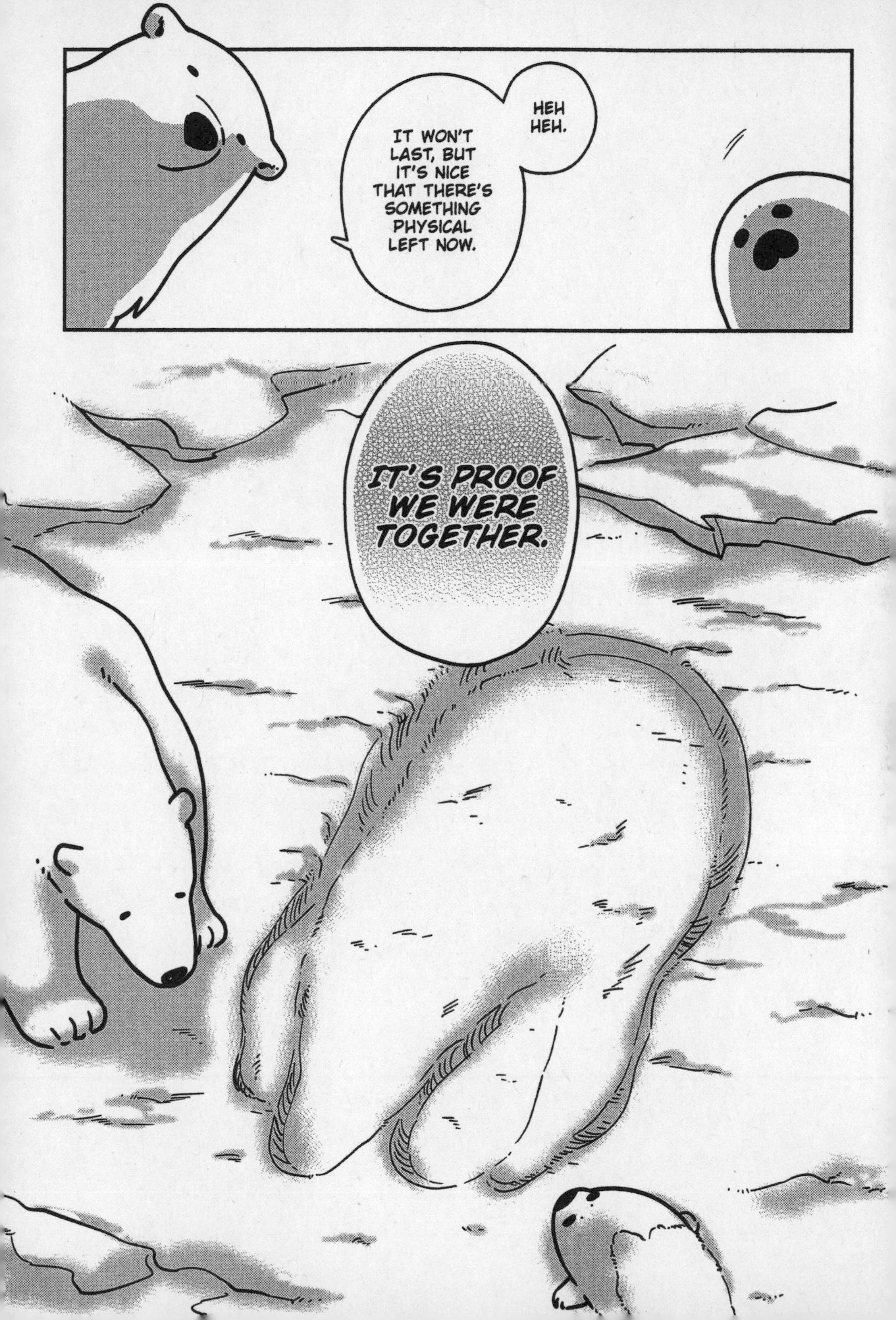
HEH HEH.
IT WON'T LAST, BUT IT'S NICE THAT THERE'S SOMETHING PHYSICAL LEFT NOW.
IT'S PROOF WE WERE TOGETHER.

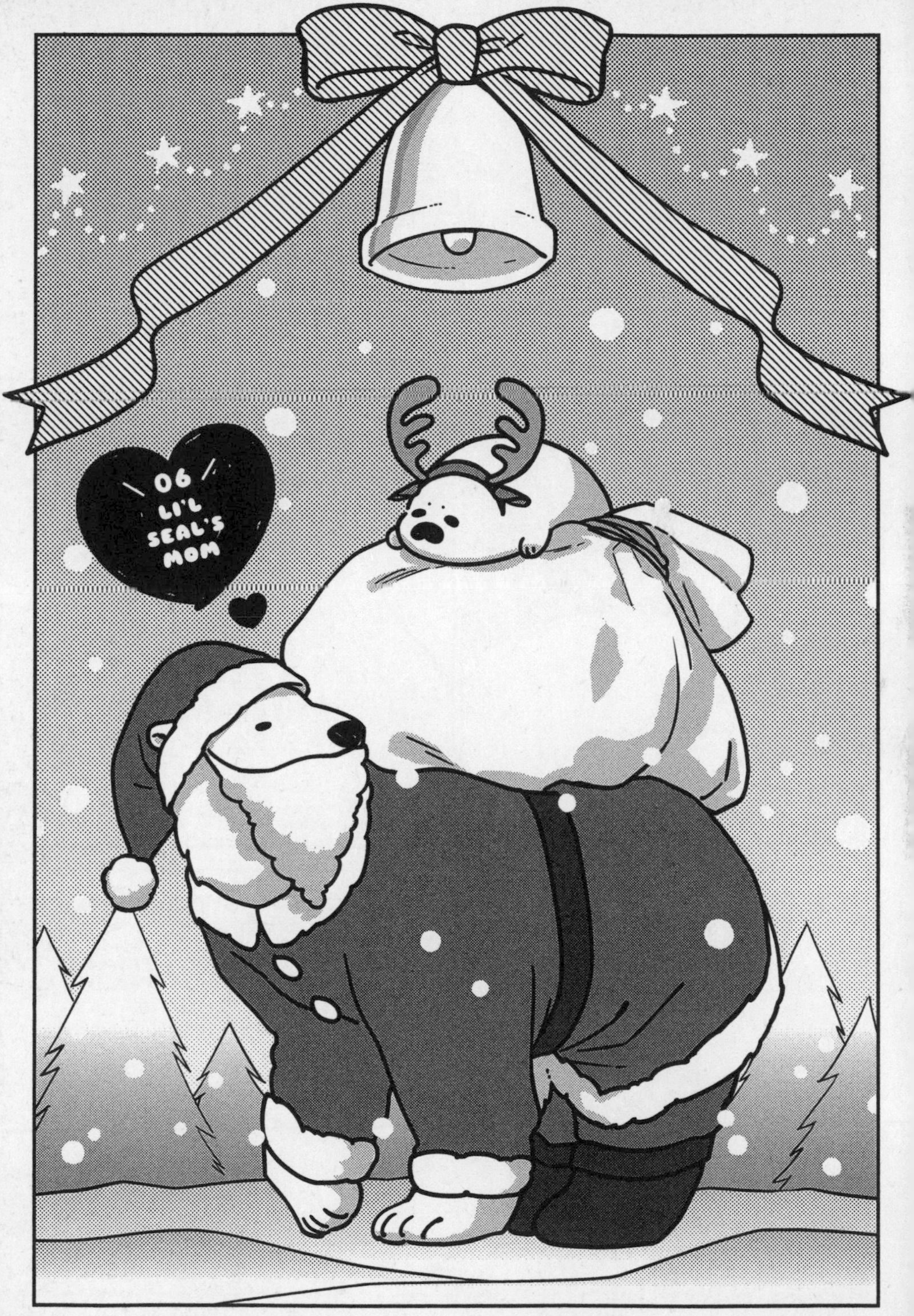
06
LI'L SEAL'S MOM

EVIDENCE

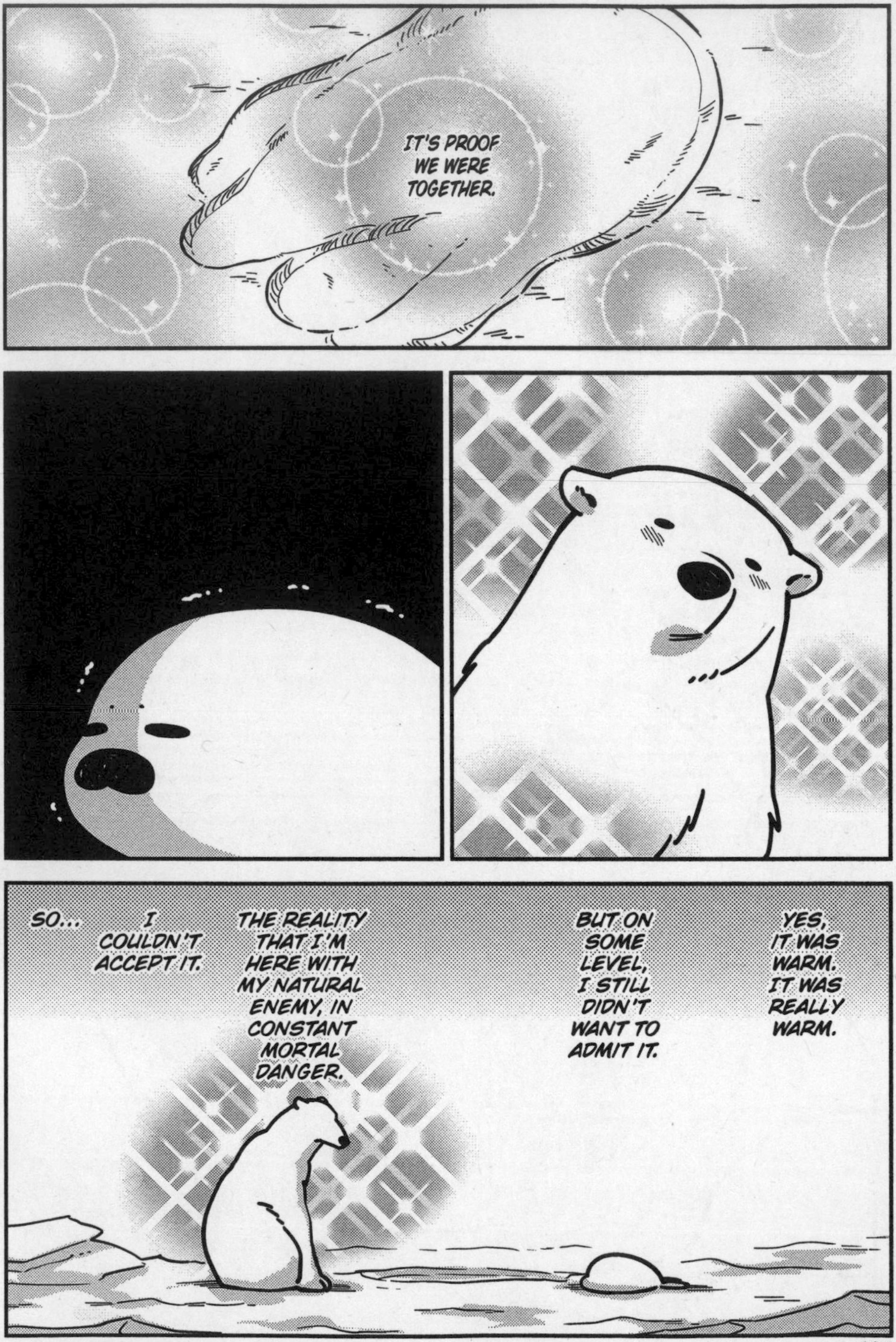
IT'S PROOF WE WERE TOGETHER.
SO...
I COULDN'T ACCEPT IT.
THE REALITY THAT I'M HERE WITH MY NATURAL ENEMY, IN CONSTANT MORTAL DANGER.
BUT ON SOME LEVEL, I STILL DIDN'T WANT TO ADMIT IT.
YES, IT WAS WARM. IT WAS REALLY WARM.

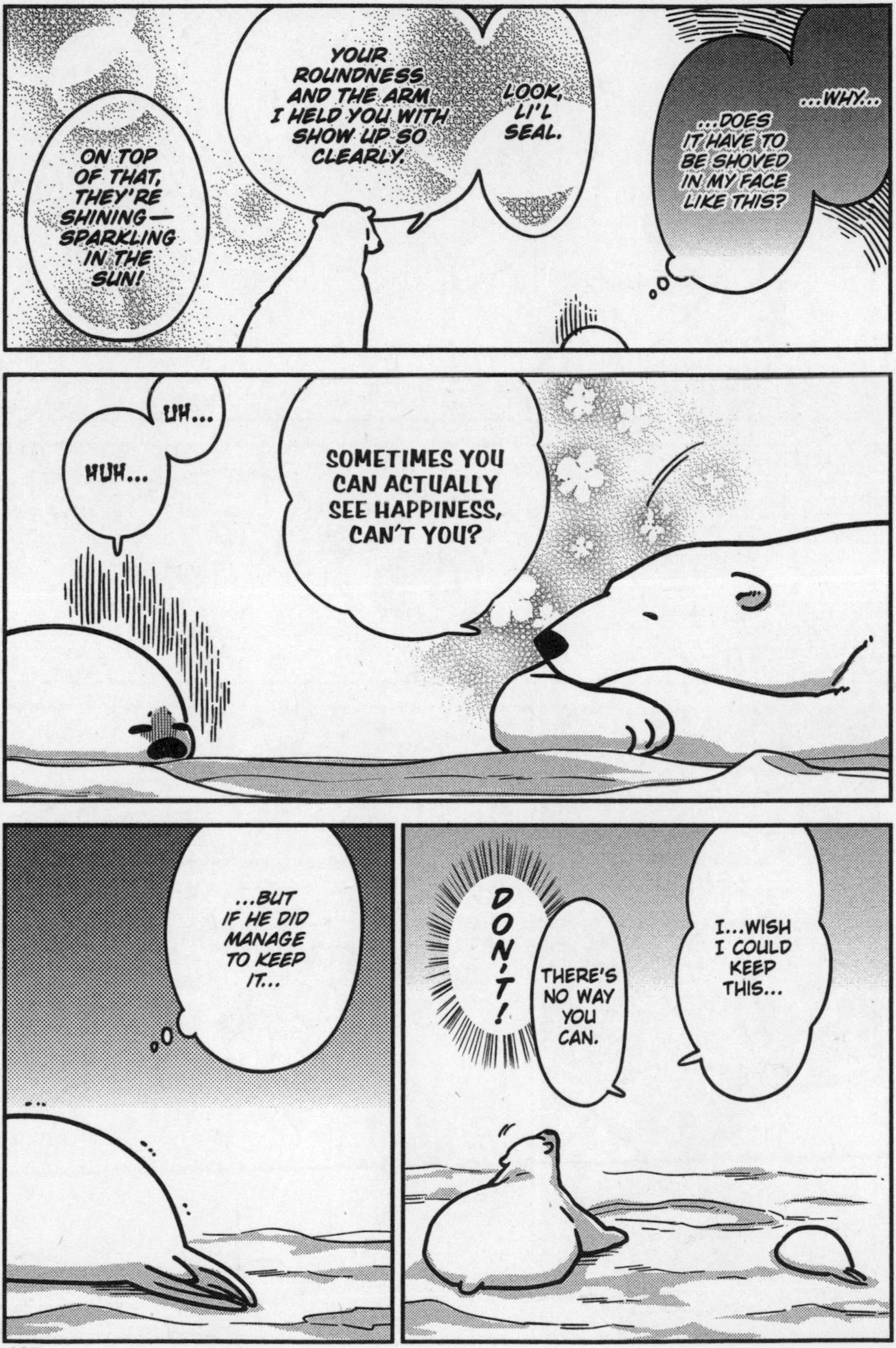
...WHY...
...DOES IT HAVE TO BE SHOVED IN MY FACE LIKE THIS?
LOOK, LI'L SEAL.
YOUR ROUNDNESS AND THE ARM I HELD YOU WITH SHOW UP SO CLEARLY.
ON TOP OF THAT, THEY'RE SHINING—SPARKLING IN THE SUN!
SOMETIMES YOU CAN ACTUALLY SEE HAPPINESS, CAN'T YOU?
UH...
HUH...
I...WISH I COULD KEEP THIS...
THERE'S NO WAY YOU CAN.
DON'T!
...BUT IF HE DID MANAGE TO KEEP IT...
...

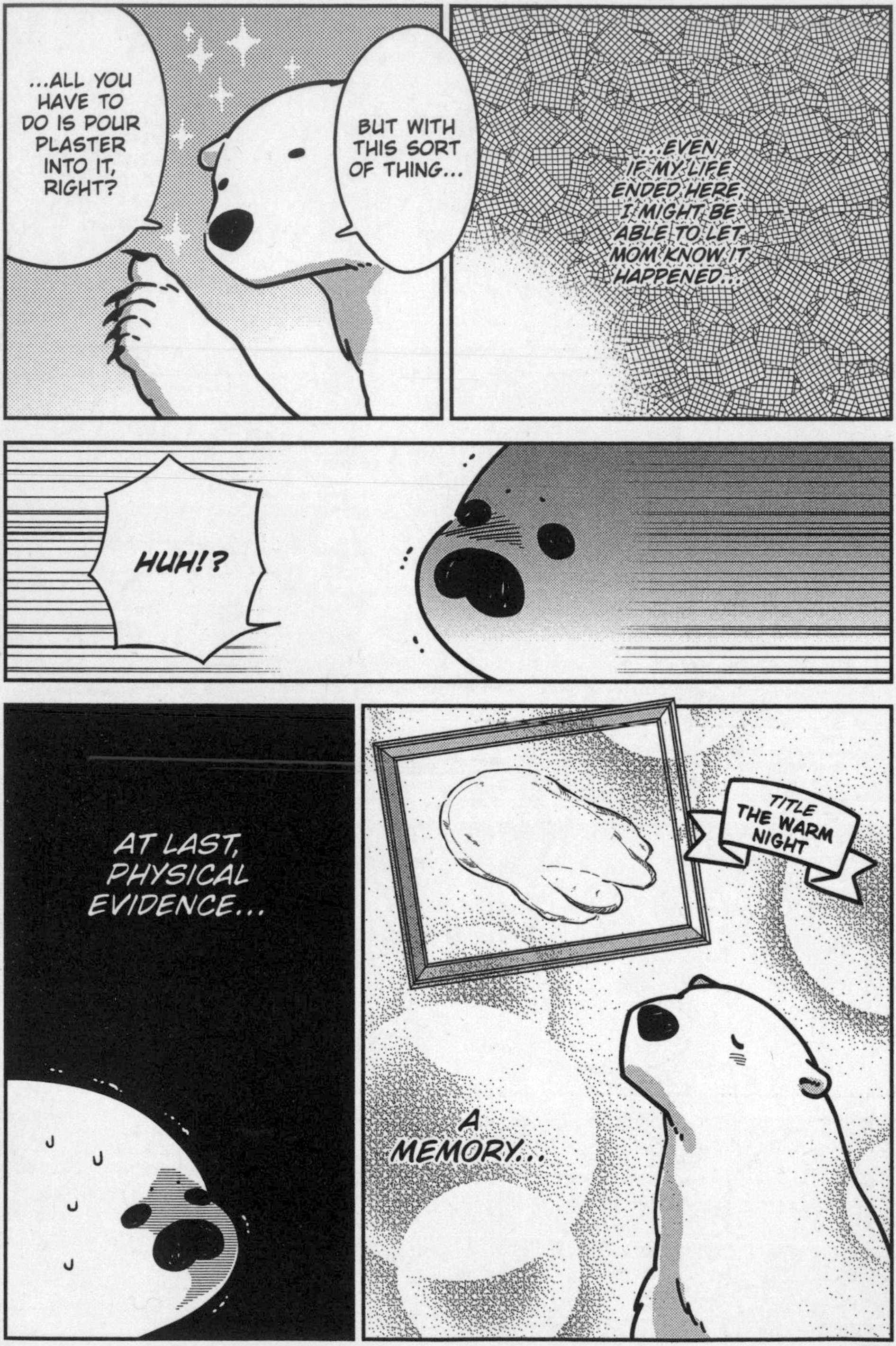
...EVEN IF MY LIFE ENDED HERE, I MIGHT BE ABLE TO LET MOM KNOW IT HAPPENED...
BUT WITH THIS SORT OF THING...
...ALL YOU HAVE TO DO IS POUR PLASTER INTO IT, RIGHT?
HUH!?
TITLE THE WARM NIGHT
A MEMORY...
AT LAST, PHYSICAL EVIDENCE...

BESIDE EXPECTATIONS

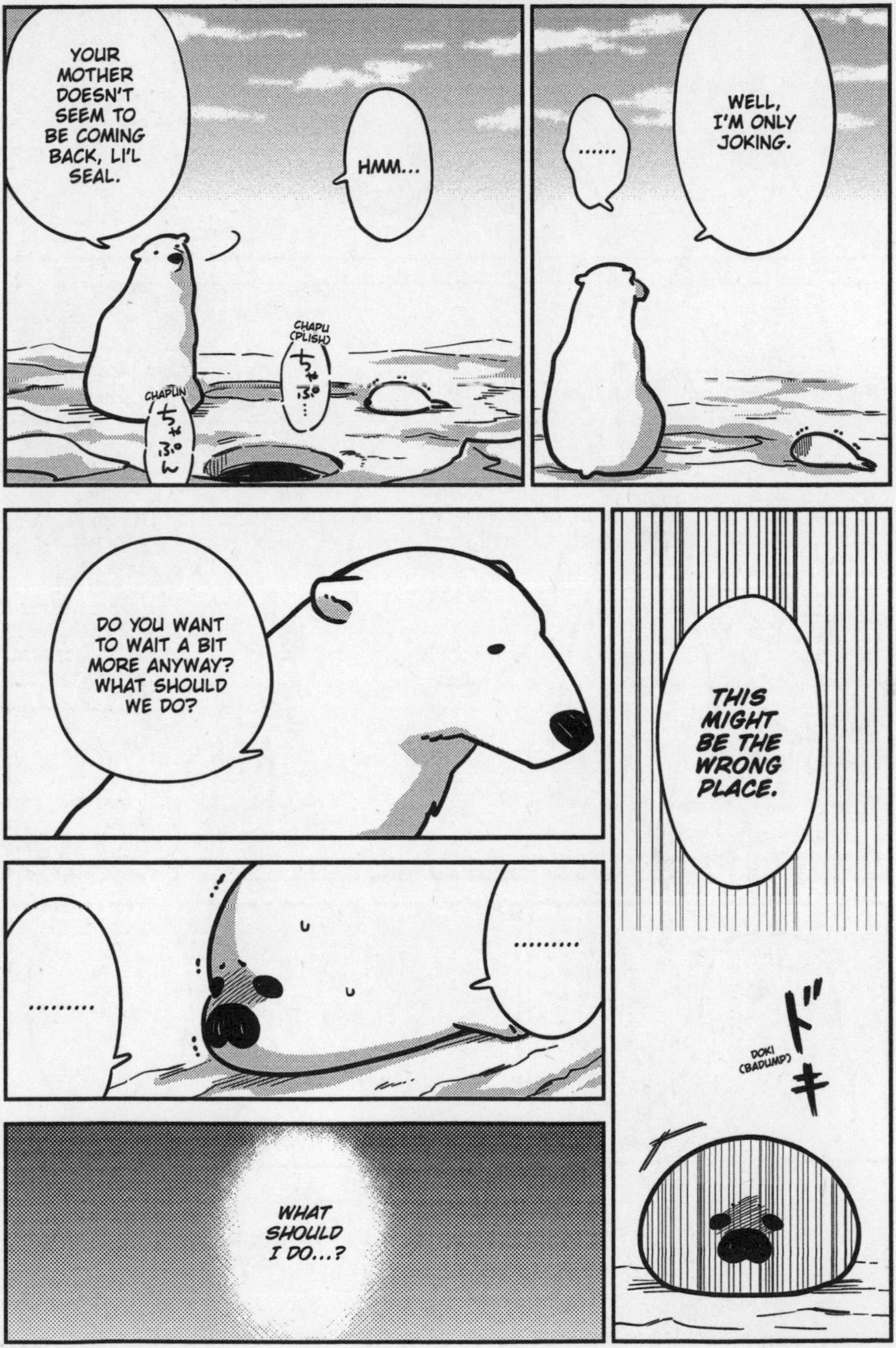
YOUR MOTHER DOESN'T SEEM TO BE COMING BACK, LI'L SEAL.
HMM...
CHAPU (PLISH)
ちゃぷ…
CHAPUN
ちゃぷん
......
WELL, I'M ONLY JOKING.
DO YOU WANT TO WAIT A BIT MORE ANYWAY? WHAT SHOULD WE DO?
....
....
WHAT SHOULD I DO...?
THIS MIGHT BE THE WRONG PLACE.
ドキ
DOKI (BADUMP)

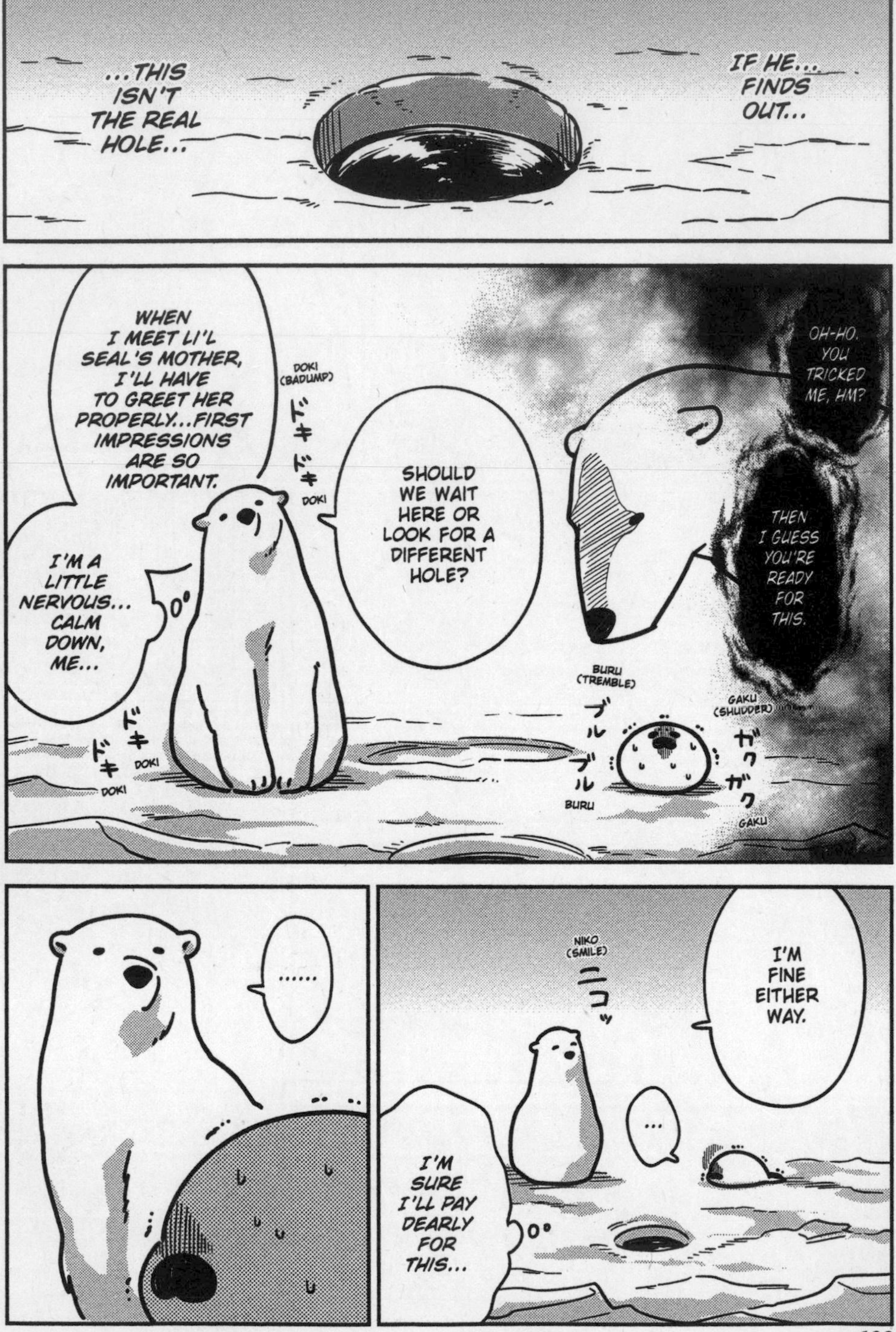

IF HE... FINDS OUT...
...THIS ISN'T THE REAL HOLE...
OH-HO. YOU TRICKED ME, HM?
THEN I GUESS YOU'RE READY FOR THIS.
GAKU (SHUDDER) ガク ガク GAKU
BURU (TREMBLE) ブル ブル BURU
SHOULD WE WAIT HERE OR LOOK FOR A DIFFERENT HOLE?
DOKI (BADUMP) ドキ ドキ DOKI
WHEN I MEET LI'L SEAL'S MOTHER, I'LL HAVE TO GREET HER PROPERLY...FIRST IMPRESSIONS ARE SO IMPORTANT.
I'M A LITTLE NERVOUS... CALM DOWN, ME...
ドキ ドキ DOKI DOKI
I'M FINE EITHER WAY.
NIKO (SMILE) ニコッ
...
I'M SURE I'LL PAY DEARLY FOR THIS...
......

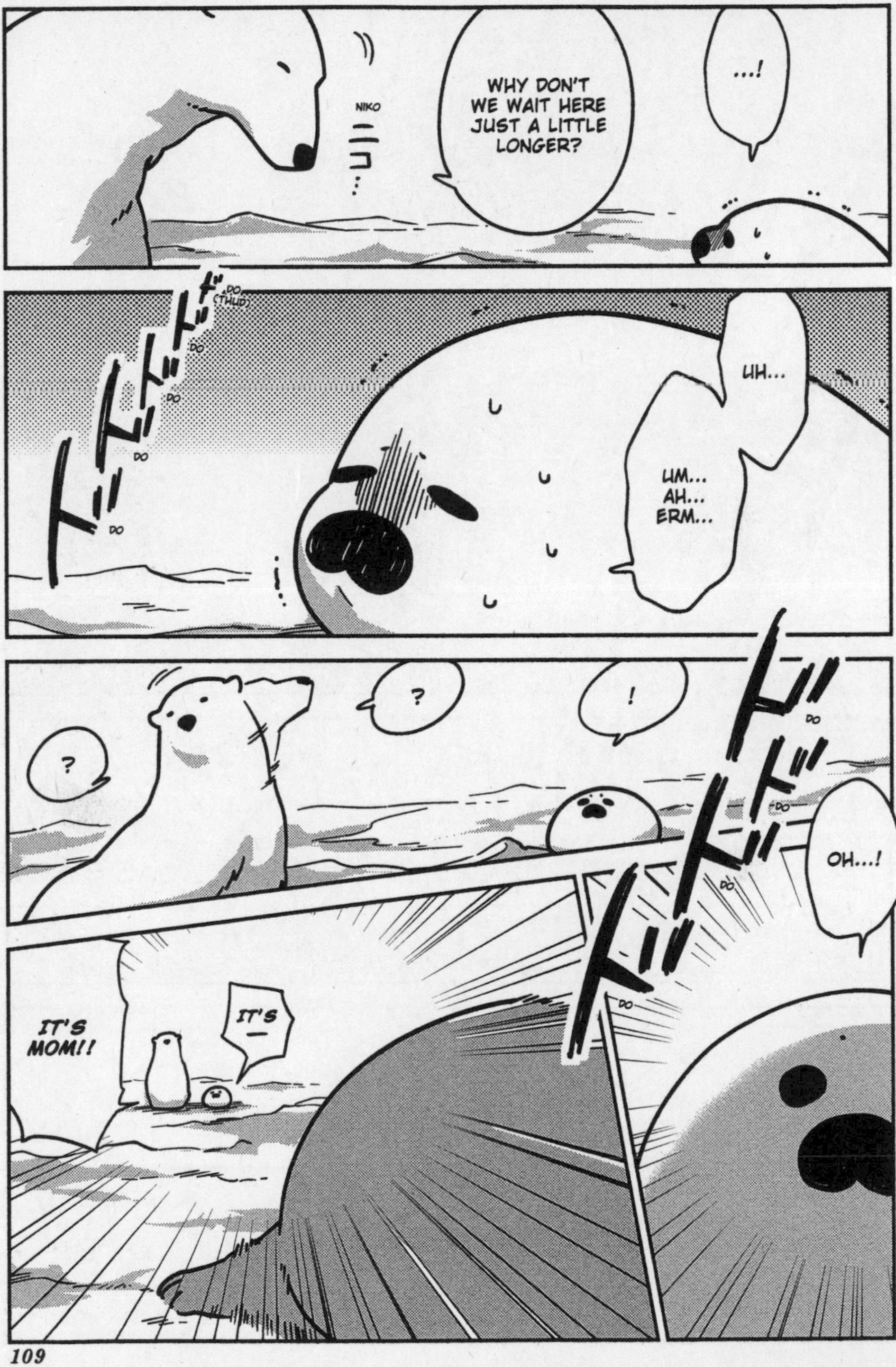

...!
WHY DON'T WE WAIT HERE JUST A LITTLE LONGER?
NIKO
UH...
UM... AH... ERM...
DO (THUD)
DO
DO
DO
DO
!
?
?
DO
DO
OH...!
DO
DO
IT'S —
IT'S MOM!!

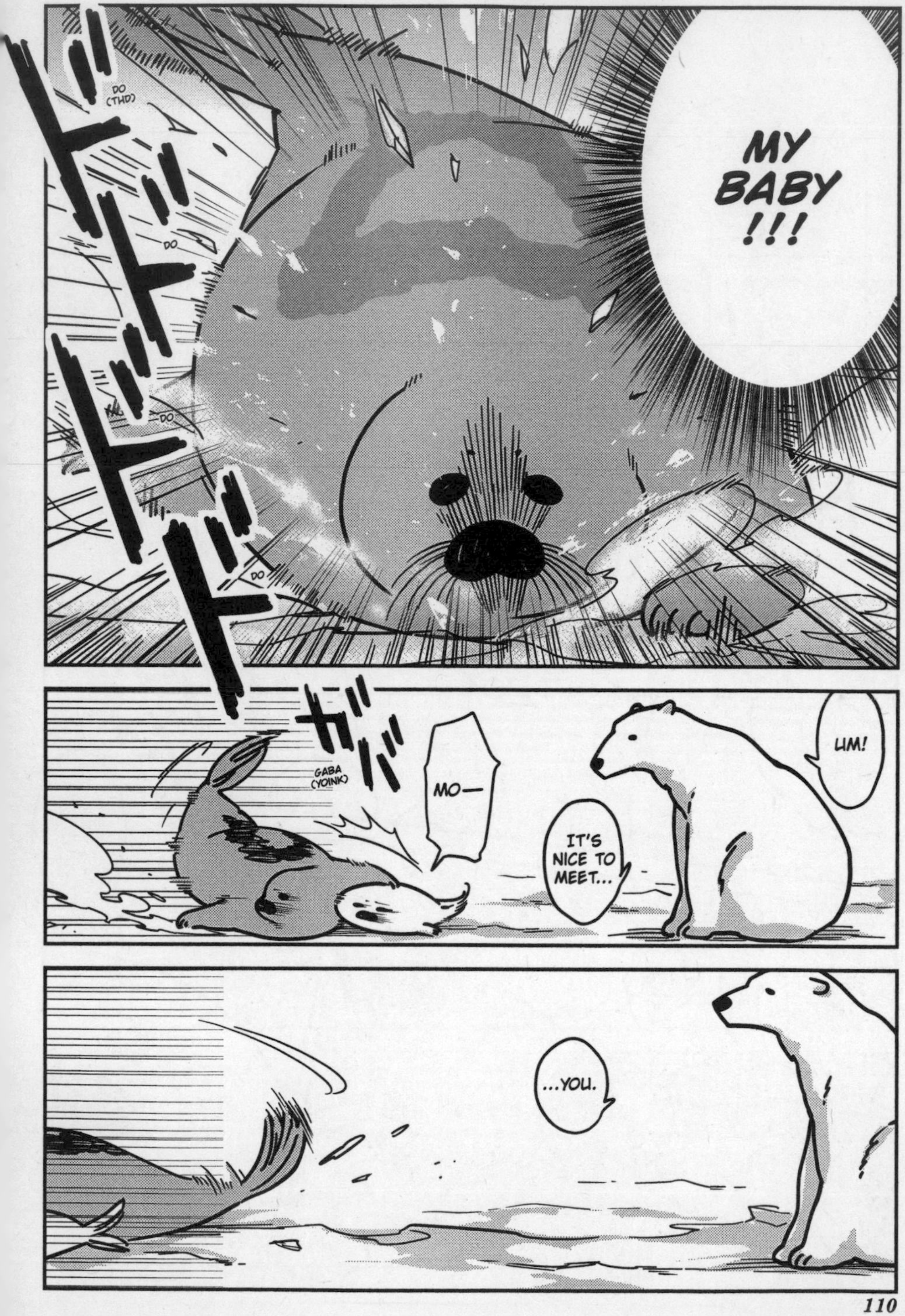
MY BABY!!!
DO (THD)
DO
DO
DO
UM!
IT'S NICE TO MEET...
MO—
GABA (YOINK)
...YOU.

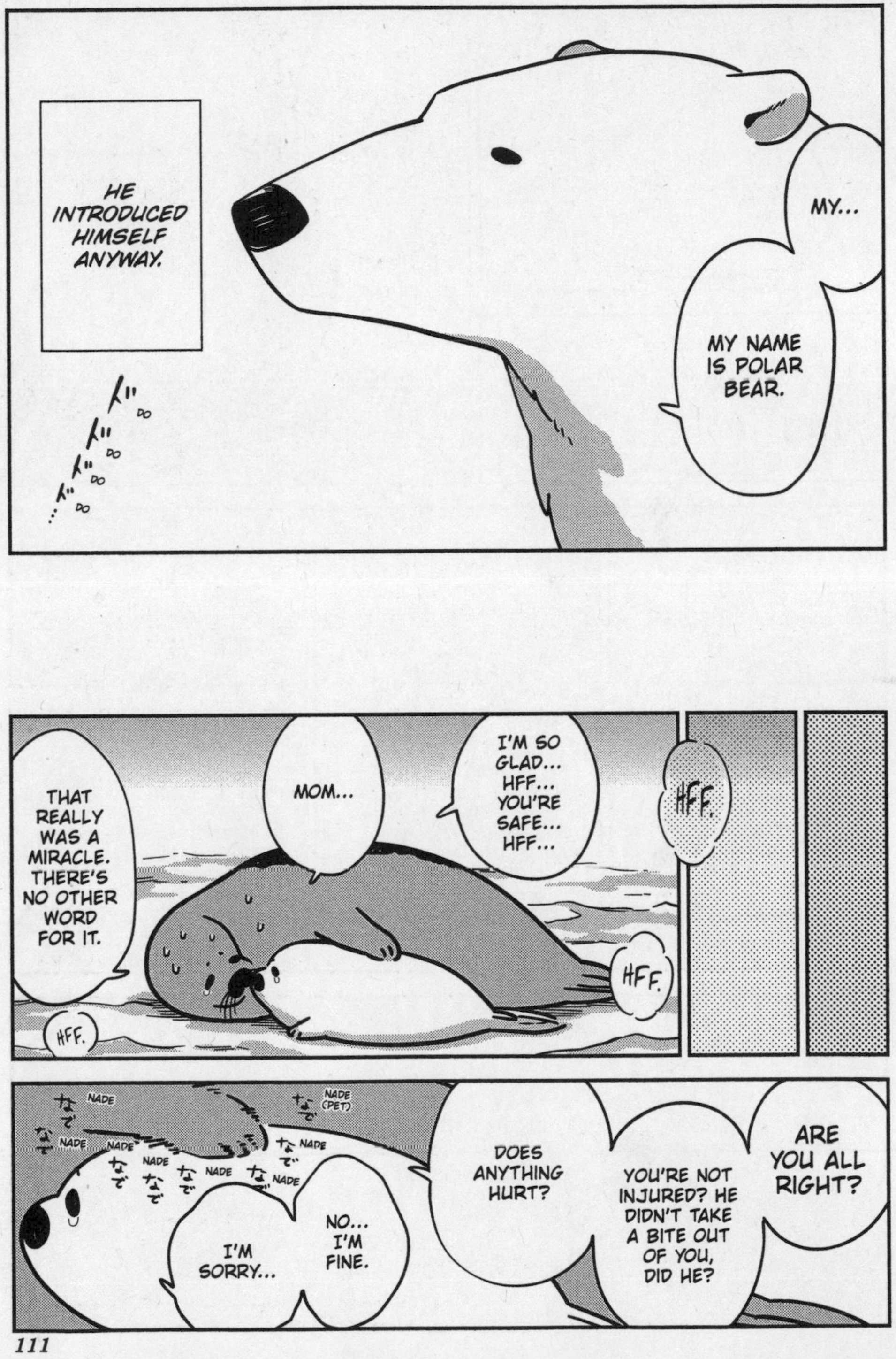
MY...
MY NAME IS POLAR BEAR.
HE INTRODUCED HIMSELF ANYWAY.
ド DO ド DO ド DO …ド DO
HFF.
I'M SO GLAD... HFF... YOU'RE SAFE... HFF...
MOM...
HFF.
THAT REALLY WAS A MIRACLE. THERE'S NO OTHER WORD FOR IT.
HFF.
ARE YOU ALL RIGHT?
YOU'RE NOT INJURED? HE DIDN'T TAKE A BITE OUT OF YOU, DID HE?
DOES ANYTHING HURT?
NO... I'M FINE.
I'M SORRY...
なで NADE (PET)
なで NADE なで NADE なで NADE なで NADE なで NADE なで NADE なで NADE

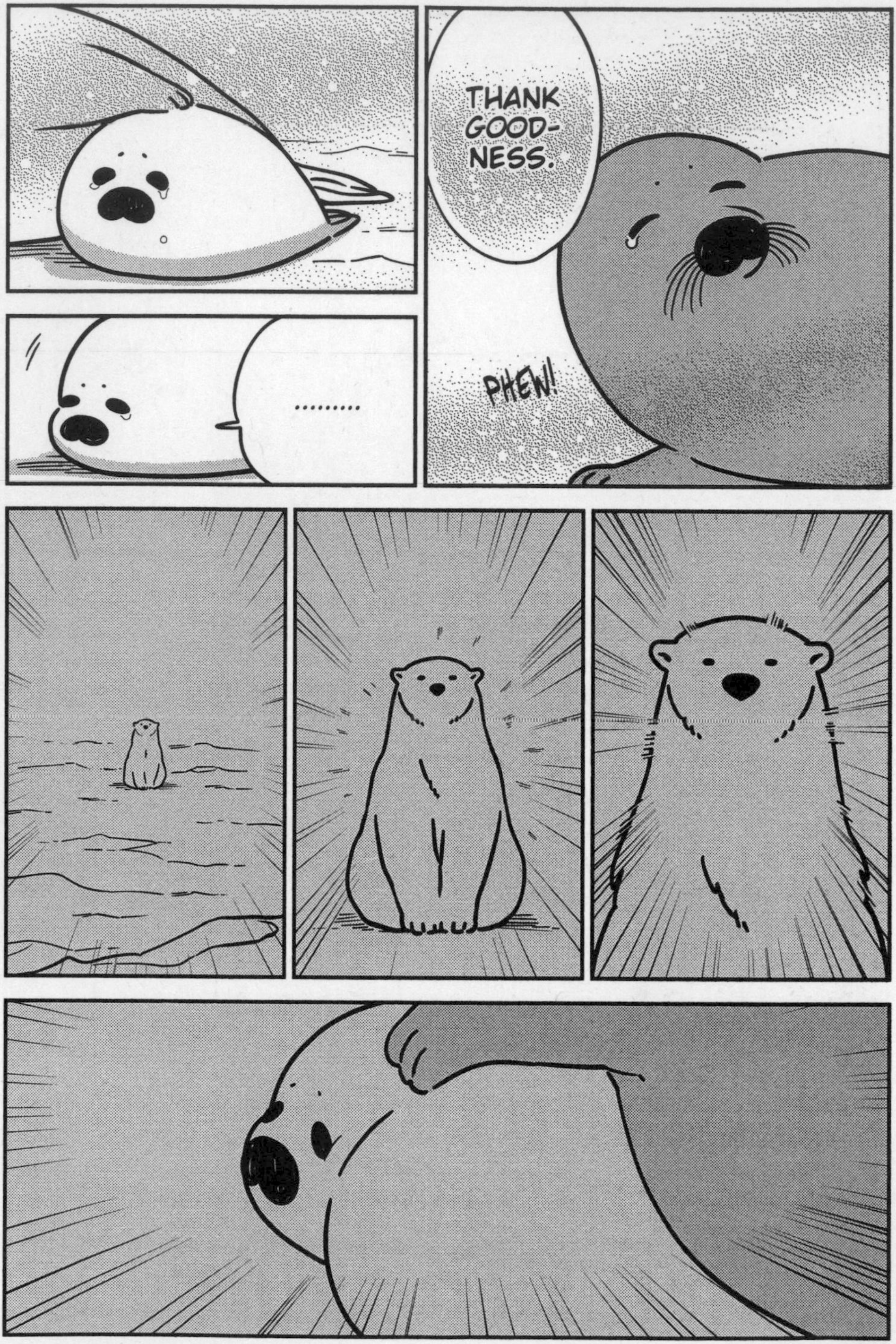
THANK GOOD-NESS.
PHEW!
....

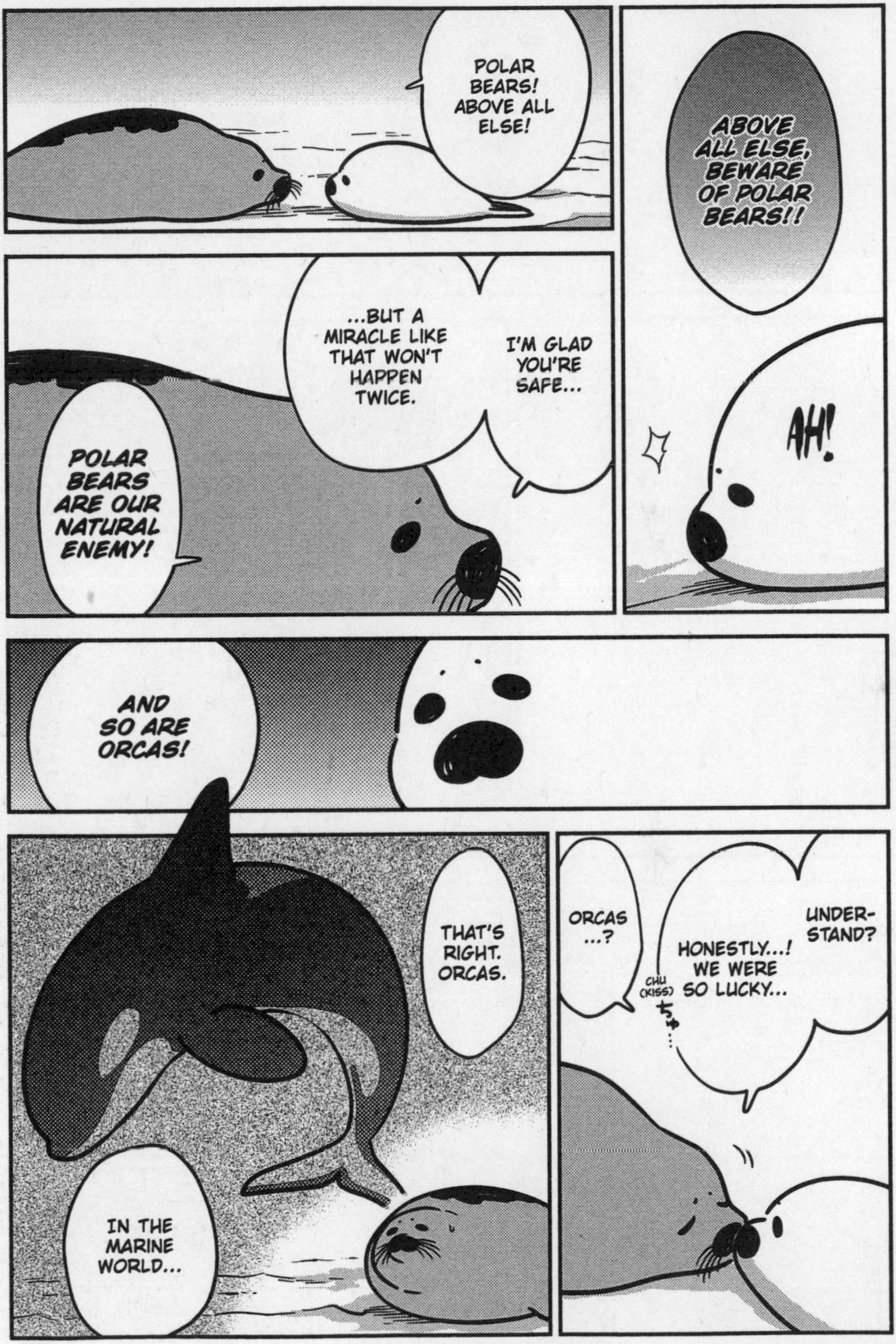

ABOVE ALL ELSE, BEWARE OF POLAR BEARS!!
AH!
POLAR BEARS! ABOVE ALL ELSE!
I'M GLAD YOU'RE SAFE...
...BUT A MIRACLE LIKE THAT WON'T HAPPEN TWICE.
POLAR BEARS ARE OUR NATURAL ENEMY!
AND SO ARE ORCAS!
UNDER-STAND?
HONESTLY...! WE WERE SO LUCKY...
CHU (KISS)
ちゅ…
ORCAS ...?
THAT'S RIGHT. ORCAS.
IN THE MARINE WORLD...

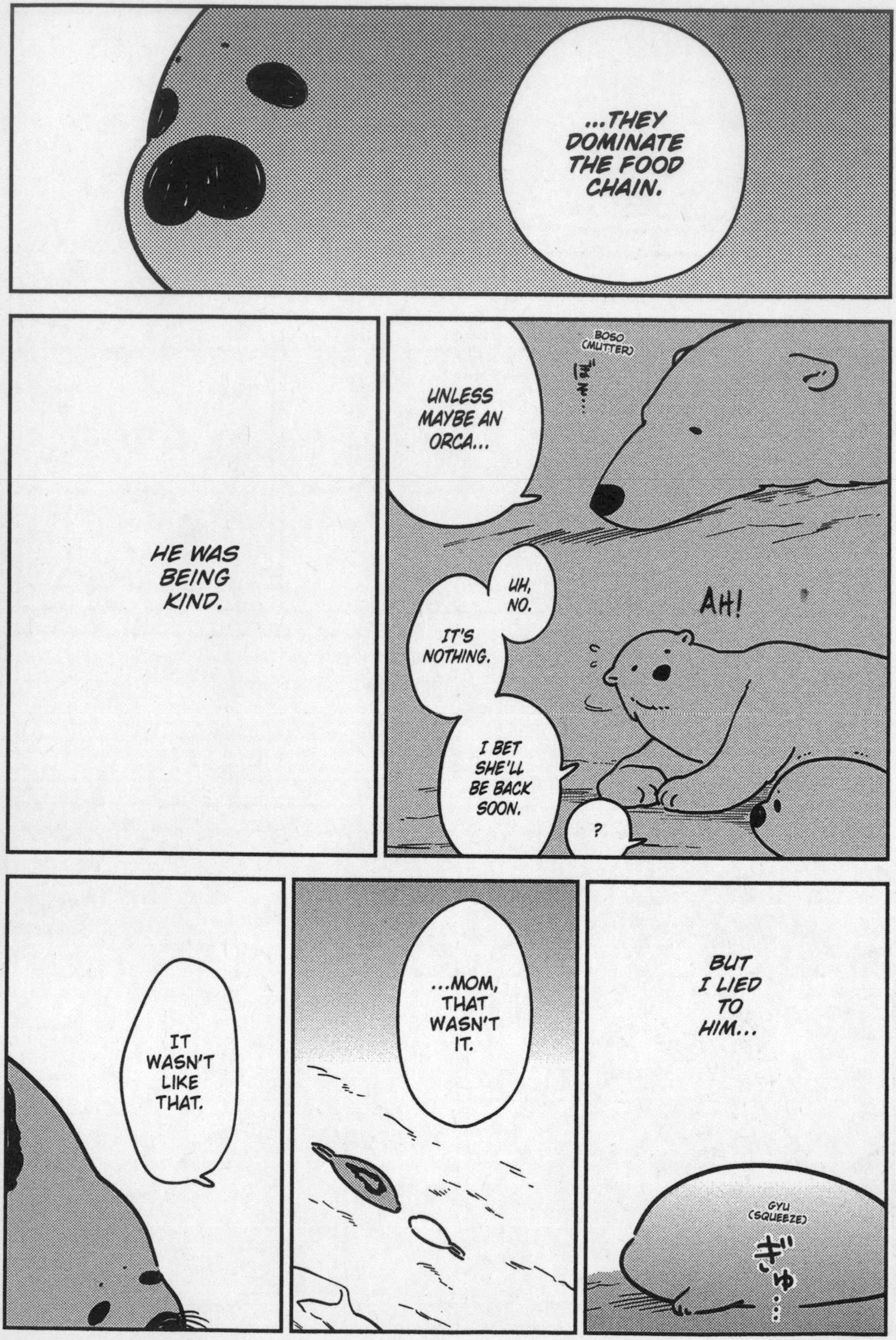
...THEY DOMINATE THE FOOD CHAIN.
BOSO (MUTTER)
UNLESS MAYBE AN ORCA...
AH!
UH, NO.
IT'S NOTHING.
I BET SHE'LL BE BACK SOON.
?
HE WAS BEING KIND.
BUT I LIED TO HIM...
GYU (SQUEEZE)
ぎゅ…
...MOM, THAT WASN'T IT.
IT WASN'T LIKE THAT.

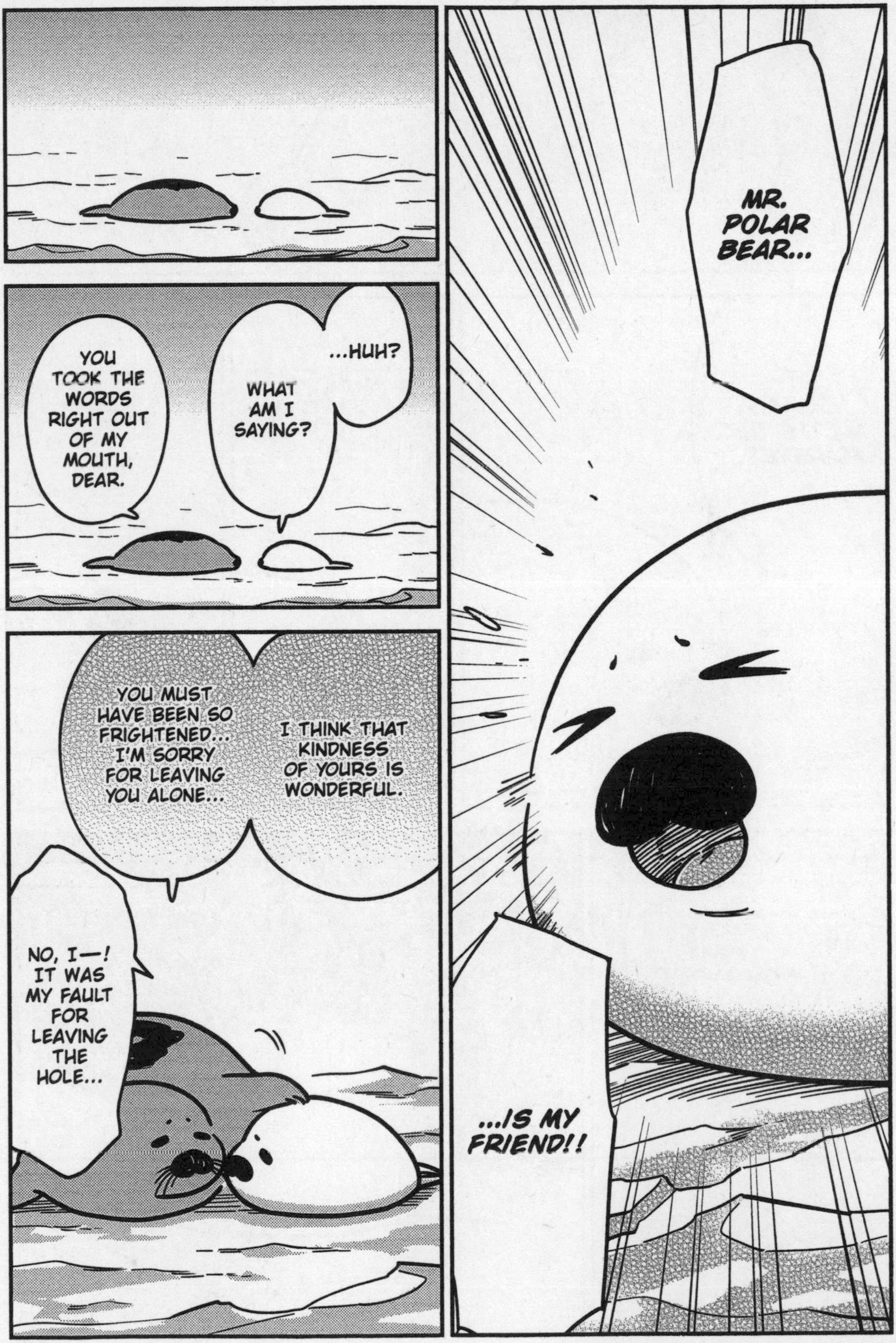
MR. POLAR BEAR...
...IS MY FRIEND!!
...HUH? WHAT AM I SAYING?
YOU TOOK THE WORDS RIGHT OUT OF MY MOUTH, DEAR.
I THINK THAT KINDNESS OF YOURS IS WONDERFUL.
YOU MUST HAVE BEEN SO FRIGHTENED... I'M SORRY FOR LEAVING YOU ALONE...
NO, I—! IT WAS MY FAULT FOR LEAVING THE HOLE...

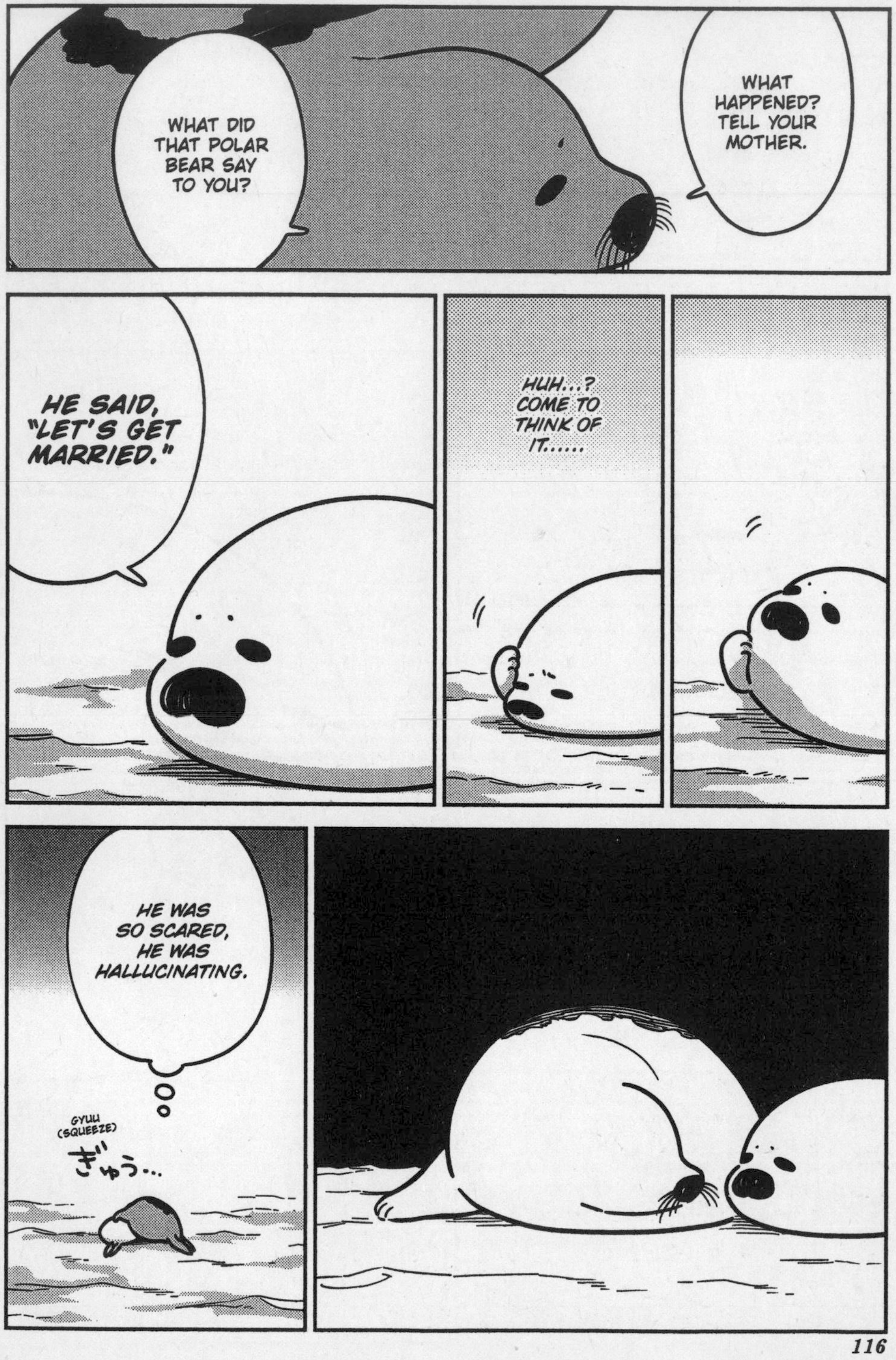
WHAT HAPPENED? TELL YOUR MOTHER.
WHAT DID THAT POLAR BEAR SAY TO YOU?
HUH...? COME TO THINK OF IT......
HE SAID, "LET'S GET MARRIED."
HE WAS SO SCARED, HE WAS HALLUCINATING.
GYUU (SQUEEZE)
ぎゅう…

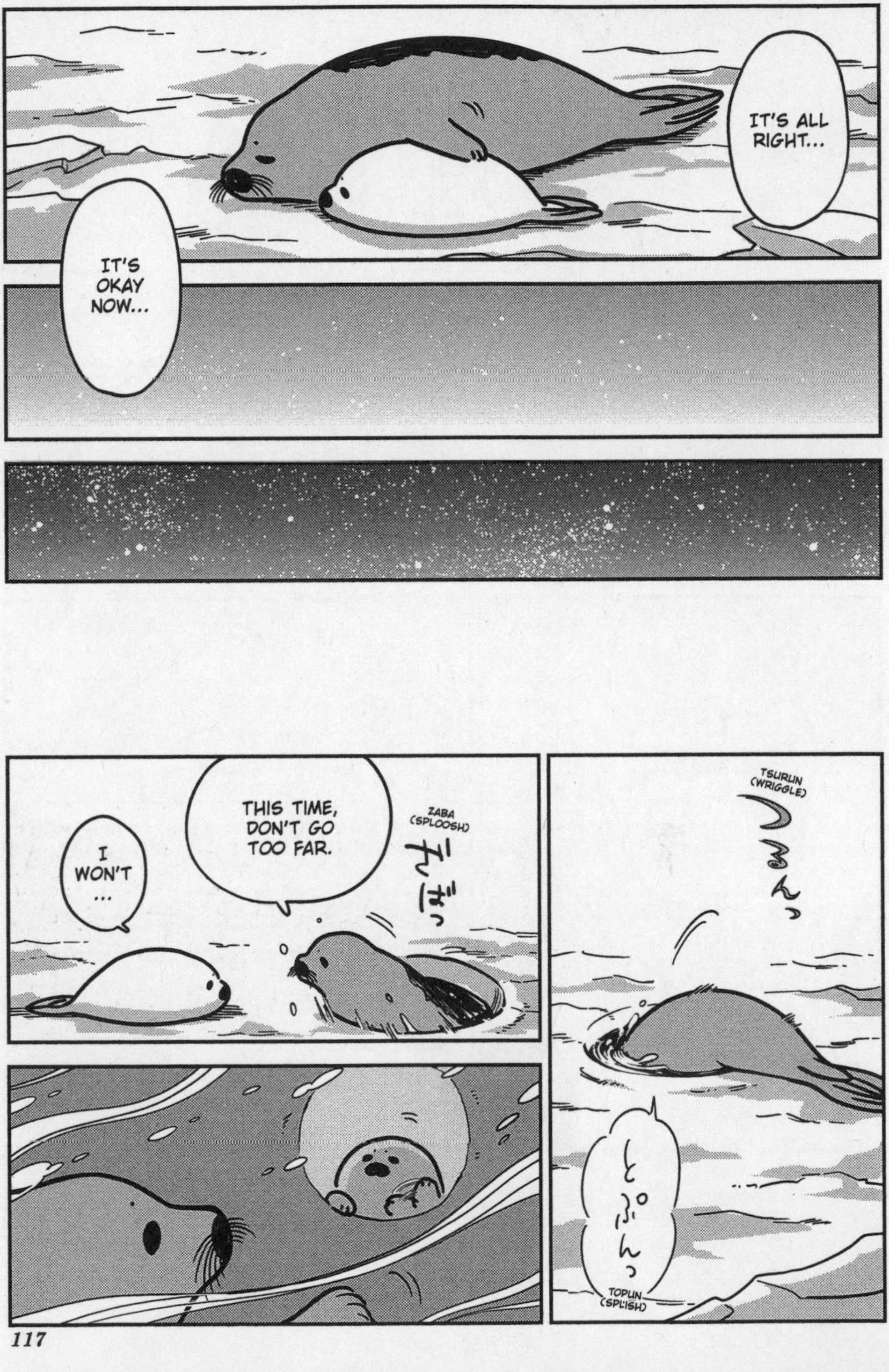
IT'S ALL RIGHT...
IT'S OKAY NOW...
TSURUN (WRIGGLE)
つるんっ
とぷんっ
TOPUN (SPLISH)
THIS TIME, DON'T GO TOO FAR.
ZABA (SPLOOSH)
ざばっ
I WON'T ...

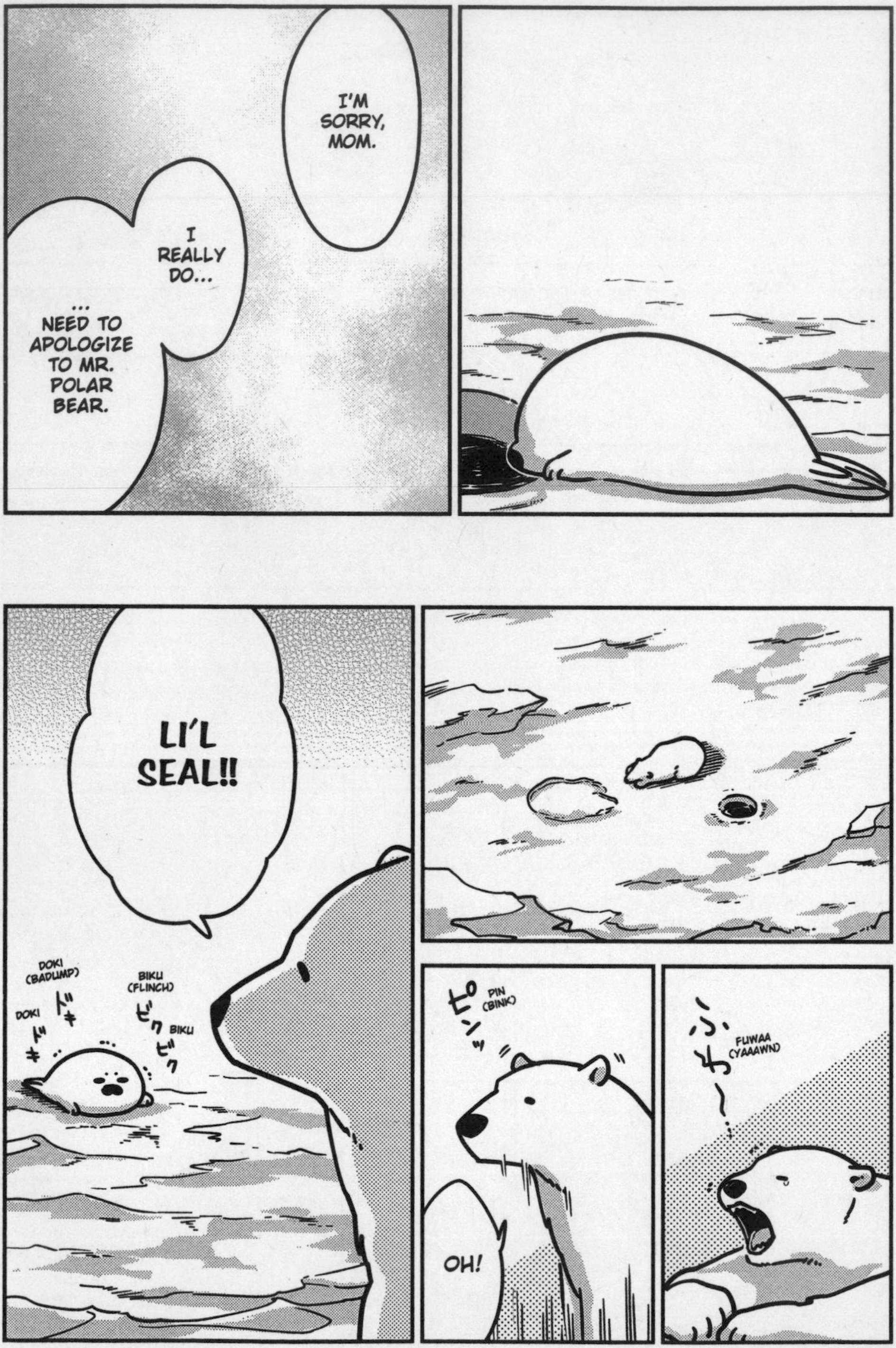
I'M SORRY, MOM.
I REALLY DO...
...NEED TO APOLOGIZE TO MR. POLAR BEAR.
ふわ~
FUWAA (YAAAWN)
ピンッ
PIN (BINK)
OH!
LI'L SEAL!!
ビク
BIKU (FLINCH)
ビク
BIKU
ドキ
DOKI (BADUMP)
ドキ
DOKI

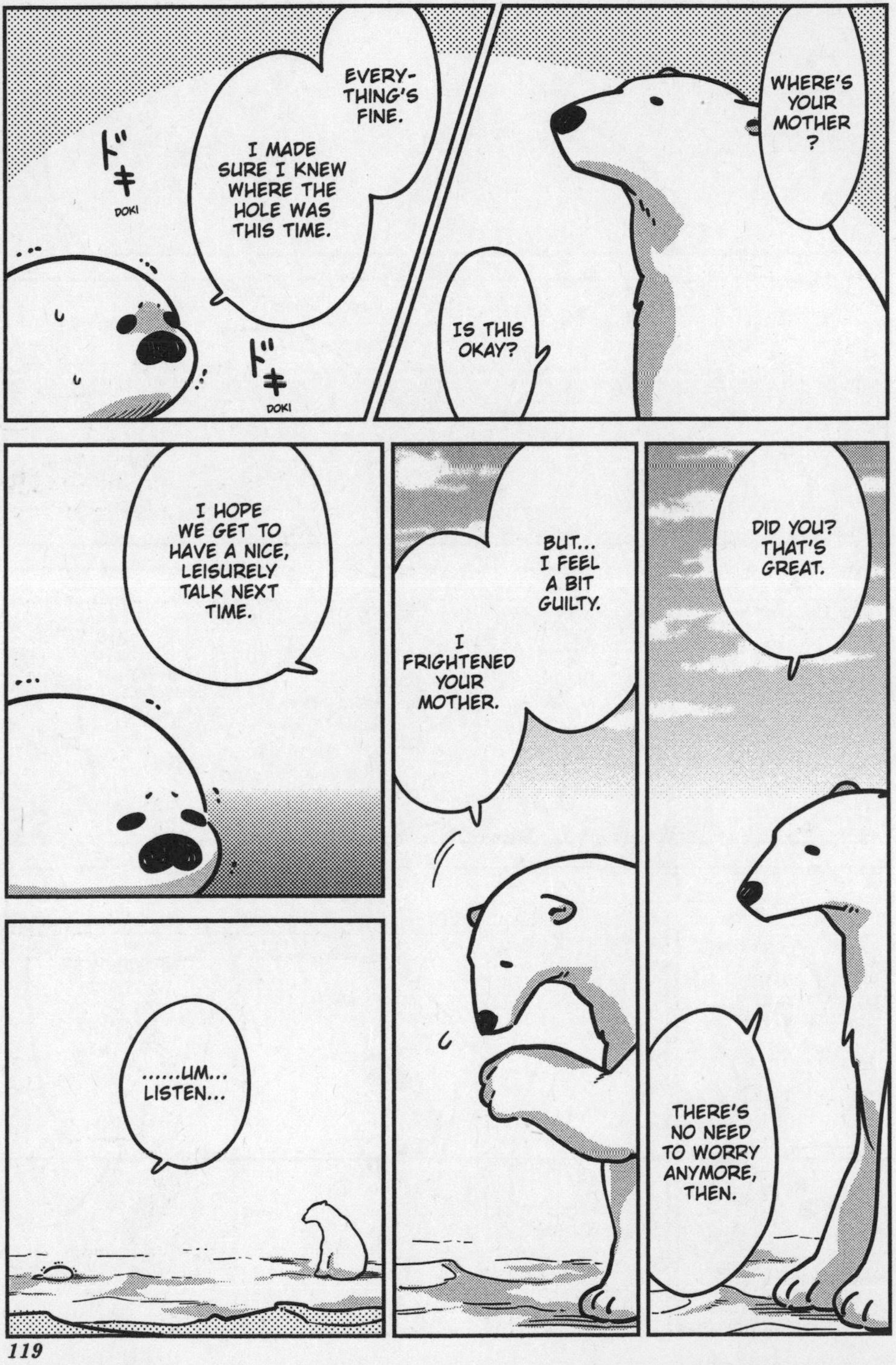
WHERE'S YOUR MOTHER?
IS THIS OKAY?
EVERY-THING'S FINE.
I MADE SURE I KNEW WHERE THE HOLE WAS THIS TIME.
ドキ DOKI
ドキ DOKI
DID YOU? THAT'S GREAT.
THERE'S NO NEED TO WORRY ANYMORE, THEN.
BUT... I FEEL A BIT GUILTY.
I FRIGHTENED YOUR MOTHER.
I HOPE WE GET TO HAVE A NICE, LEISURELY TALK NEXT TIME.
......UM... LISTEN...

I NEED TO APOLOGIZE TO YOU, MR. POLAR BEAR.
?
I...LIED.
THE HOLE I SAID MY MOM WOULD COME BACK TO...
...WASN'T THE RIGHT HOLE AT ALL.
WELL, THERE ARE LOTS OF HOLES. IT'S EASY TO GET THEM CONFUSED.
I WOULDN'T CALL THAT A LIE.
!
N-NO, THAT'S NOT IT.

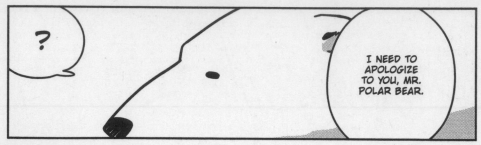

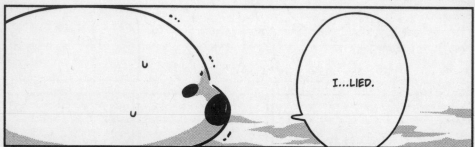

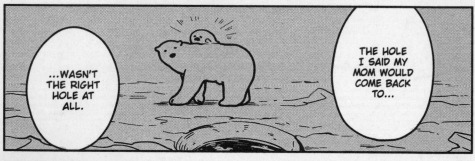

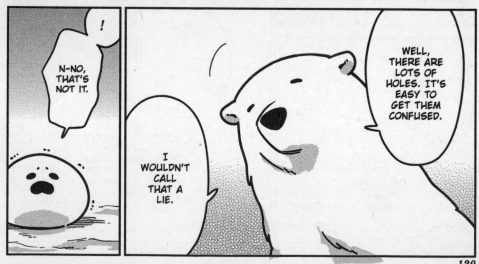

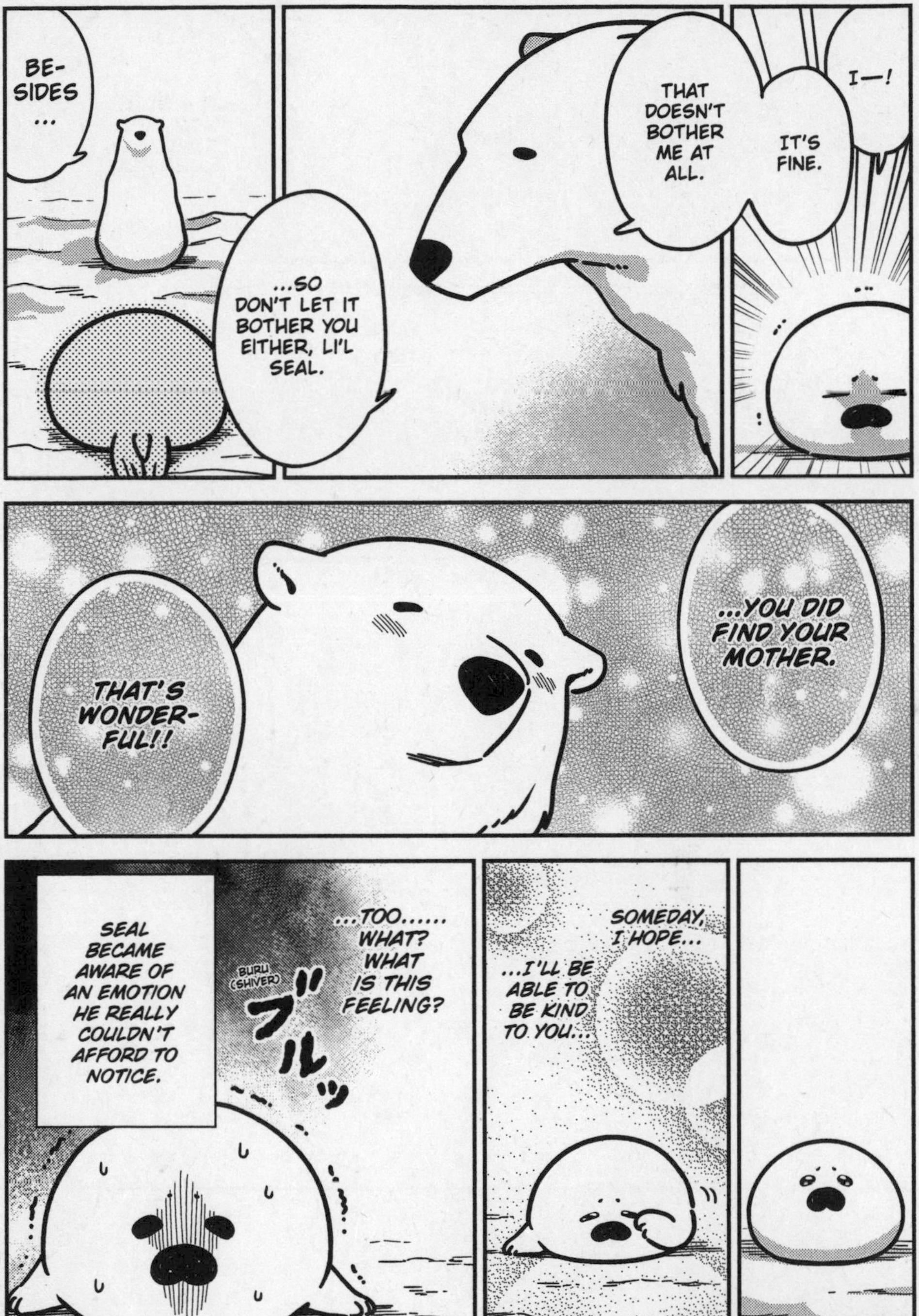
I—!
IT'S FINE.
THAT DOESN'T BOTHER ME AT ALL.
BE-SIDES...
...SO DON'T LET IT BOTHER YOU EITHER, LI'L SEAL.
...YOU DID FIND YOUR MOTHER.
THAT'S WONDER-FUL!!
SOMEDAY, I HOPE...
...I'LL BE ABLE TO BE KIND TO YOU...
...TOO...... WHAT? WHAT IS THIS FEELING?
BURU (SHIVER)
ブルッ
SEAL BECAME AWARE OF AN EMOTION HE REALLY COULDN'T AFFORD TO NOTICE.

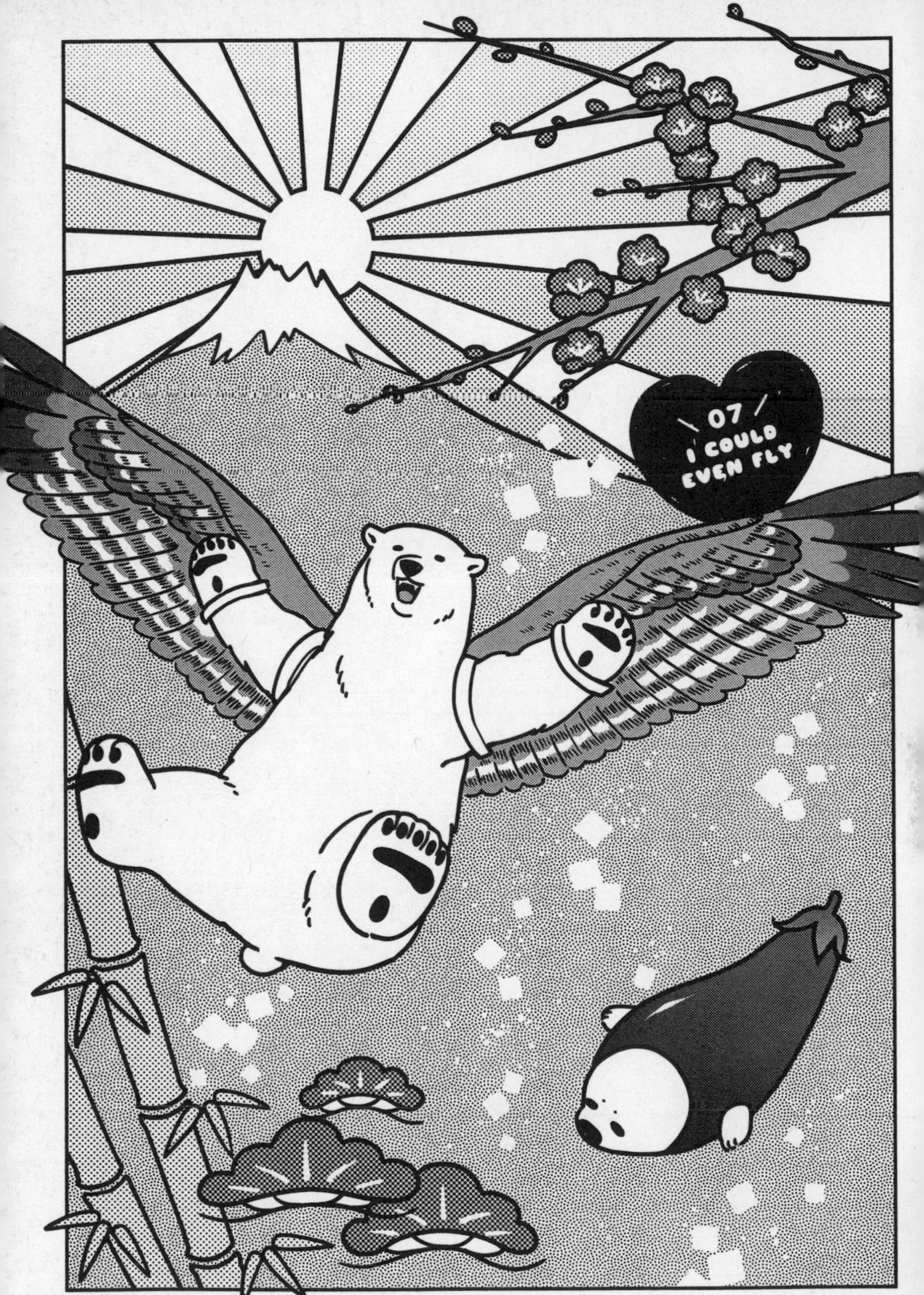
07
I COULD
EVEN FLY

LUCKY SEAGULL

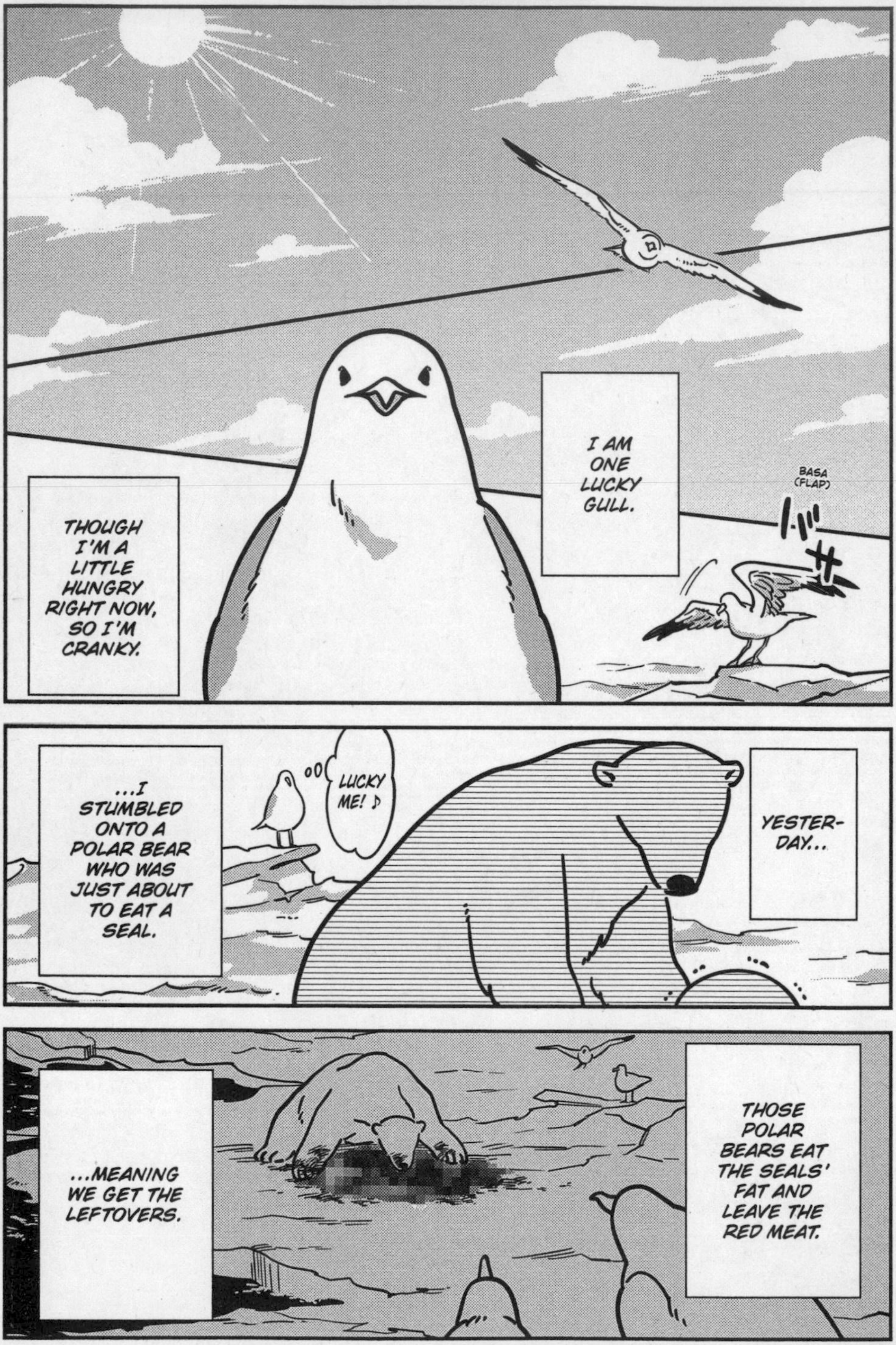
I AM ONE LUCKY GULL.
BASA (FLAP)
THOUGH I'M A LITTLE HUNGRY RIGHT NOW, SO I'M CRANKY.
YESTER-DAY...
...I STUMBLED ONTO A POLAR BEAR WHO WAS JUST ABOUT TO EAT A SEAL.
LUCKY ME! ♪
THOSE POLAR BEARS EAT THE SEALS' FAT AND LEAVE THE RED MEAT.
...MEANING WE GET THE LEFTOVERS.

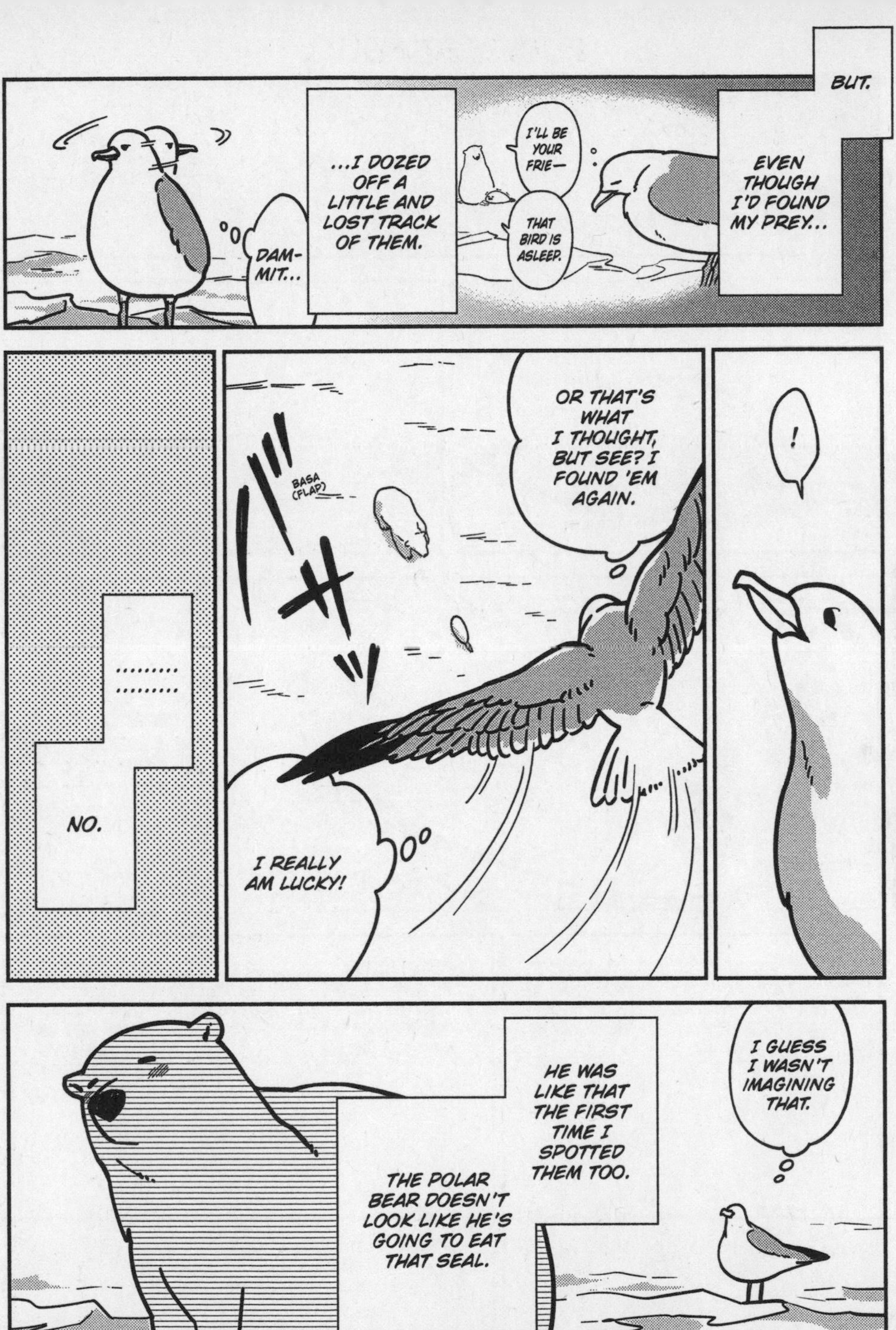
BUT.
EVEN THOUGH I'D FOUND MY PREY...
I'LL BE YOUR FRIE—
THAT BIRD IS ASLEEP.
...I DOZED OFF A LITTLE AND LOST TRACK OF THEM.
DAM-MIT...
!
OR THAT'S WHAT I THOUGHT, BUT SEE? I FOUND 'EM AGAIN.
BASA (FLAP)
I REALLY AM LUCKY!
....
....
NO.
I GUESS I WASN'T IMAGINING THAT.
HE WAS LIKE THAT THE FIRST TIME I SPOTTED THEM TOO.
THE POLAR BEAR DOESN'T LOOK LIKE HE'S GOING TO EAT THAT SEAL.

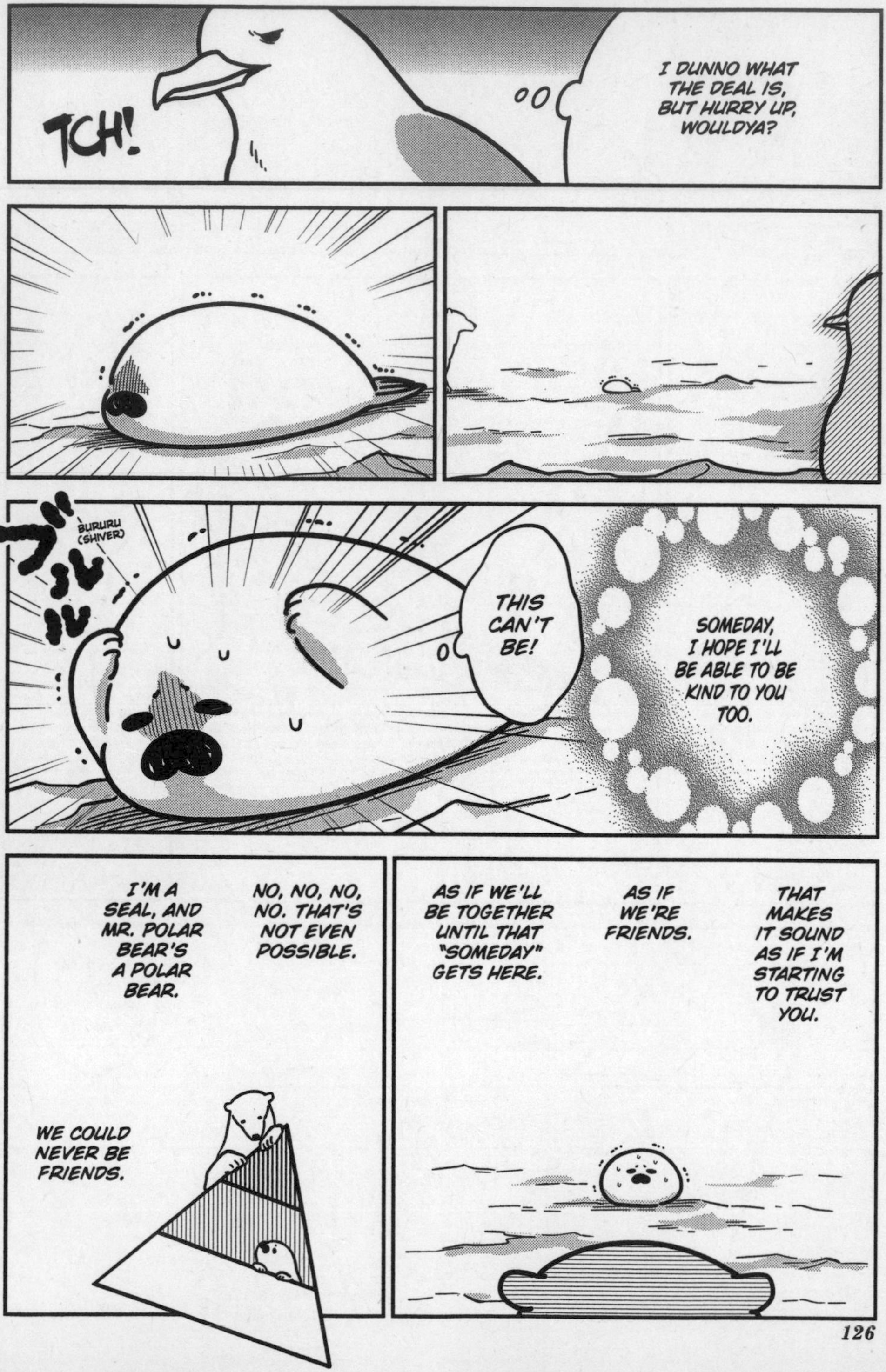
I DUNNO WHAT THE DEAL IS, BUT HURRY UP, WOULDYA?
TCH!
SOMEDAY, I HOPE I'LL BE ABLE TO BE KIND TO YOU TOO.
THIS CAN'T BE!
ブルル
BURURU (SHIVER)
THAT MAKES IT SOUND AS IF I'M STARTING TO TRUST YOU.
AS IF WE'RE FRIENDS.
AS IF WE'LL BE TOGETHER UNTIL THAT "SOMEDAY" GETS HERE.
NO, NO, NO, NO. THAT'S NOT EVEN POSSIBLE.
I'M A SEAL, AND MR. POLAR BEAR'S A POLAR BEAR.
WE COULD NEVER BE FRIENDS.

INSTINCT AND TERROR

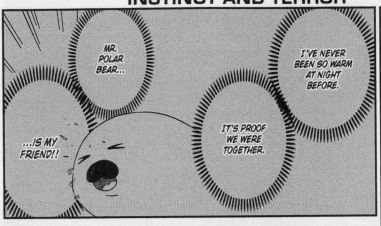

......
I'VE NEVER BEEN SO WARM AT NIGHT BEFORE.
IT'S PROOF WE WERE TOGETHER.
MR. POLAR BEAR...
...IS MY FRIEND!!
NO, NO, NO! WE COULD NEVER BE LIKE THAT.
BUN (SHAKE)
BUN
HE CAME BACK.
I BET THAT MEANS...
...WE CAN BE LOVERS.
"FRIENDS"? IT WOULD TAKE A MIRACLE FOR THAT TO...
THAT REALLY WAS A MIRACLE. THERE'S NO OTHER WORD FOR IT.
......
SEAL'S HEART WAS WAVERING.

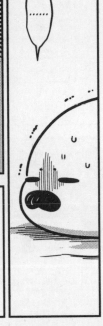

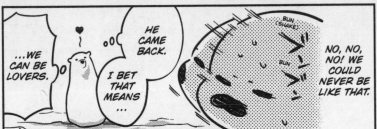

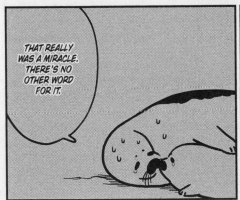

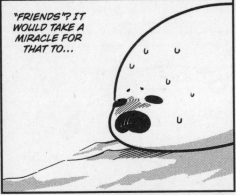

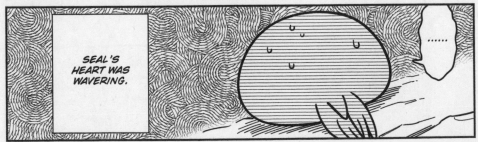

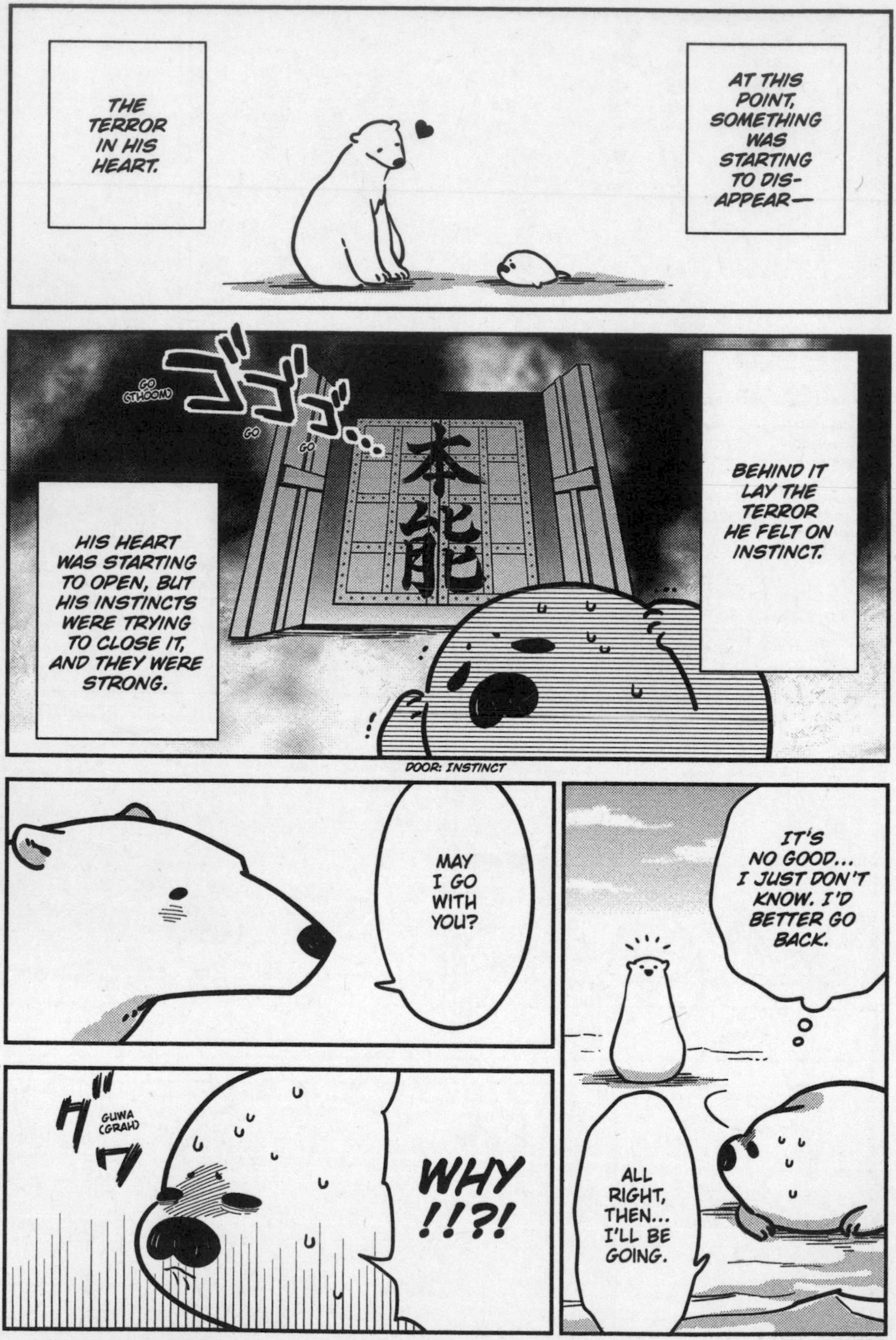
AT THIS POINT, SOMETHING WAS STARTING TO DIS-APPEAR—
THE TERROR IN HIS HEART.
BEHIND IT LAY THE TERROR HE FELT ON INSTINCT.
GO (THOOM)
GO
GO
HIS HEART WAS STARTING TO OPEN, BUT HIS INSTINCTS WERE TRYING TO CLOSE IT, AND THEY WERE STRONG.
DOOR: INSTINCT
IT'S NO GOOD... I JUST DON'T KNOW. I'D BETTER GO BACK.
ALL RIGHT, THEN... I'LL BE GOING.
MAY I GO WITH YOU?
GUWA (GRAH)
WHY!!?!

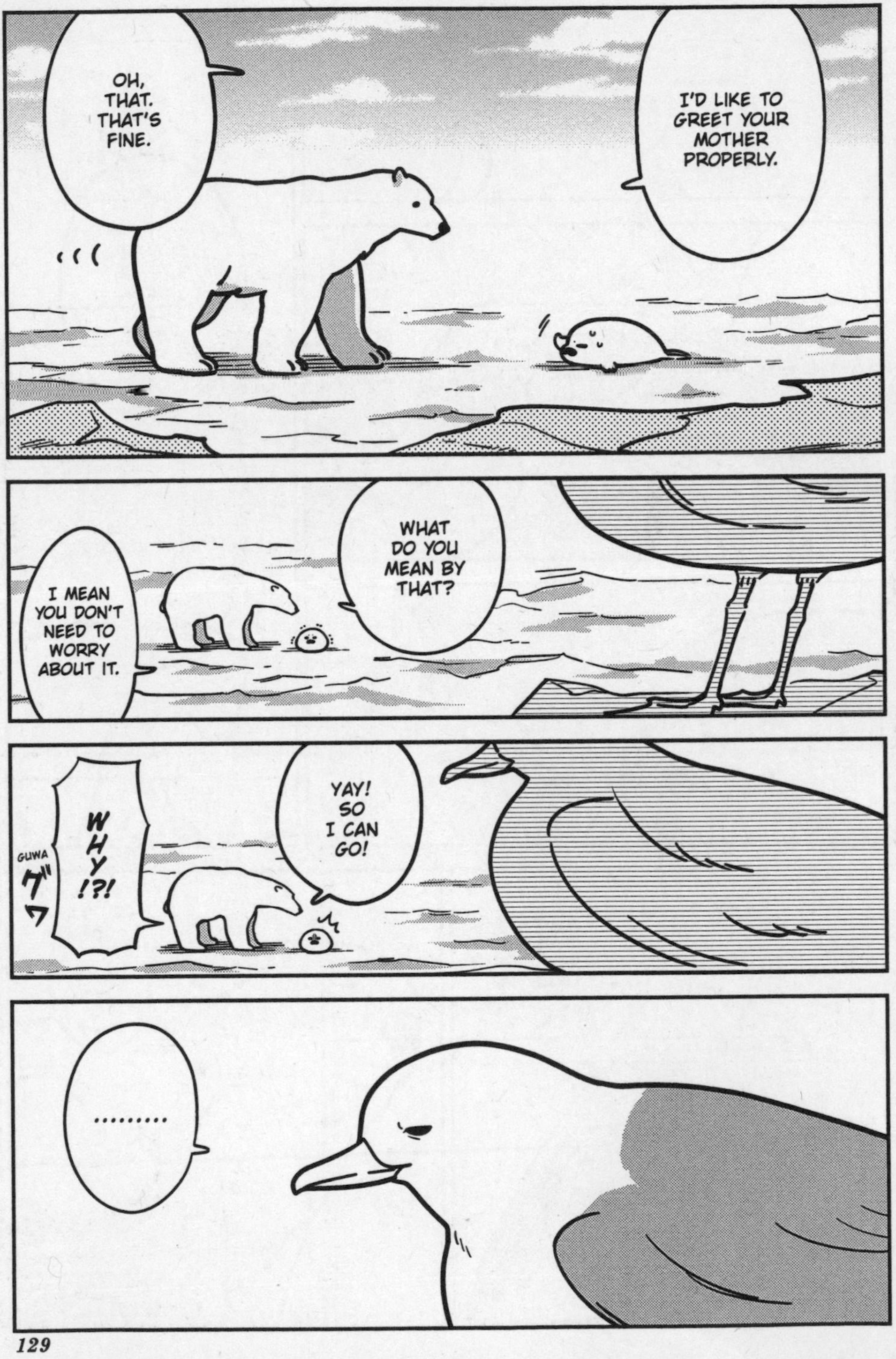
I'D LIKE TO GREET YOUR MOTHER PROPERLY.
OH, THAT. THAT'S FINE.
WHAT DO YOU MEAN BY THAT?
I MEAN YOU DON'T NEED TO WORRY ABOUT IT.
YAY! SO I CAN GO!
WHY!?!
GUWA
....

BIRD, STOP

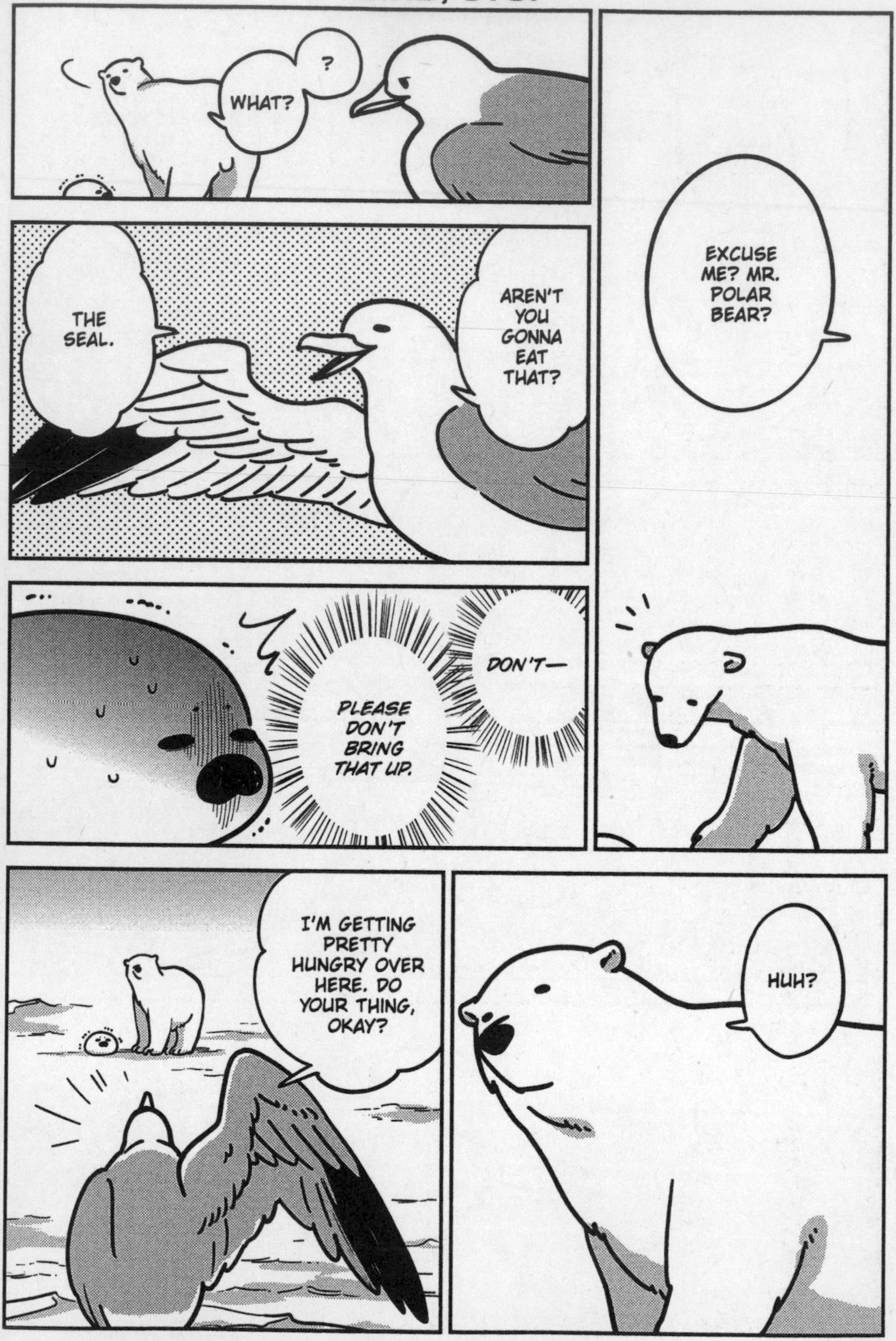

EXCUSE ME? MR. POLAR BEAR?
?
WHAT?
AREN'T YOU GONNA EAT THAT?
THE SEAL.
DON'T—
PLEASE DON'T BRING THAT UP.
HUH?
I'M GETTING PRETTY HUNGRY OVER HERE. DO YOUR THING, OKAY?

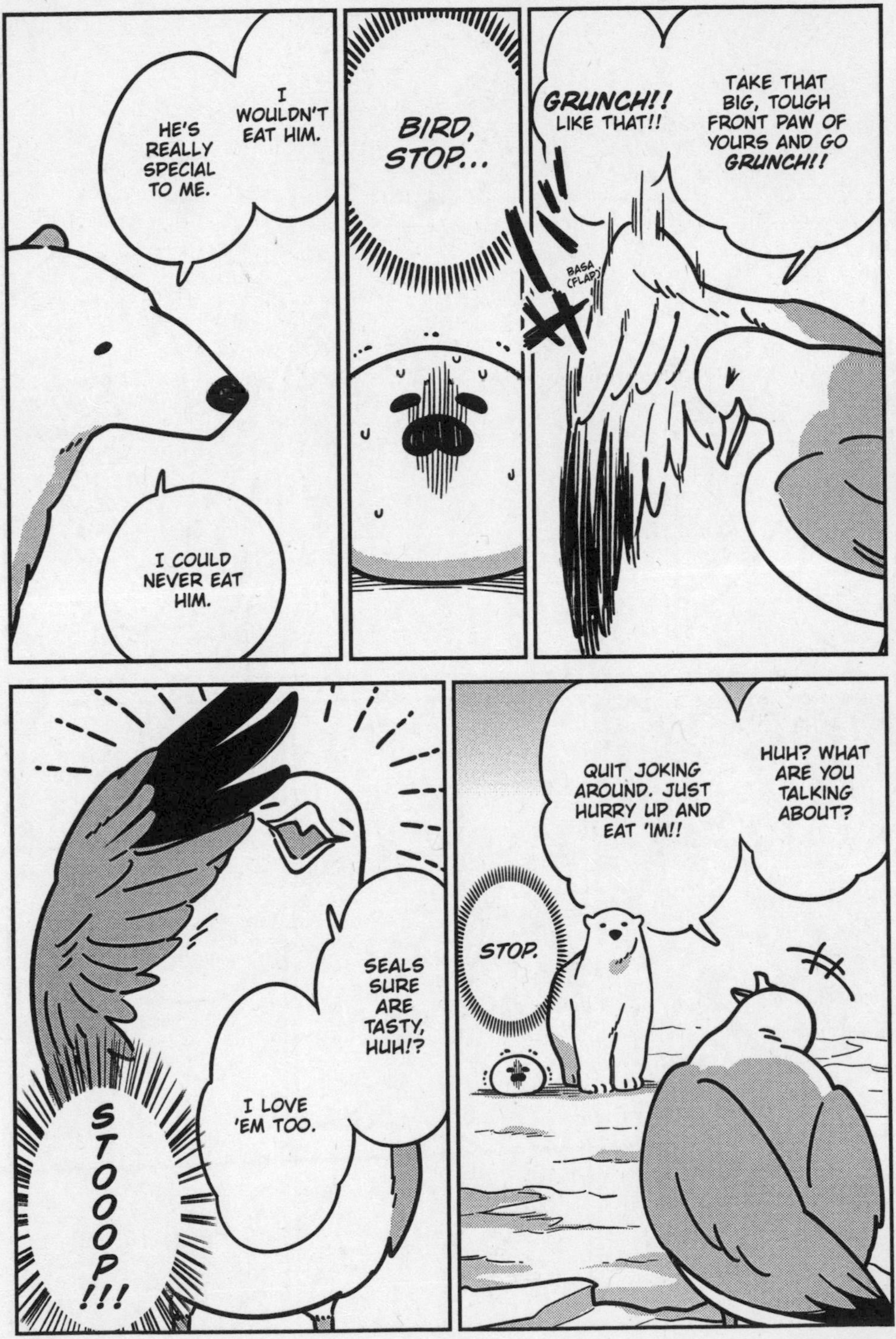
TAKE THAT BIG, TOUGH FRONT PAW OF YOURS AND GO GRUNCH!!
GRUNCH!! LIKE THAT!!
BASA (FLAP)
BIRD, STOP...
I WOULDN'T EAT HIM.
HE'S REALLY SPECIAL TO ME.
I COULD NEVER EAT HIM.
HUH? WHAT ARE YOU TALKING ABOUT?
QUIT JOKING AROUND. JUST HURRY UP AND EAT 'IM!!
STOP.
SEALS SURE ARE TASTY, HUH!?
I LOVE 'EM TOO.
STOOOOP!!!

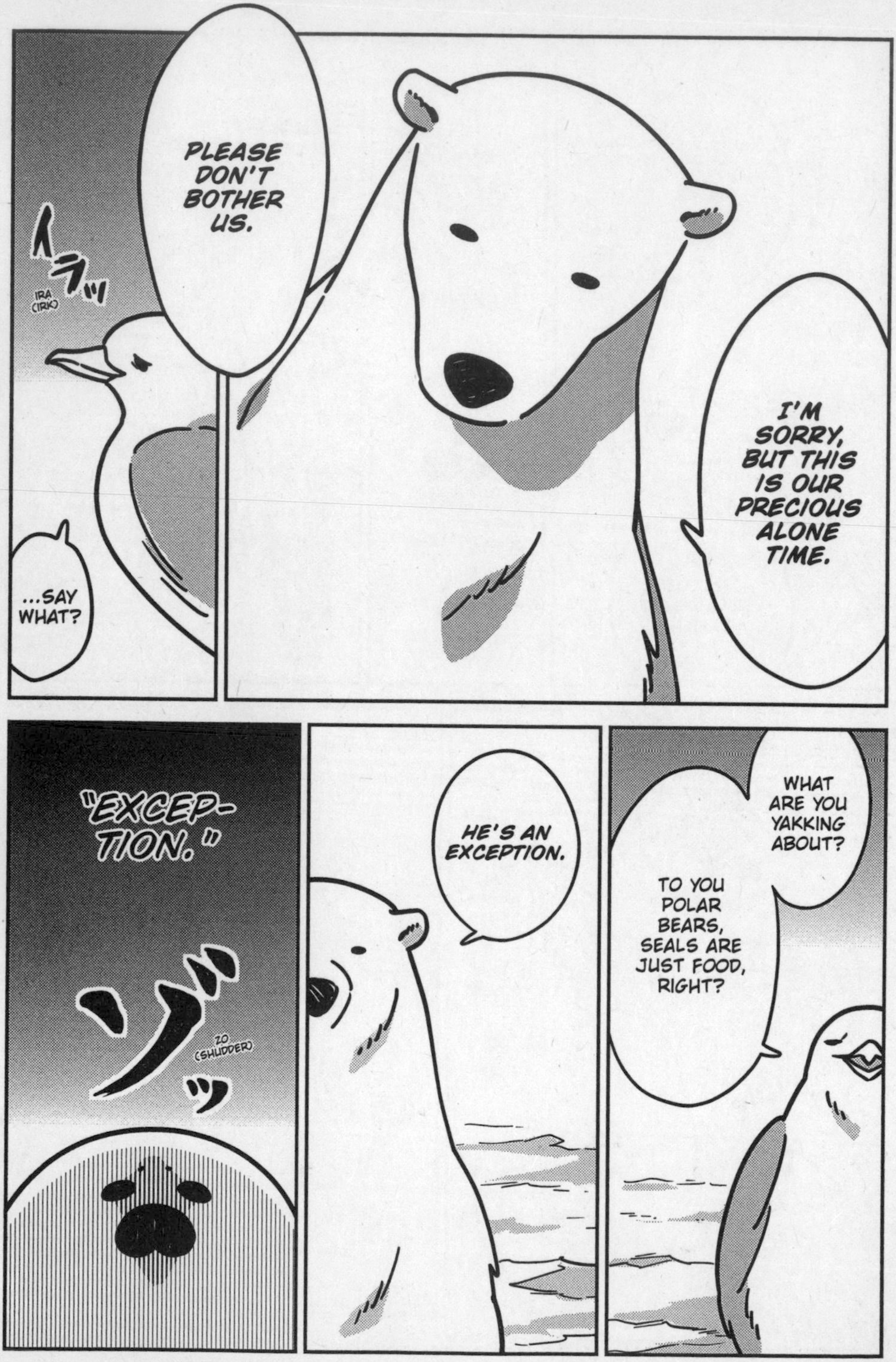
PLEASE DON'T BOTHER US.
I'M SORRY, BUT THIS IS OUR PRECIOUS ALONE TIME.
IRA (IRK)
...SAY WHAT?
WHAT ARE YOU YAKKING ABOUT?
TO YOU POLAR BEARS, SEALS ARE JUST FOOD, RIGHT?
HE'S AN EXCEPTION.
"EXCEP-TION."
ZO (SHUDDER)

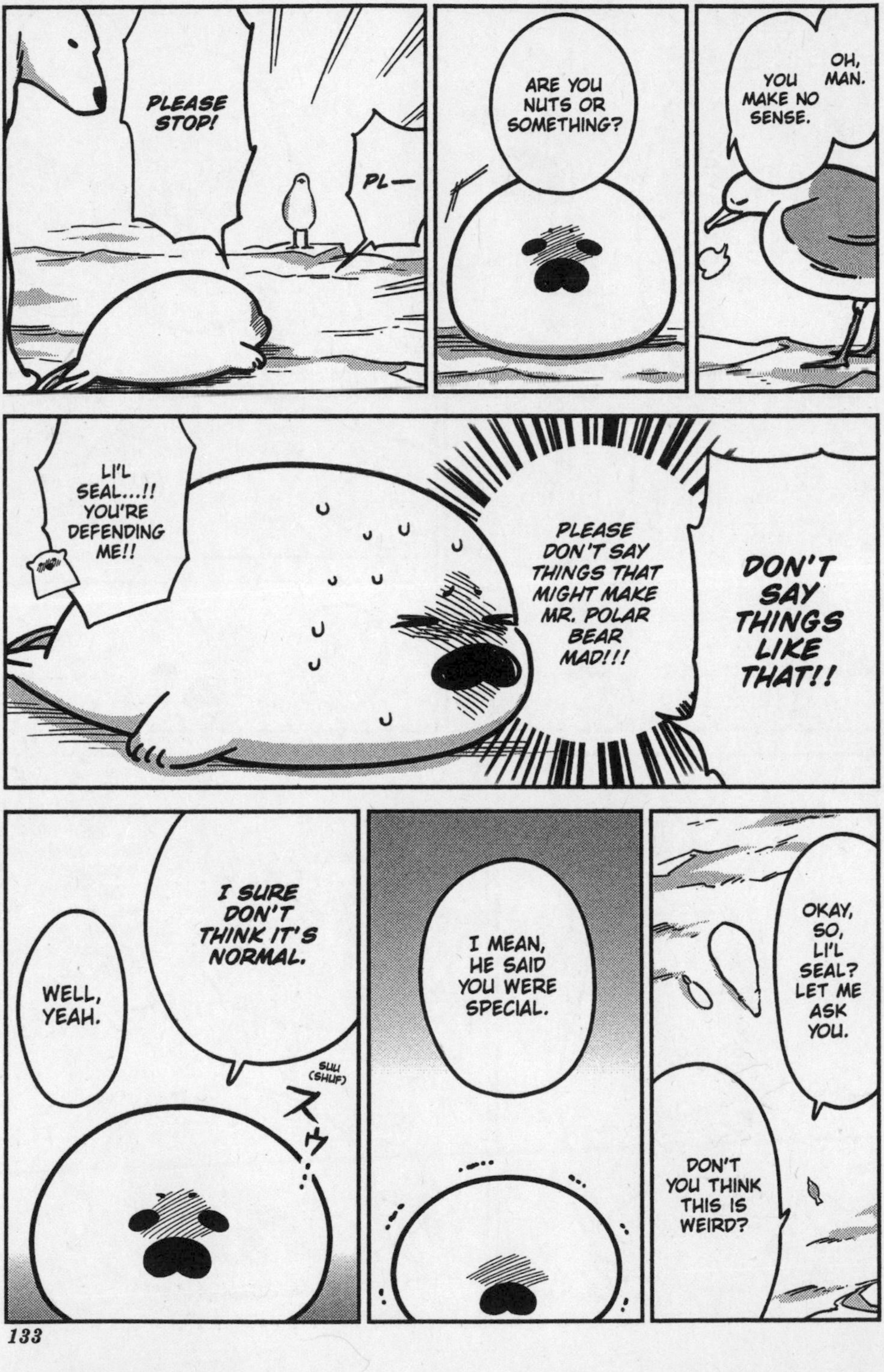
OH, MAN.
YOU MAKE NO SENSE.
ARE YOU NUTS OR SOMETHING?
PL—
PLEASE STOP!
DON'T SAY THINGS LIKE THAT!!
PLEASE DON'T SAY THINGS THAT MIGHT MAKE MR. POLAR BEAR MAD!!!
LI'L SEAL...!! YOU'RE DEFENDING ME!!
OKAY, SO, LI'L SEAL? LET ME ASK YOU.
DON'T YOU THINK THIS IS WEIRD?
I MEAN, HE SAID YOU WERE SPECIAL.
I SURE DON'T THINK IT'S NORMAL.
SUU (SHUF)
スゥ
WELL, YEAH.

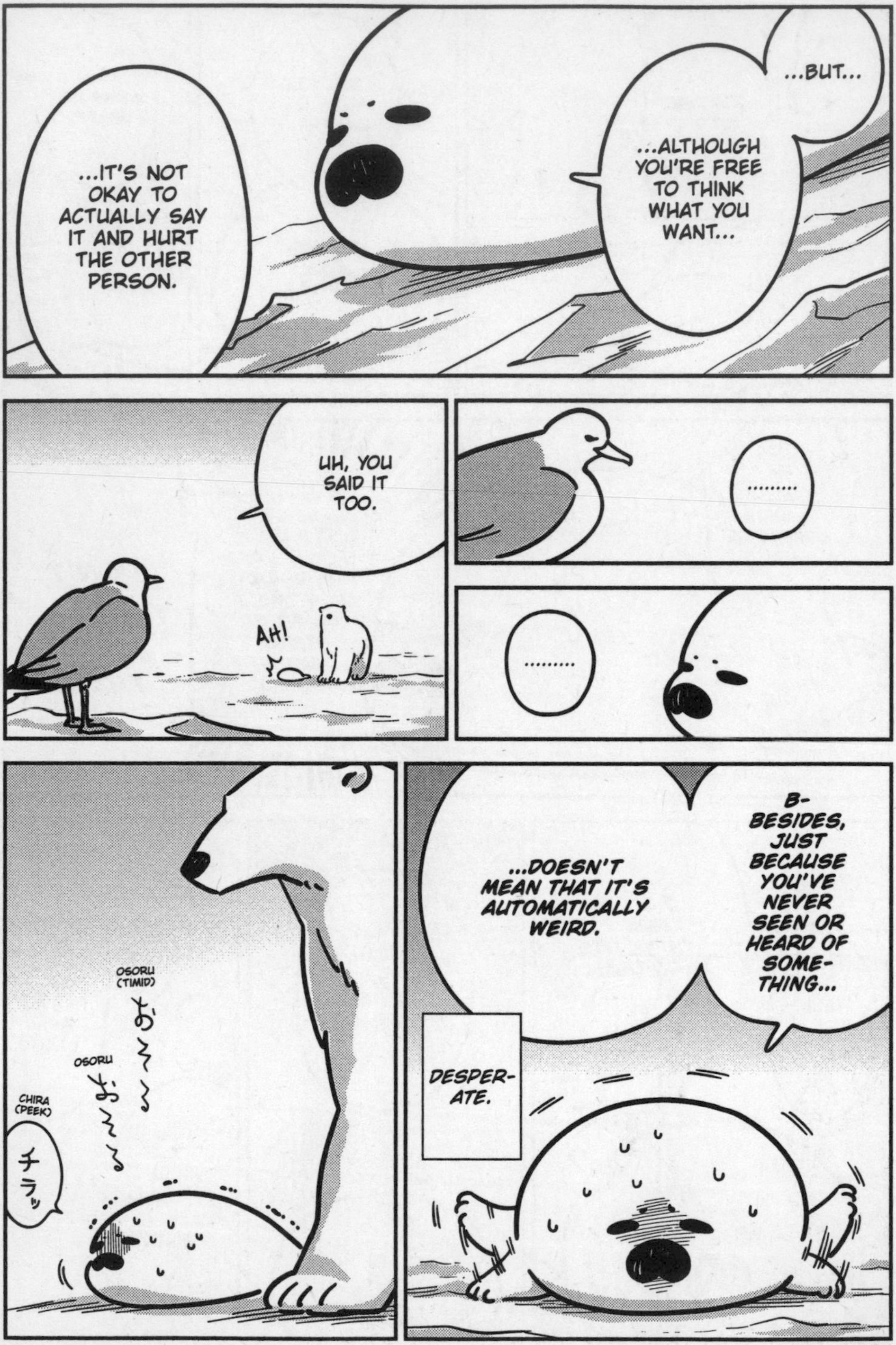
...BUT...
...ALTHOUGH YOU'RE FREE TO THINK WHAT YOU WANT...
...IT'S NOT OKAY TO ACTUALLY SAY IT AND HURT THE OTHER PERSON.
....
....
UH, YOU SAID IT TOO.
AH!
B-BESIDES, JUST BECAUSE YOU'VE NEVER SEEN OR HEARD OF SOME-THING...
...DOESN'T MEAN THAT IT'S AUTOMATICALLY WEIRD.
DESPER-ATE.
おそる
OSORU (TIMID)
おそる
OSORU
チラッ
CHIRA (PEEK)

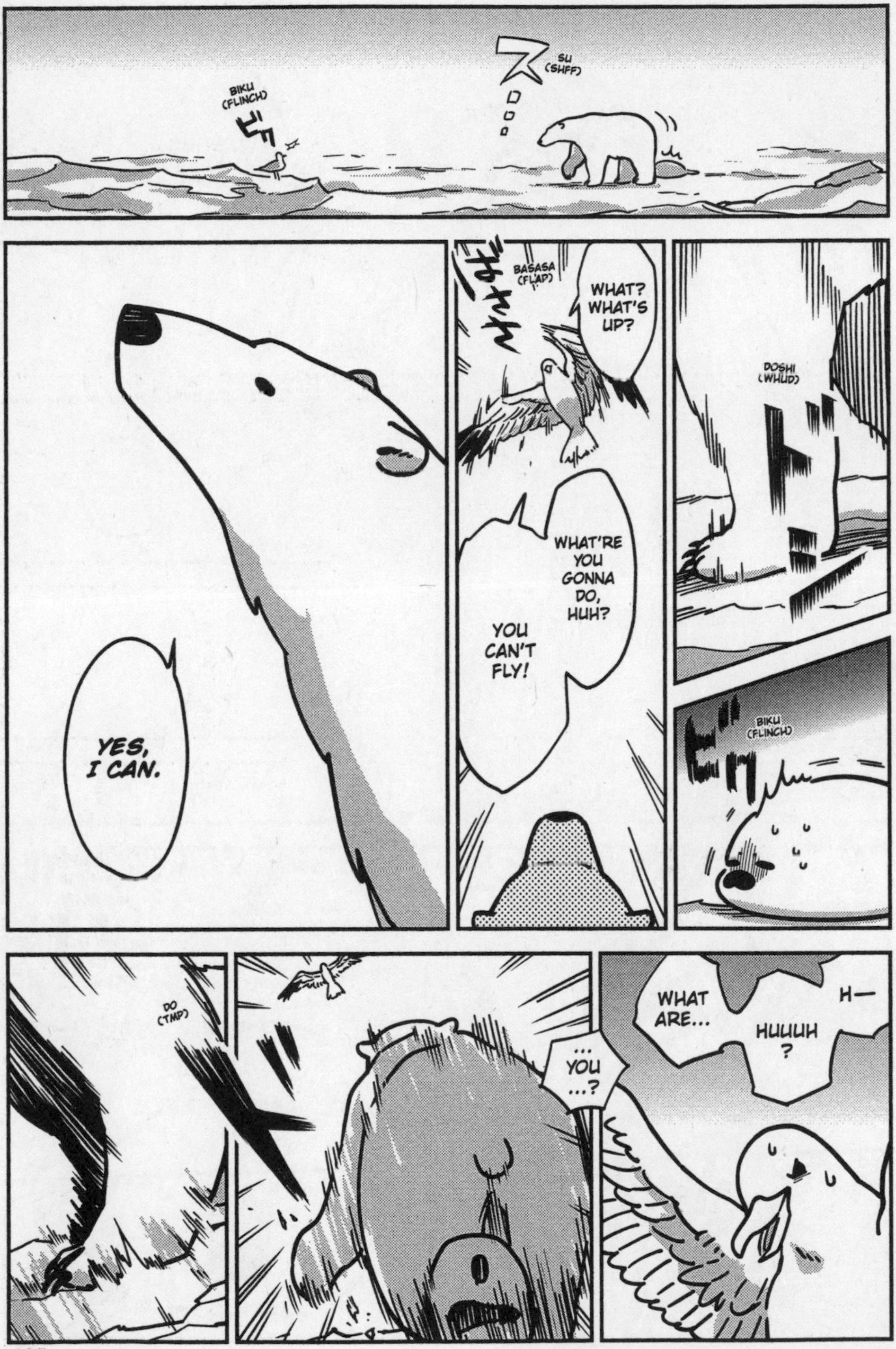
SU (SHFF)
BIKU (FLINCH)
DOSHI (WHUD)
BIKU (FLINCH)
WHAT? WHAT'S UP?
BASASA (FLAP)
WHAT'RE YOU GONNA DO, HUH?
YOU CAN'T FLY!
YES, I CAN.
H—
HUUUH?
WHAT ARE...
... YOU ...?
DO (TMP)

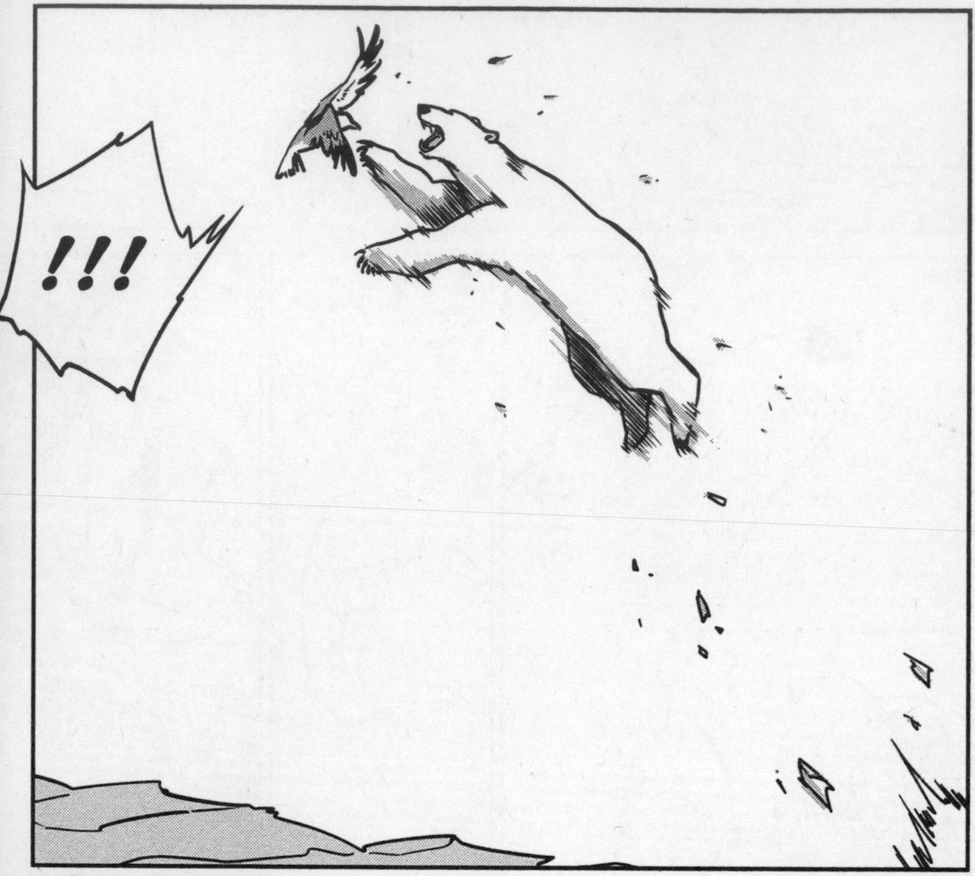
!!!

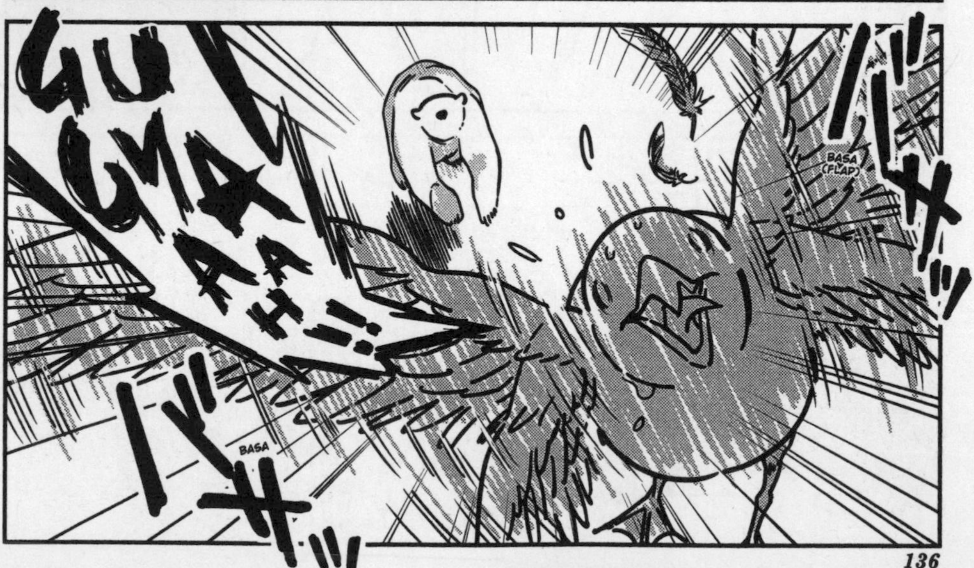
バサッ
BASA (FLAP)
GUGYAAAH--!!
バサッ
BASA

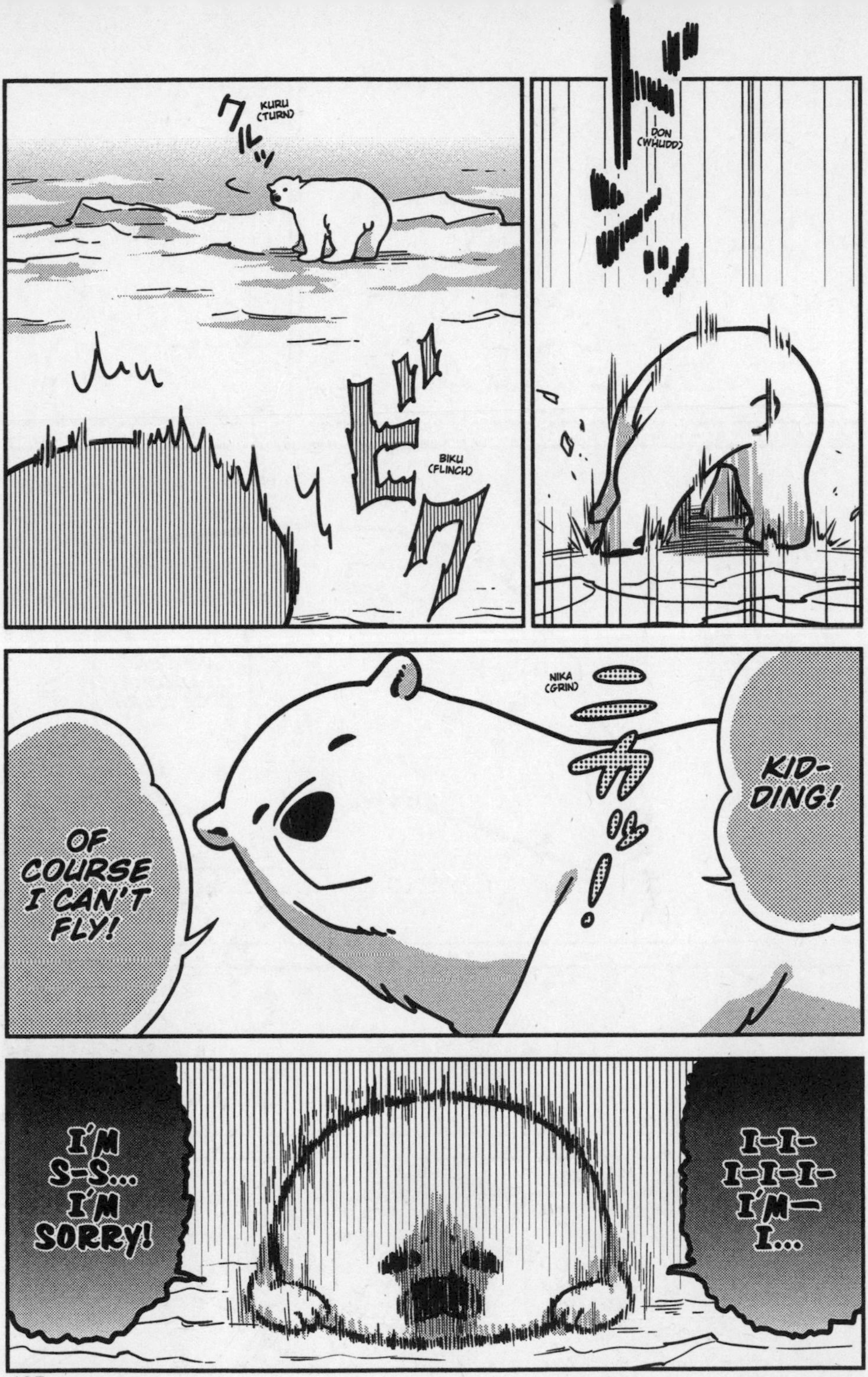

DON (WHUDD)
KURU (TURN)
BIKU (FLINCH)
NIKA (GRIN)
KID-DING!
OF COURSE I CAN'T FLY!
I-I- I-I-I- I'M— I...
I'M S-S... I'M SORRY!

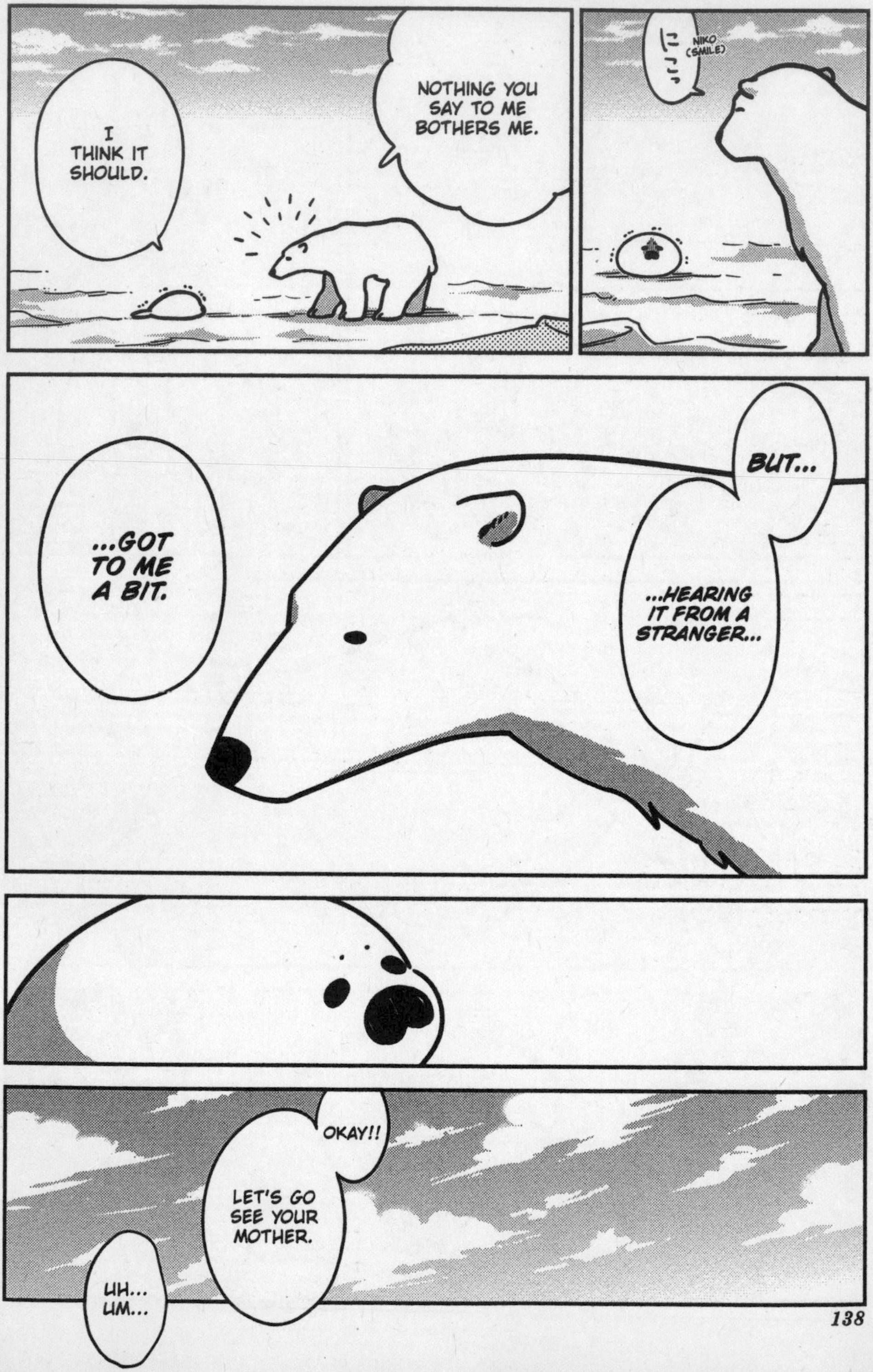
にこっ
NIKO (SMILE)
NOTHING YOU SAY TO ME BOTHERS ME.
I THINK IT SHOULD.
BUT...
...HEARING IT FROM A STRANGER...
...GOT TO ME A BIT.
OKAY!!
LET'S GO SEE YOUR MOTHER.
UH... UM...

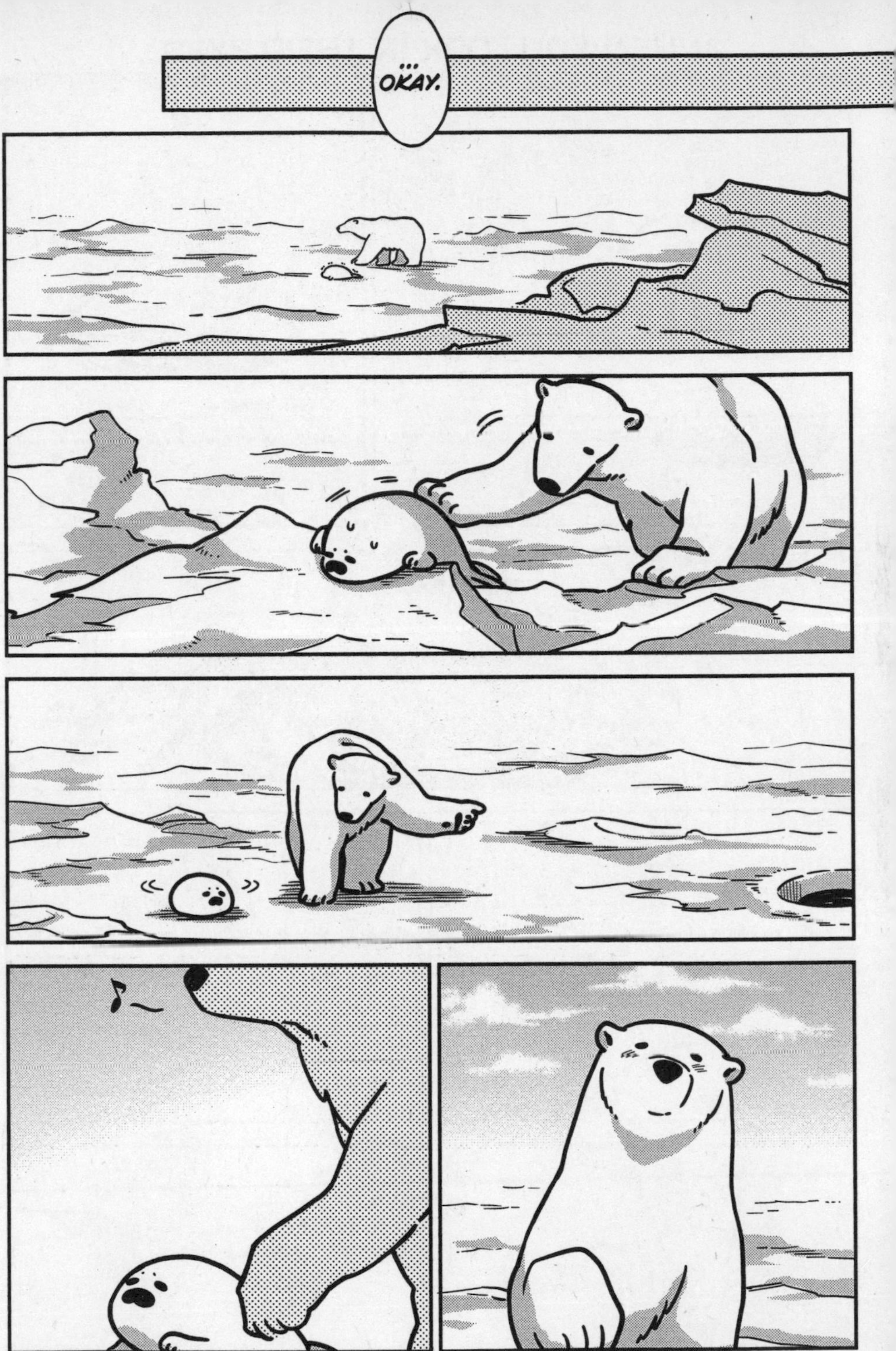
...OKAY.
♪~

WHEN YOU LOOK IN THEIR EYES...

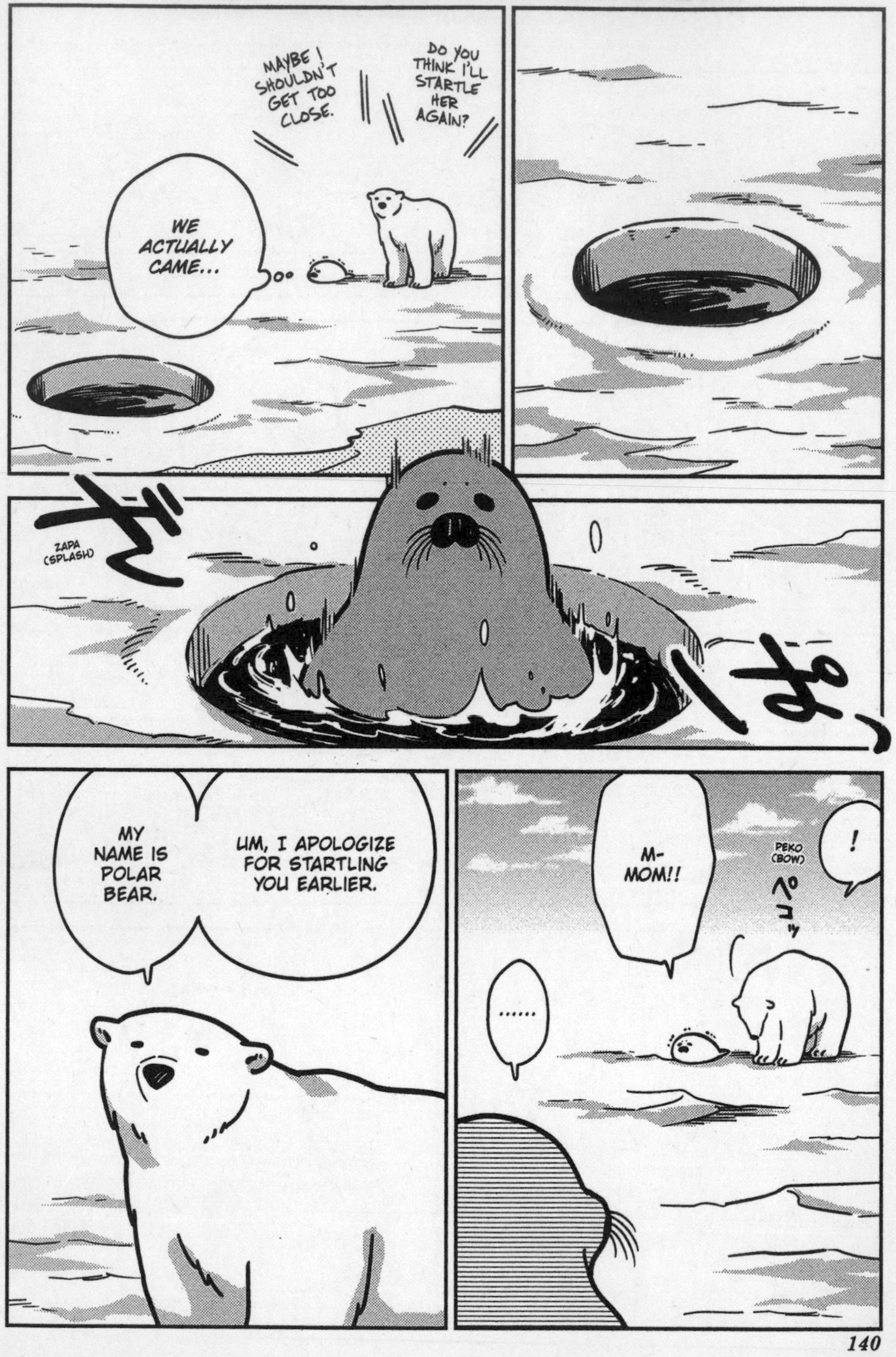
DO YOU THINK I'LL STARTLE HER AGAIN?
MAYBE I SHOULDN'T GET TOO CLOSE.
WE ACTUALLY CAME...
ZAPA (SPLASH)
!
PEKO (BOW)
M-MOM!!
......
UM, I APOLOGIZE FOR STARTLING YOU EARLIER.
MY NAME IS POLAR BEAR.

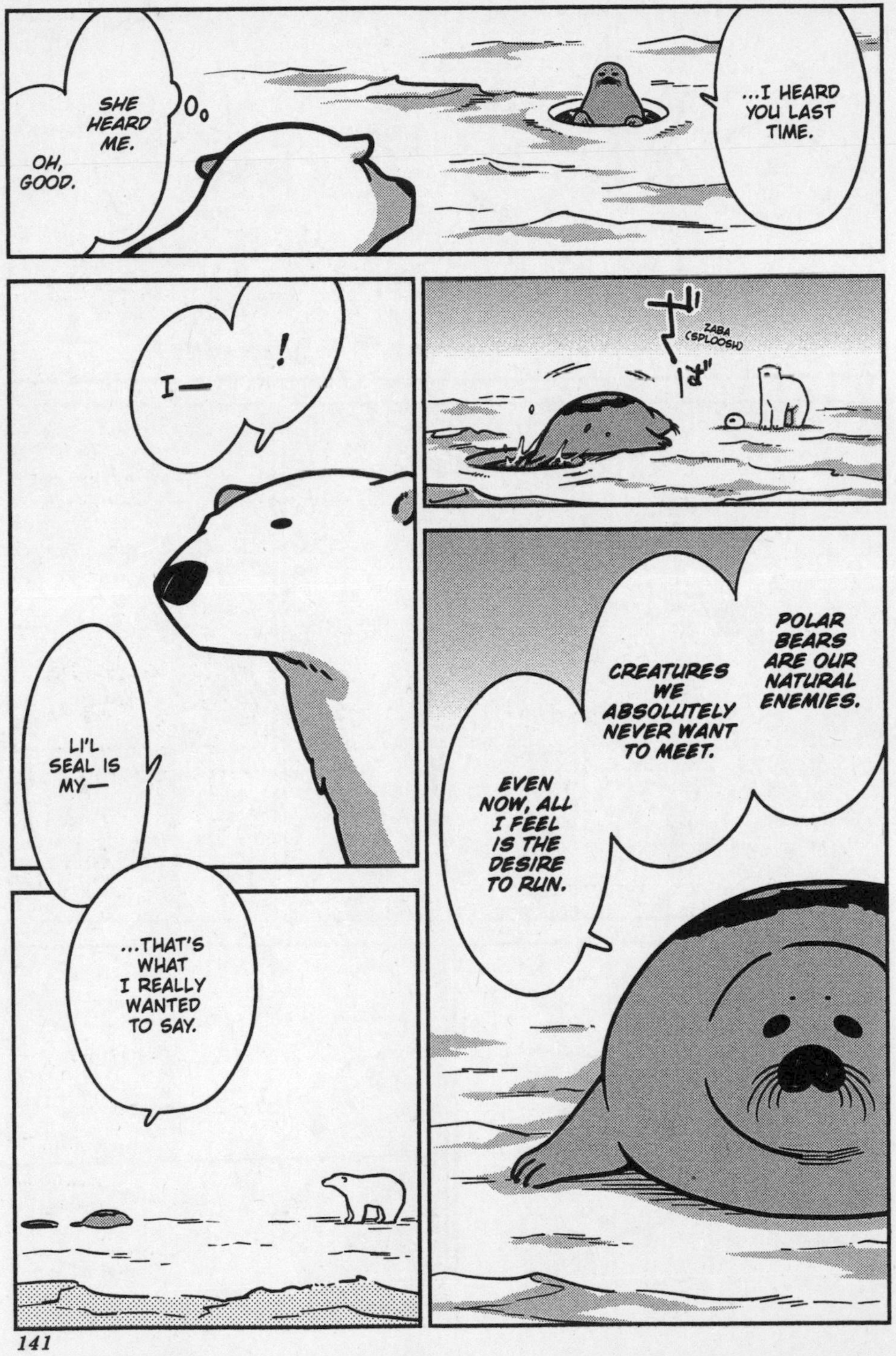
...I HEARD YOU LAST TIME.
SHE HEARD ME.
OH, GOOD.
ZABA (SPLOOSH)
POLAR BEARS ARE OUR NATURAL ENEMIES.
CREATURES WE ABSOLUTELY NEVER WANT TO MEET.
EVEN NOW, ALL I FEEL IS THE DESIRE TO RUN.
I— !
LI'L SEAL IS MY—
...THAT'S WHAT I REALLY WANTED TO SAY.

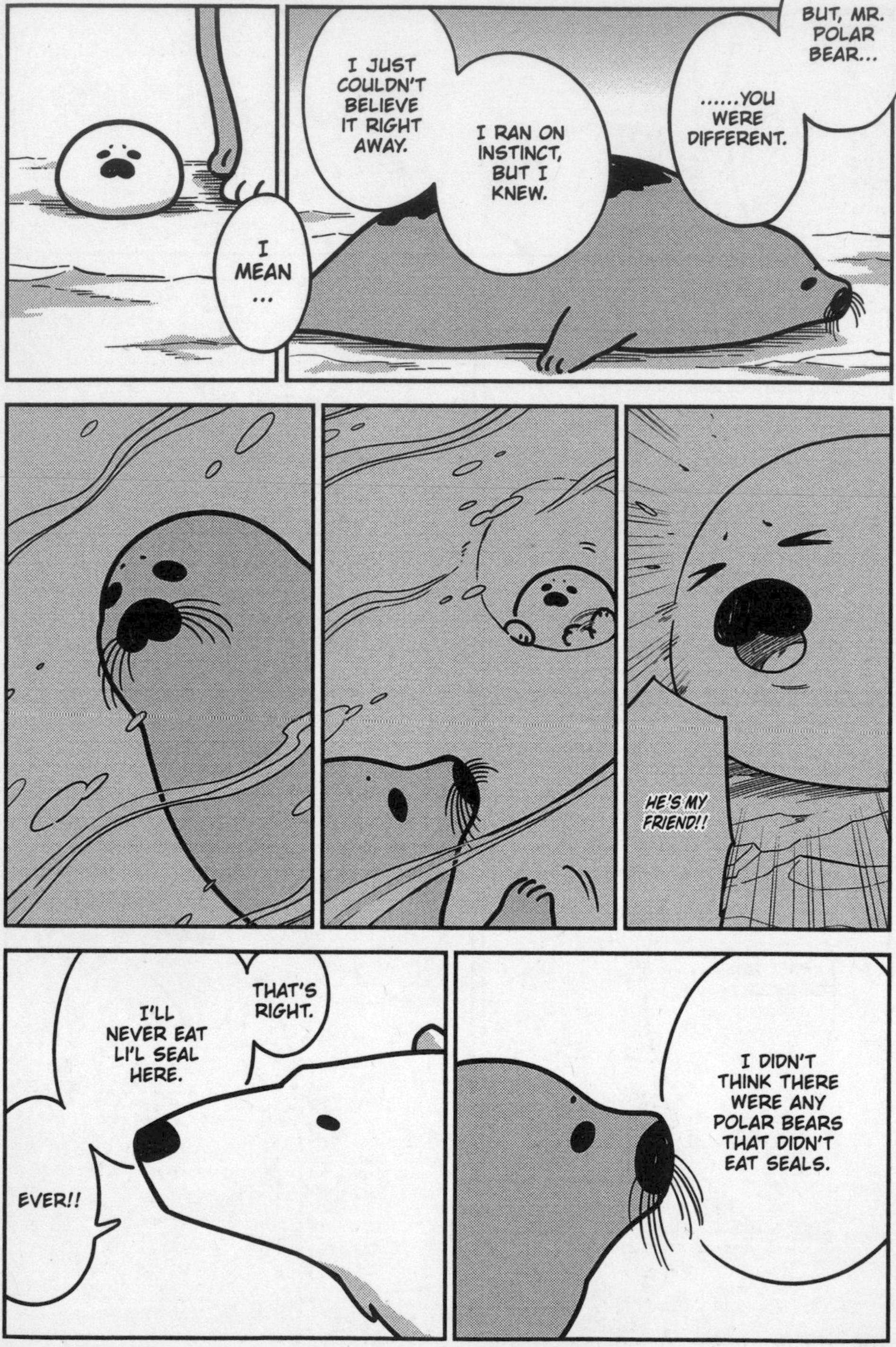
BUT, MR. POLAR BEAR...
......YOU WERE DIFFERENT.
I RAN ON INSTINCT, BUT I KNEW.
I JUST COULDN'T BELIEVE IT RIGHT AWAY.
I MEAN ...
HE'S MY FRIEND!!
I DIDN'T THINK THERE WERE ANY POLAR BEARS THAT DIDN'T EAT SEALS.
THAT'S RIGHT.
I'LL NEVER EAT LI'L SEAL HERE.
EVER!!

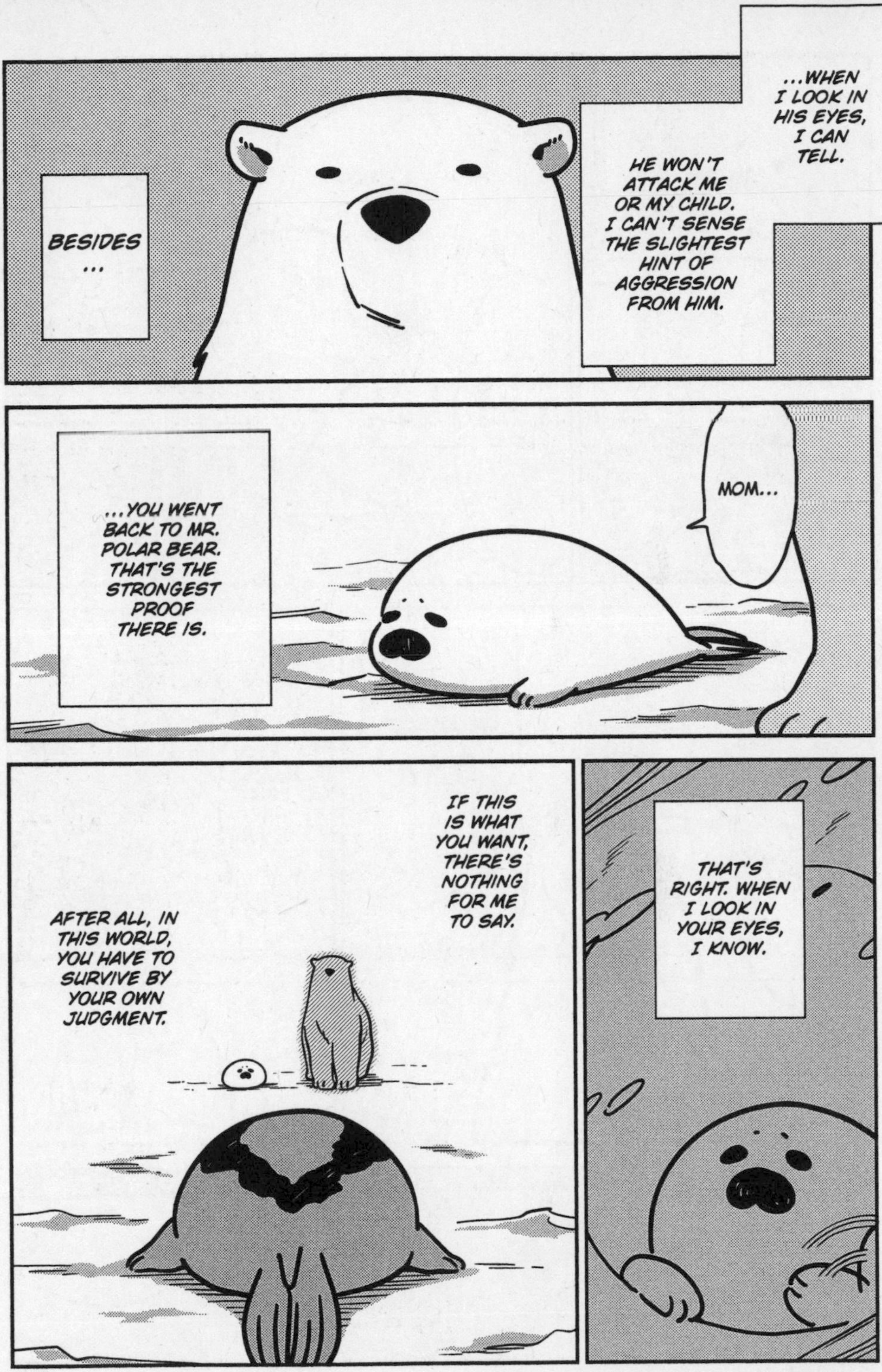
...WHEN I LOOK IN HIS EYES, I CAN TELL.
HE WON'T ATTACK ME OR MY CHILD. I CAN'T SENSE THE SLIGHTEST HINT OF AGGRESSION FROM HIM.
BESIDES...
MOM...
...YOU WENT BACK TO MR. POLAR BEAR. THAT'S THE STRONGEST PROOF THERE IS.
THAT'S RIGHT. WHEN I LOOK IN YOUR EYES, I KNOW.
IF THIS IS WHAT YOU WANT, THERE'S NOTHING FOR ME TO SAY.
AFTER ALL, IN THIS WORLD, YOU HAVE TO SURVIVE BY YOUR OWN JUDGMENT.

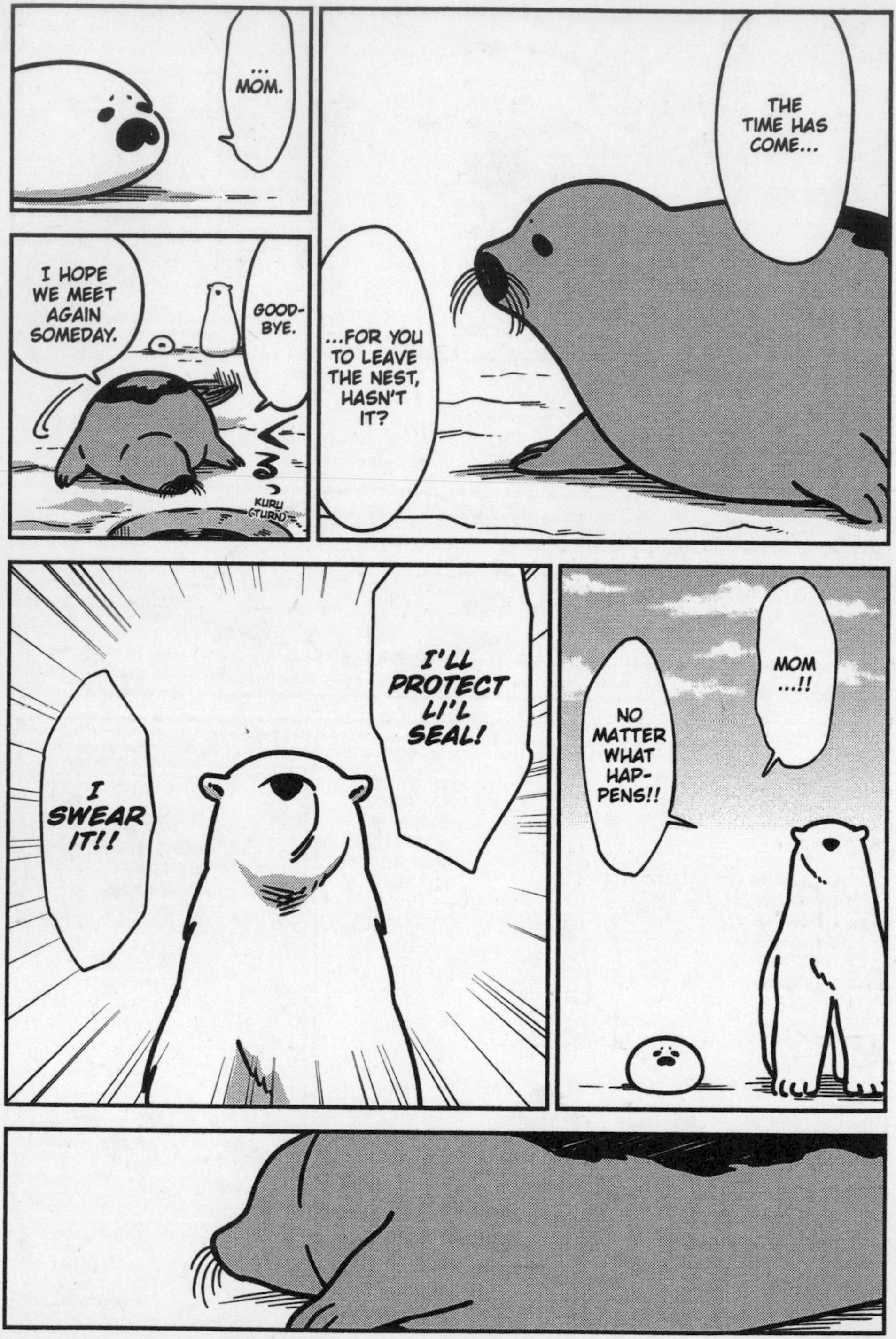
THE TIME HAS COME...
...FOR YOU TO LEAVE THE NEST, HASN'T IT?
...MOM.
GOOD-BYE.
I HOPE WE MEET AGAIN SOMEDAY.
くるっ
KURU (TURN)
MOM ...!!
NO MATTER WHAT HAP-PENS!!
I'LL PROTECT LI'L SEAL!
I SWEAR IT!!

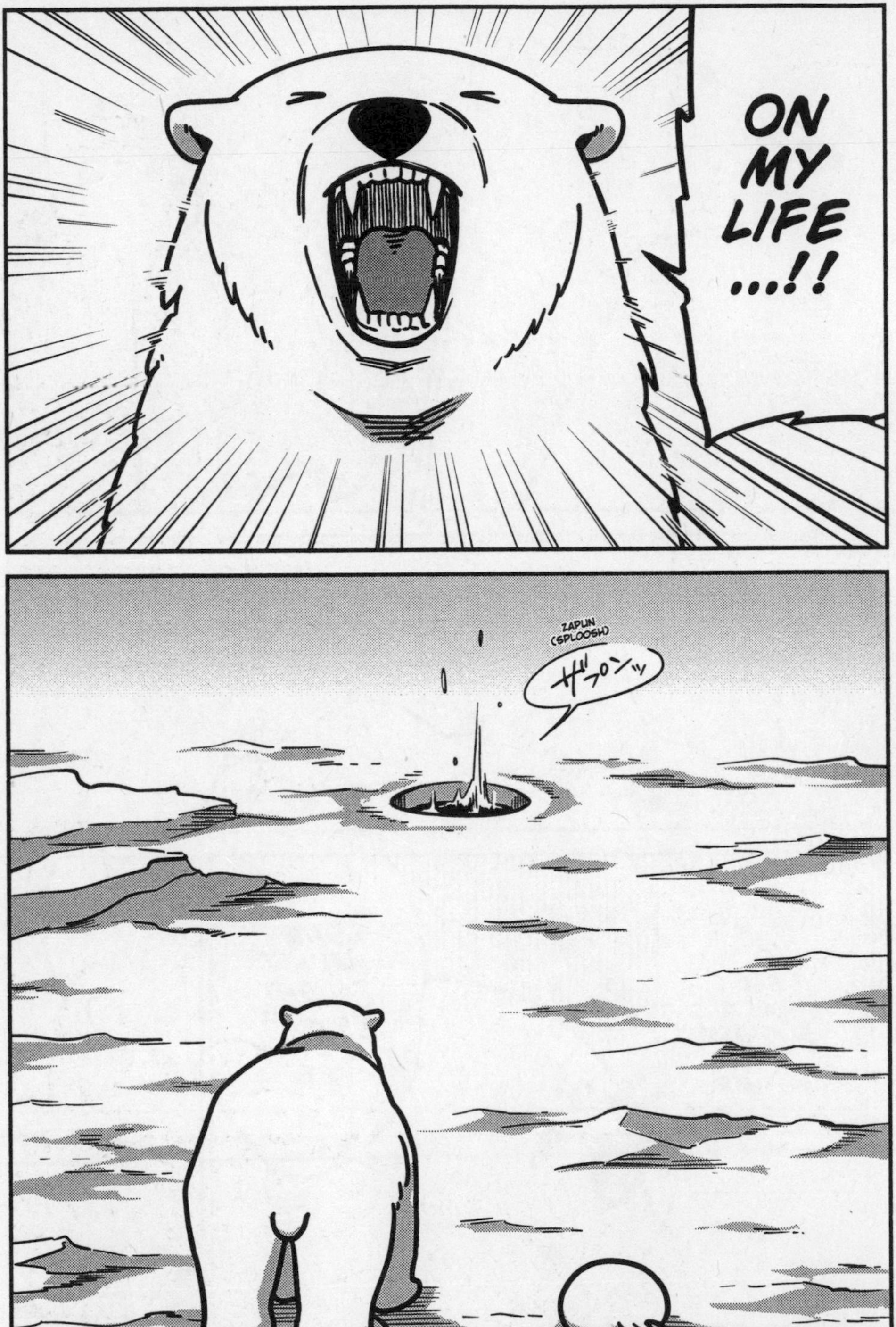
ON MY LIFE ...!!
ZAPUN (SPLOOSH)
ザブンッ

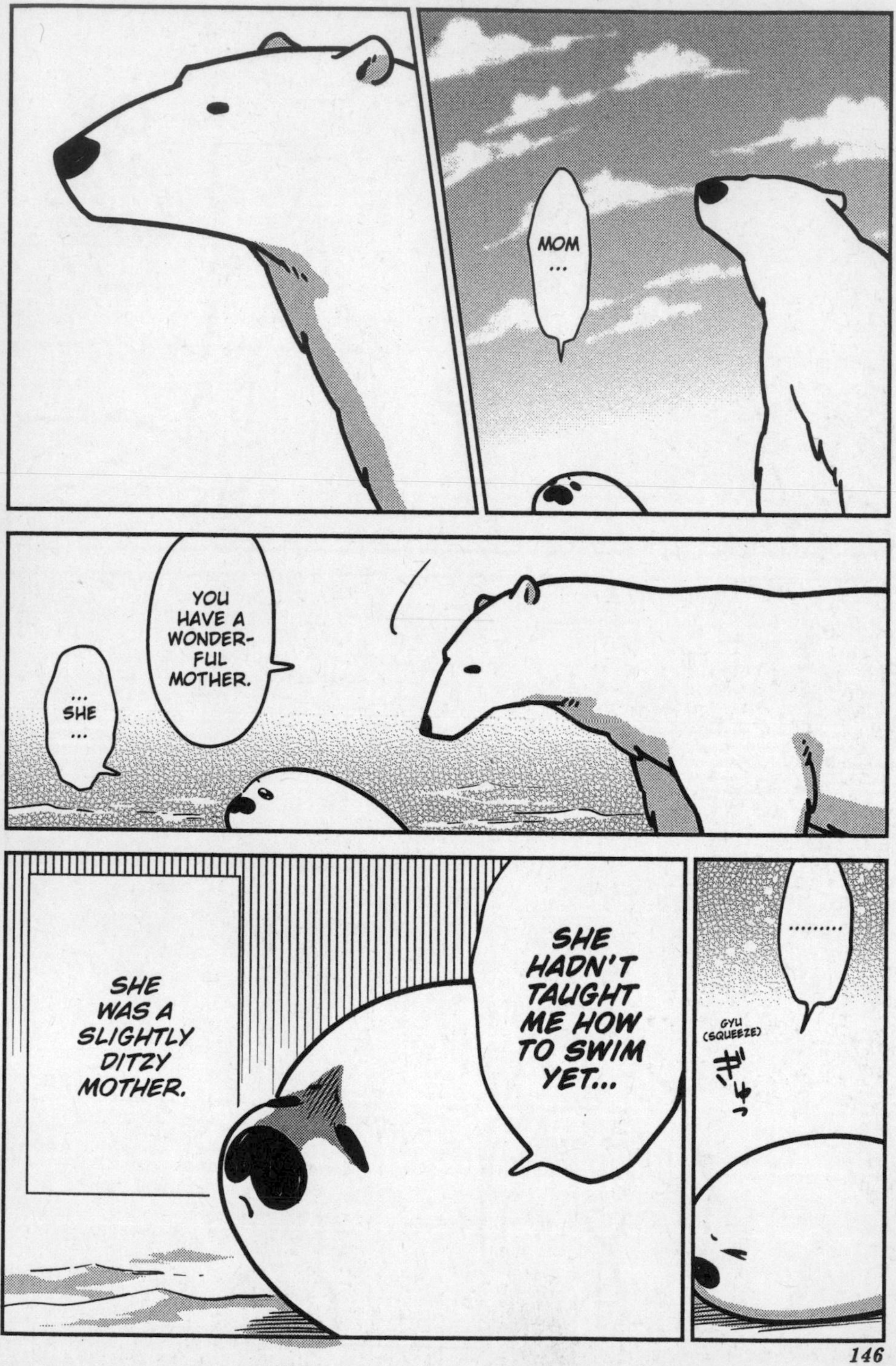
MOM ...
YOU HAVE A WONDERFUL MOTHER.
... SHE ...
....
GYU (SQUEEZE)
ぎゅっ
SHE HADN'T TAUGHT ME HOW TO SWIM YET...
SHE WAS A SLIGHTLY DITZY MOTHER.

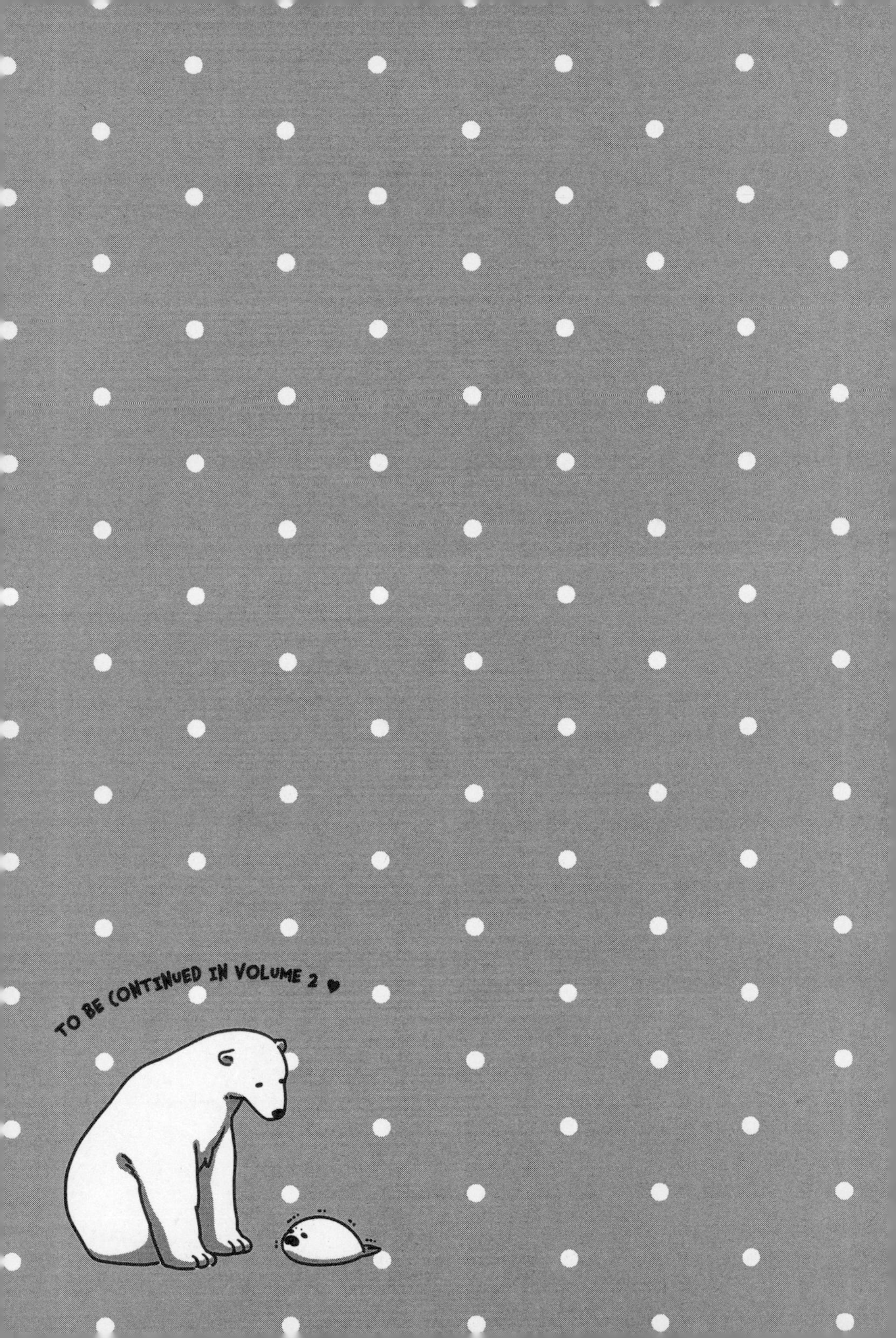
TO BE CONTINUED IN VOLUME 2 ♥

BACKGROUND MANGA FOR THE
CHAPTER SPLASH PAGES

SUMMER

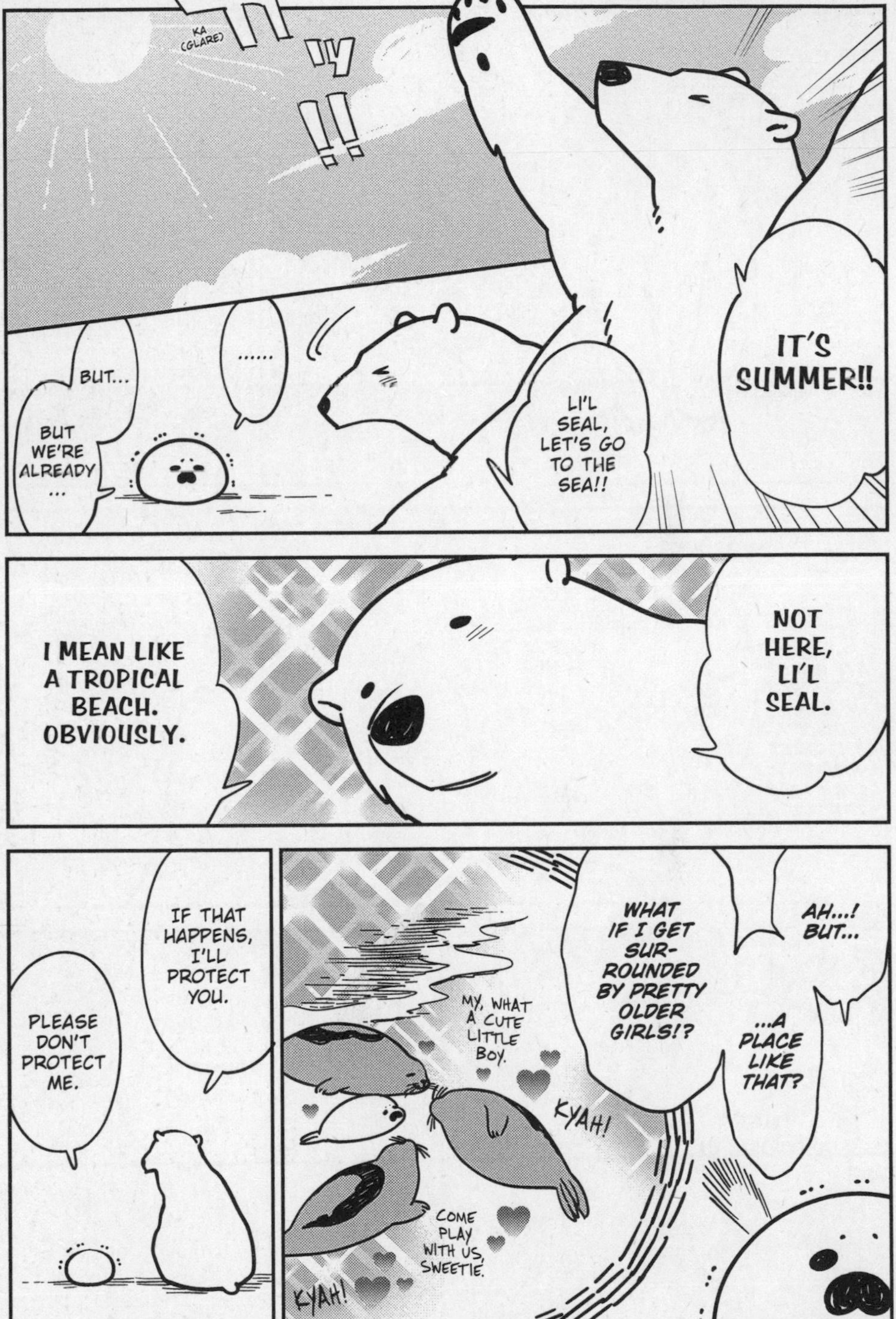
IT'S SUMMER!!
KA (GLARE)
LI'L SEAL, LET'S GO TO THE SEA!!
......
BUT...
BUT WE'RE ALREADY ...
NOT HERE, LI'L SEAL.
I MEAN LIKE A TROPICAL BEACH. OBVIOUSLY.
AH...! BUT...
...A PLACE LIKE THAT?
WHAT IF I GET SUR-ROUNDED BY PRETTY OLDER GIRLS!?
MY, WHAT A CUTE LITTLE BOY.
KYAH!
COME PLAY WITH US, SWEETIE.
KYAH!
IF THAT HAPPENS, I'LL PROTECT YOU.
PLEASE DON'T PROTECT ME.

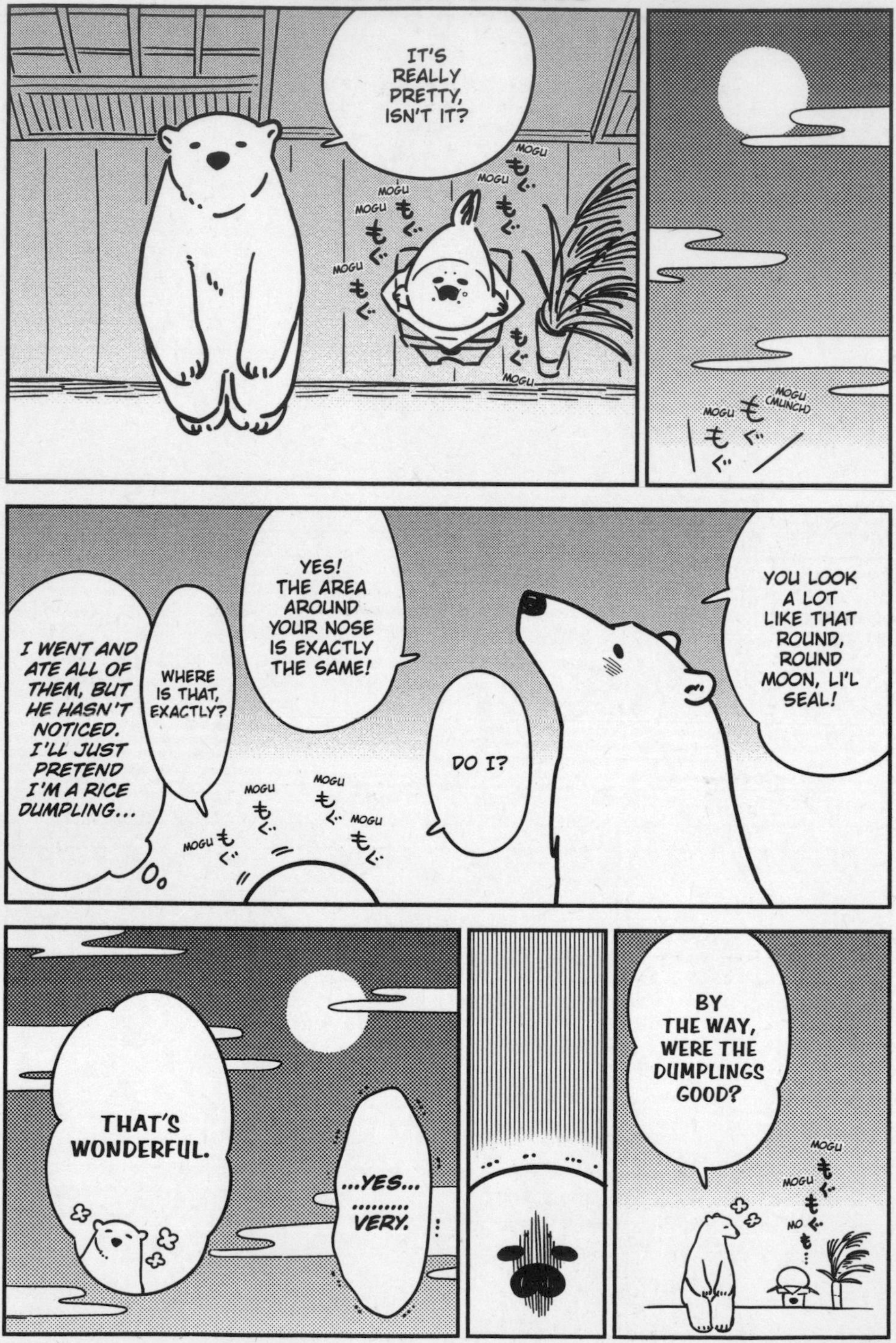
MOGU (MUNCH) もぐ
MOGU もぐ
IT'S REALLY PRETTY, ISN'T IT?
MOGU もぐ
MOGU もぐ
MOGU もぐ
MOGU もぐ
MOGU もぐ
MOGU もぐ
YOU LOOK A LOT LIKE THAT ROUND, ROUND MOON, LI'L SEAL!
DO I?
YES! THE AREA AROUND YOUR NOSE IS EXACTLY THE SAME!
WHERE IS THAT, EXACTLY?
I WENT AND ATE ALL OF THEM, BUT HE HASN'T NOTICED. I'LL JUST PRETEND I'M A RICE DUMPLING...
MOGU もぐ
MOGU もぐ
MOGU もぐ
MOGU もぐ
BY THE WAY, WERE THE DUMPLINGS GOOD?
MOGU もぐ
MOGU もぐ
MO も...
...YES... .... VERY.
THAT'S WONDERFUL.

HALLOWEEN

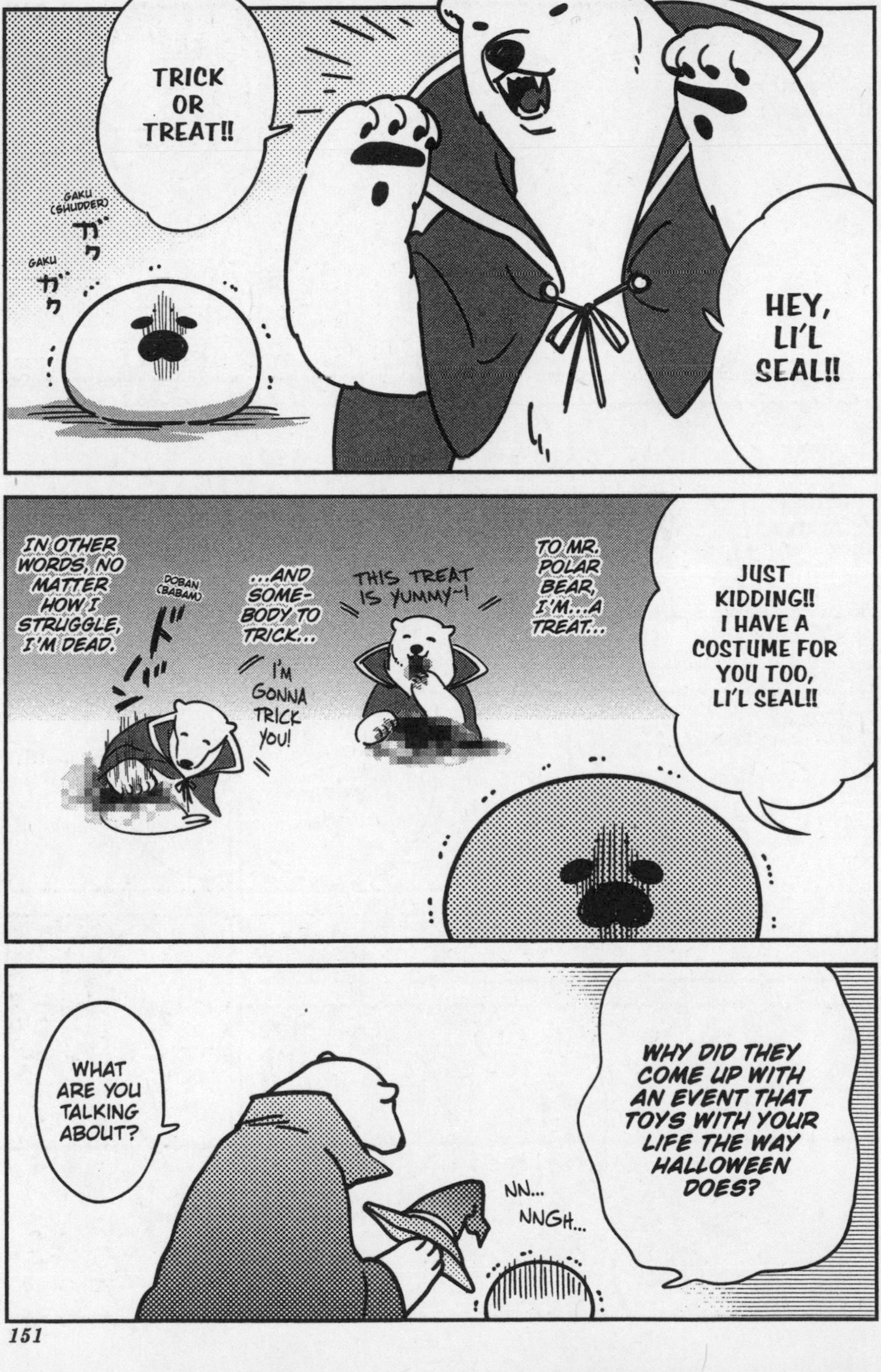
HEY, LI'L SEAL!!
TRICK OR TREAT!!
GAKU (SHUDDER)
GAKU
JUST KIDDING!! I HAVE A COSTUME FOR YOU TOO, LI'L SEAL!!
TO MR. POLAR BEAR, I'M...A TREAT...
THIS TREAT IS YUMMY~!
...AND SOME-BODY TO TRICK...
I'M GONNA TRICK YOU!
DOBAN (BABAM)
IN OTHER WORDS, NO MATTER HOW I STRUGGLE, I'M DEAD.
WHY DID THEY COME UP WITH AN EVENT THAT TOYS WITH YOUR LIFE THE WAY HALLOWEEN DOES?
NN... NNGH...
WHAT ARE YOU TALKING ABOUT?

AUTUMN IS FOR EATING

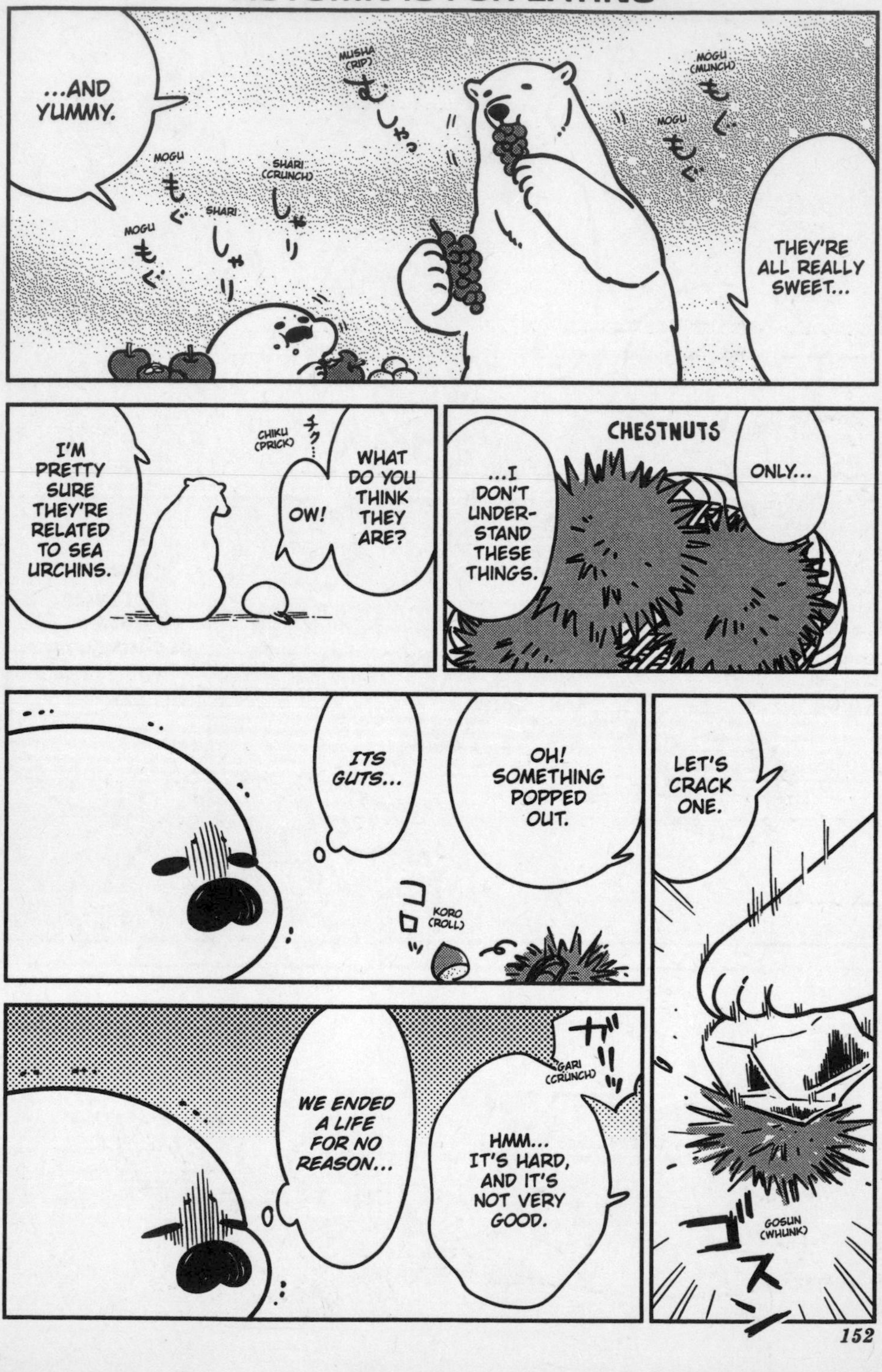
THEY'RE ALL REALLY SWEET...
MOGU (MUNCH)
MOGU
MUSHA (RIP)
SHARI (CRUNCH)
SHARI
MOGU
MOGU
...AND YUMMY.
ONLY...
CHESTNUTS
...I DON'T UNDERSTAND THESE THINGS.
WHAT DO YOU THINK THEY ARE?
CHIKU (PRICK)
OW!
I'M PRETTY SURE THEY'RE RELATED TO SEA URCHINS.
LET'S CRACK ONE.
GOSUN (WHUNK)
OH! SOMETHING POPPED OUT.
ITS GUTS...
KORO (ROLL)
...
GARI (CRUNCH)
HMM... IT'S HARD, AND IT'S NOT VERY GOOD.
WE ENDED A LIFE FOR NO REASON...
...

CHRISTMAS

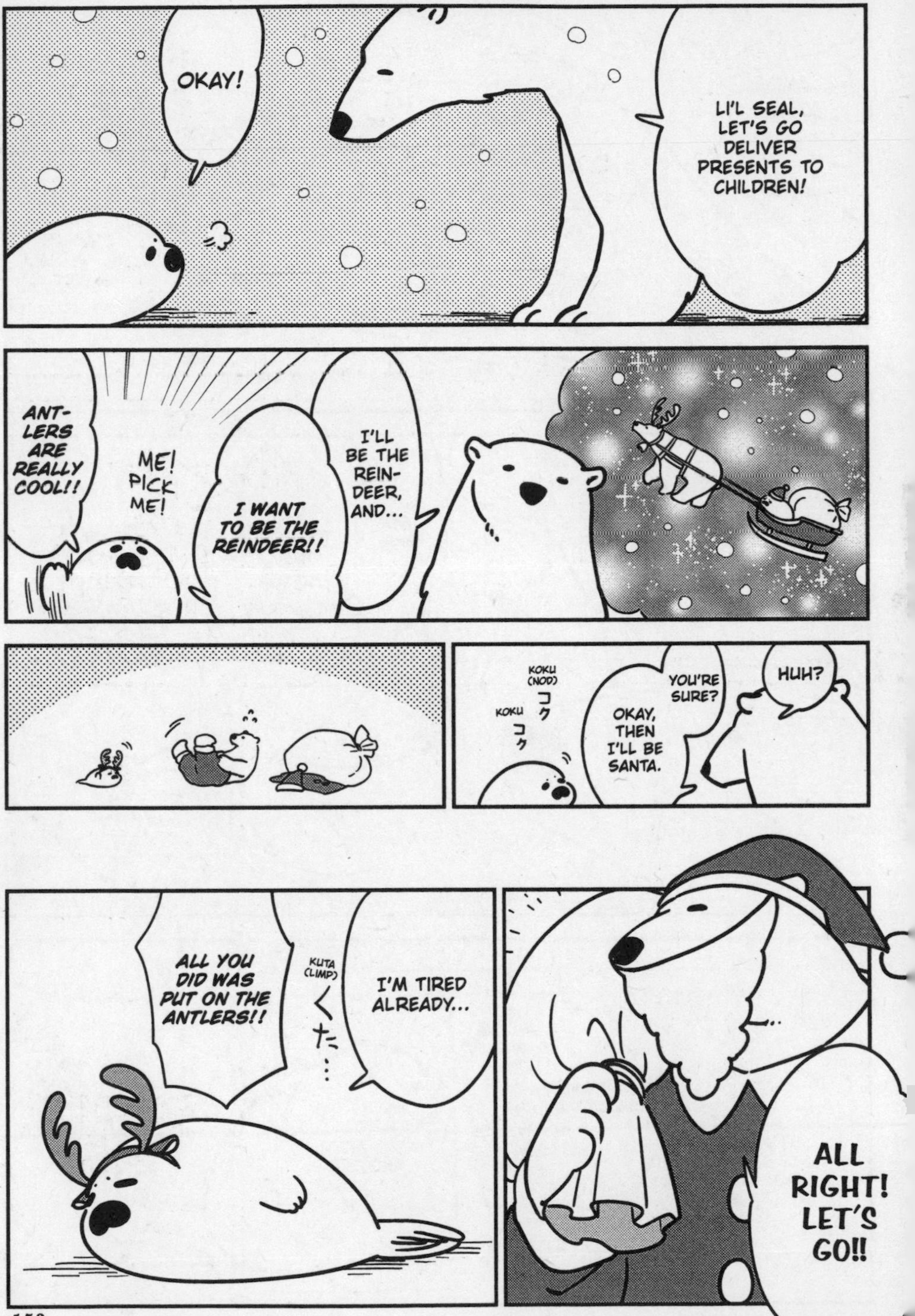
LI'L SEAL, LET'S GO DELIVER PRESENTS TO CHILDREN!
OKAY!
I'LL BE THE REIN-DEER, AND...
I WANT TO BE THE REINDEER!!
ME! PICK ME!
ANT-LERS ARE REALLY COOL!!
HUH?
YOU'RE SURE?
KOKU (NOD)
コク
KOKU
コク
OKAY, THEN I'LL BE SANTA.
ALL RIGHT! LET'S GO!!
I'M TIRED ALREADY...
KUTA (LIMP)
くた…
ALL YOU DID WAS PUT ON THE ANTLERS!!

NEW YEAR'S

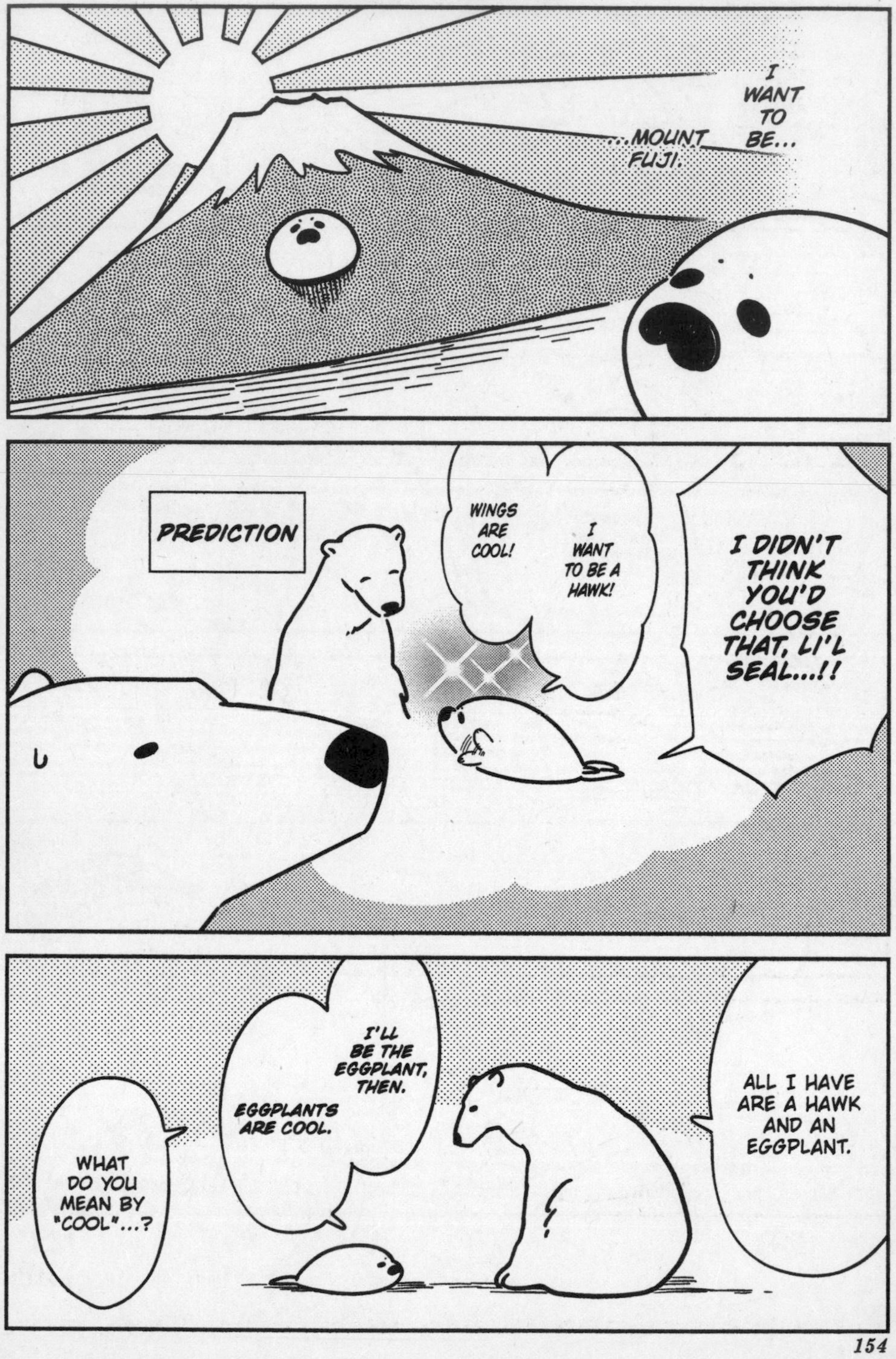
I WANT TO BE...
...MOUNT FUJI.
I DIDN'T THINK YOU'D CHOOSE THAT, LI'L SEAL...!!
I WANT TO BE A HAWK!
WINGS ARE COOL!
PREDICTION
ALL I HAVE ARE A HAWK AND AN EGGPLANT.
I'LL BE THE EGGPLANT, THEN.
EGGPLANTS ARE COOL.
WHAT DO YOU MEAN BY "COOL"...?

THE WEIGHT OF LOVE

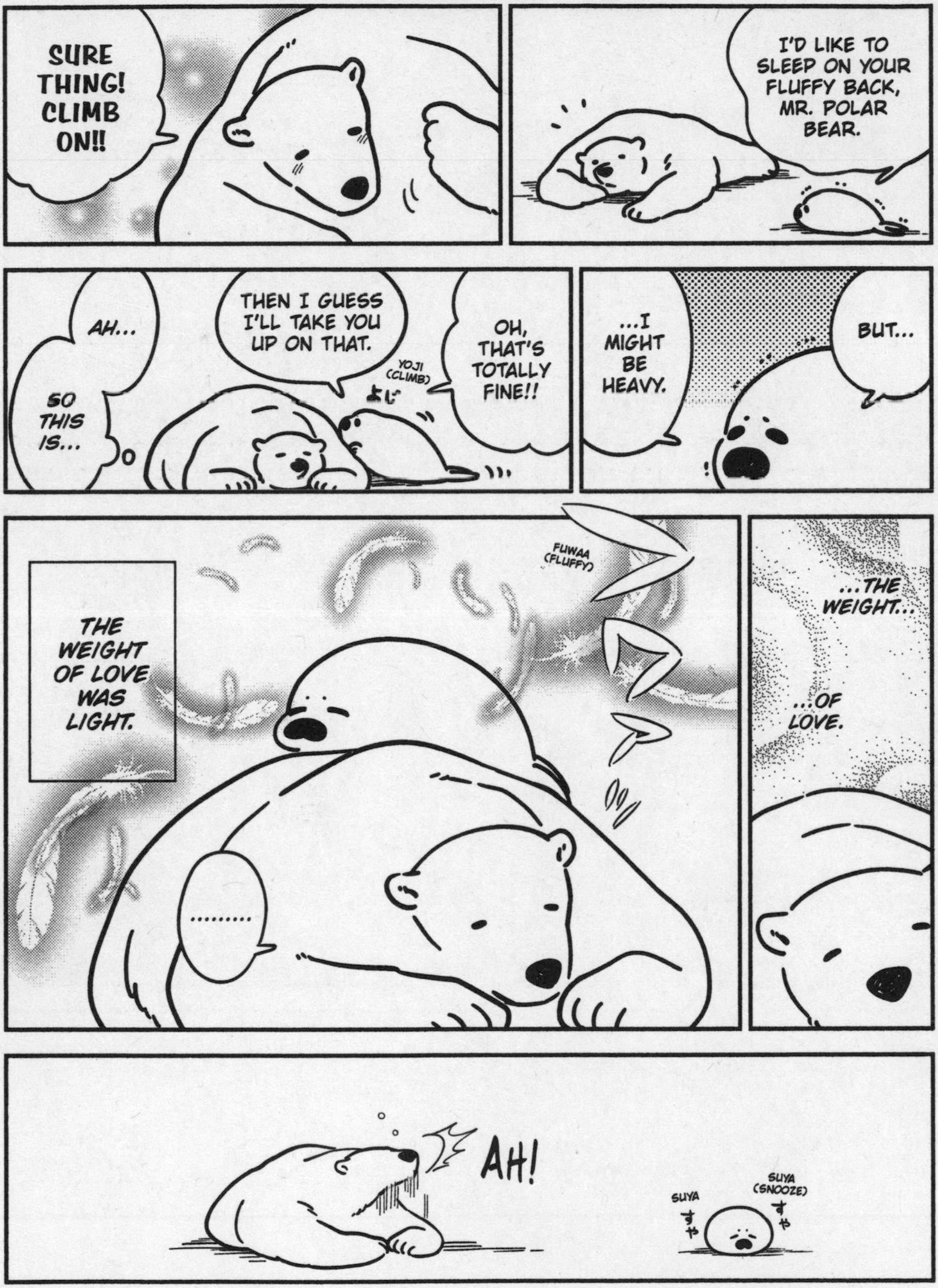
I'D LIKE TO SLEEP ON YOUR FLUFFY BACK, MR. POLAR BEAR.
SURE THING! CLIMB ON!!
BUT...
...I MIGHT BE HEAVY.
OH, THAT'S TOTALLY FINE!!
YOJI (CLIMB)
THEN I GUESS I'LL TAKE YOU UP ON THAT.
AH...
SO THIS IS...
...THE WEIGHT...
...OF LOVE.
FUWAA (FLUFFY)
THE WEIGHT OF LOVE WAS LIGHT.
....
AH!
SUYA (SNOOZE)
SUYA

I'M GRATEFUL TO EVERYONE WHO HELPED WITH THIS BOOK AND EVERYONE WHO READ IT. THANK YOU SO MUCH!

THE SPARKLE OF
COUNTLESS SHINING
STARS CAN'T COMPARE
TO YOUR BEAUTY.
HOWEVER, I SWEAR ON
THIS NIGHT SKY THAT
I'LL PROTECT YOU WITH
MY LIFE...

FROM
MR. POLAR
BEAR'S
LETTER.

COMING FEBRUARY 2018

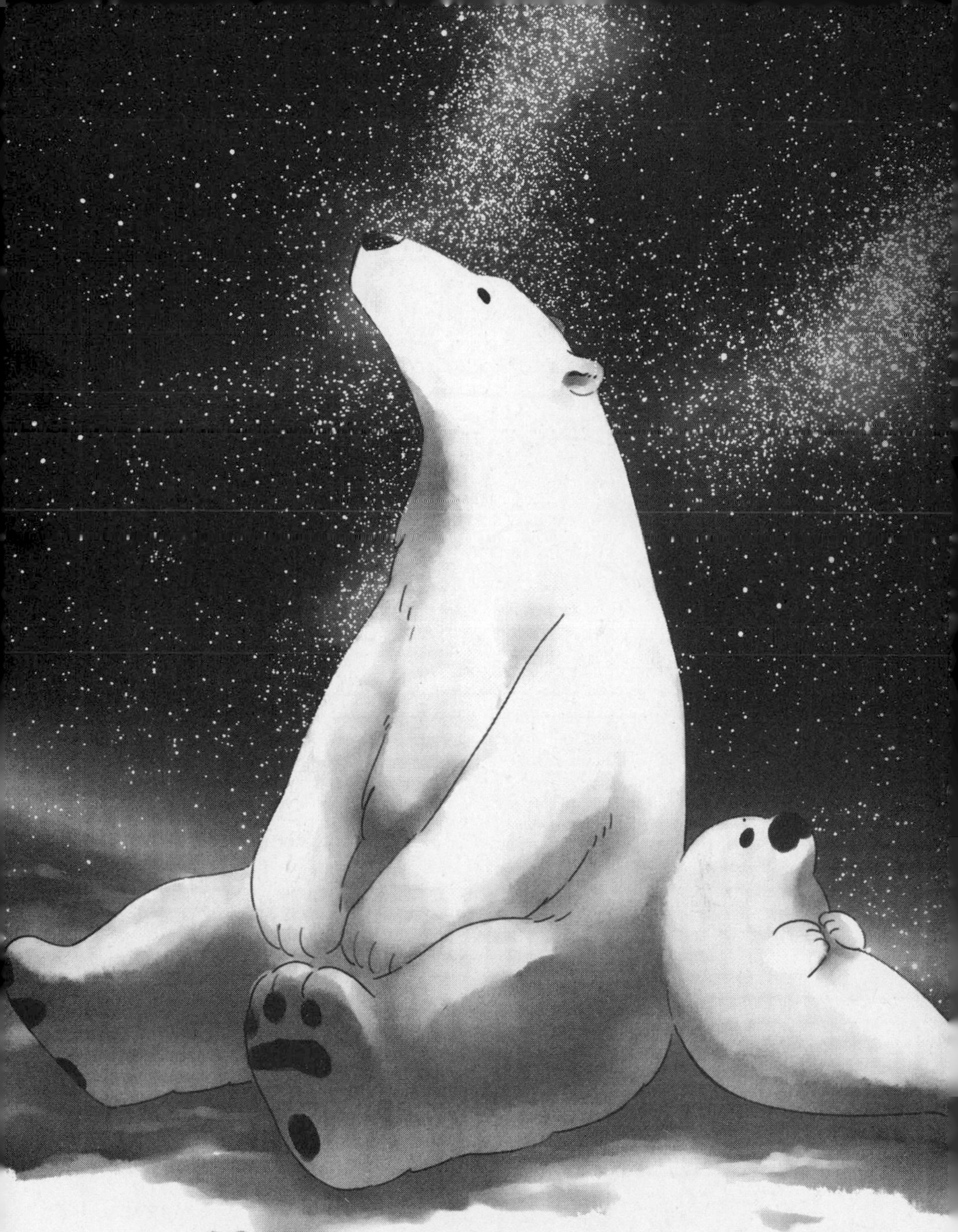

A POLAR BEAR in LOVE 2

CONTINUED FROM THE FRONT COVER...

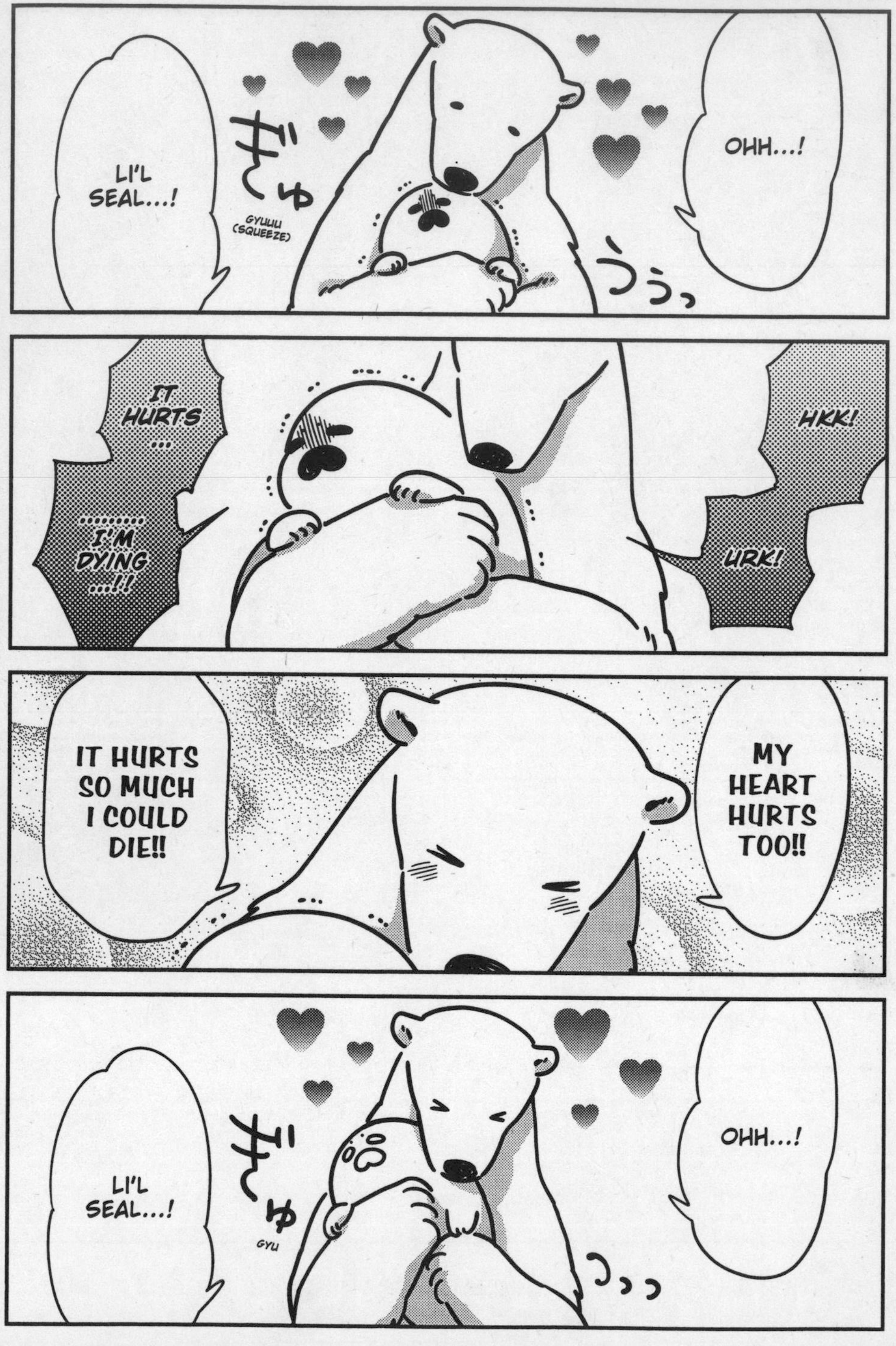

OHH...!
うぅっ
ぎゅ
GYUUU (SQUEEZE)
LI'L SEAL...!
HKK!
URK!
IT HURTS...
........I'M DYING...!!
MY HEART HURTS TOO!!
IT HURTS SO MUCH I COULD DIE!!
OHH...!
ぎゅ
GYU
LI'L SEAL...!

CONTINUED FROM THE LAST PAGE...

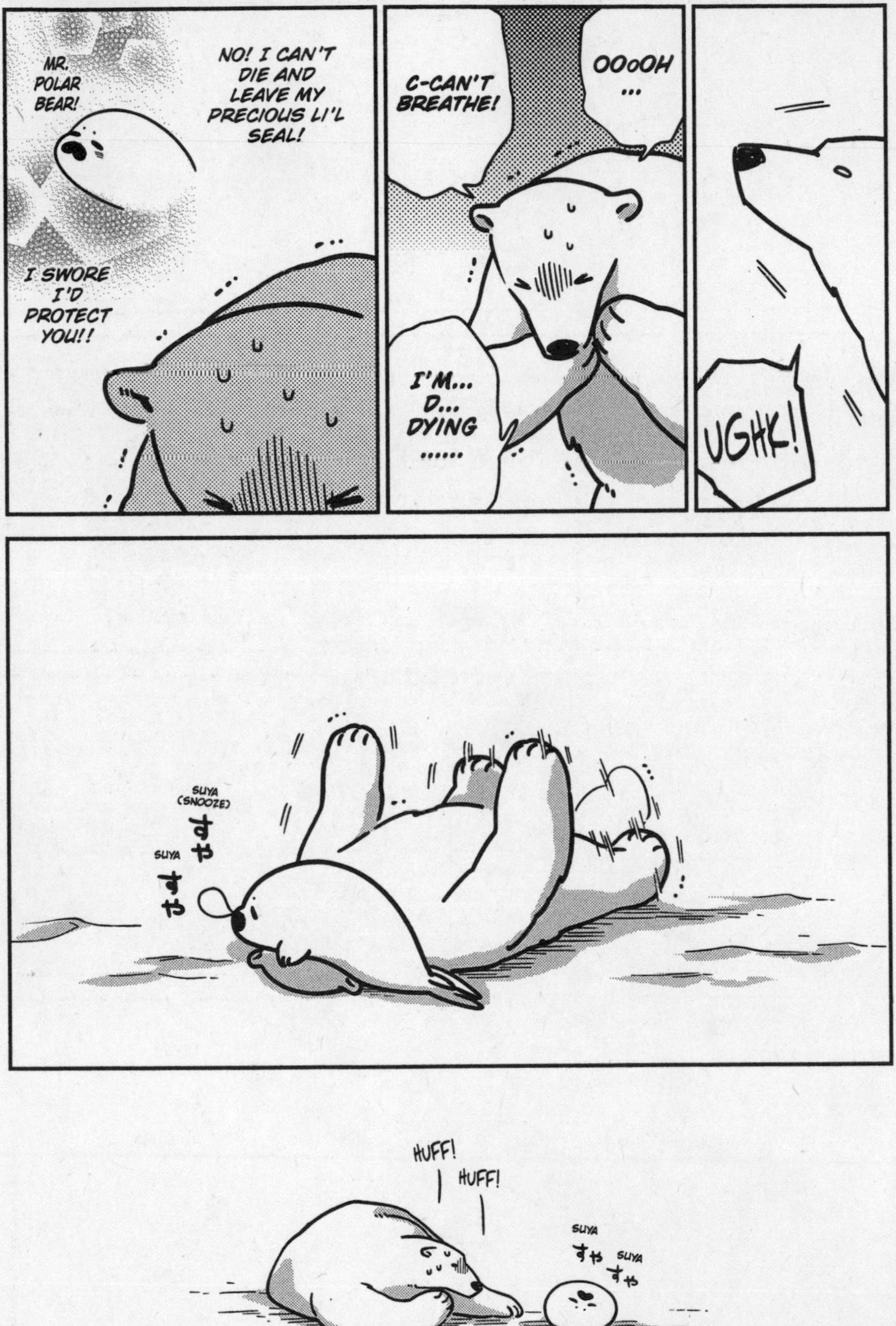
UGHK!
OOoOH ...
C-CAN'T BREATHE!
I'M... D... DYING ......
NO! I CAN'T DIE AND LEAVE MY PRECIOUS LI'L SEAL!
MR. POLAR BEAR!
I SWORE I'D PROTECT YOU!!
SUYA (SNOOZE) すや
SUYA すや
HUFF!
HUFF!
SUYA すや
SUYA すや

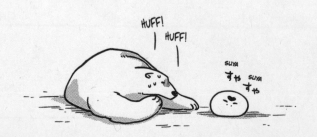

AUTHOR'S NOTE

RIBBON SEAL

Koromo

I'M DRAWING LI'L SEAL AS A HARP SEAL—THEY'RE MY FAVORITE KIND. BUT I ALSO LIKE THE RIBBON SEAL'S MARKINGS THAT SAY, "THE PRESENT IS M-O-I. ♥"

TRANSLATION NOTES

PAGE 150
"The moon is beautiful" is a traditionally poetic way to say "I love you" in Japanese, so Mr. Polar Bear is playfully suggesting that the moment is quite romantic.

PAGE 154
Having a dream on the evening of January 1 that contains an eggplant, a hawk, and Mount Fuji is a sign of good luck in Japanese culture.

ENJOY EVERYTHING.

Hello! This is YOTSUBA!

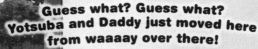

Guess what? Guess what?
Yotsuba and Daddy just moved here
from waaaay over there!

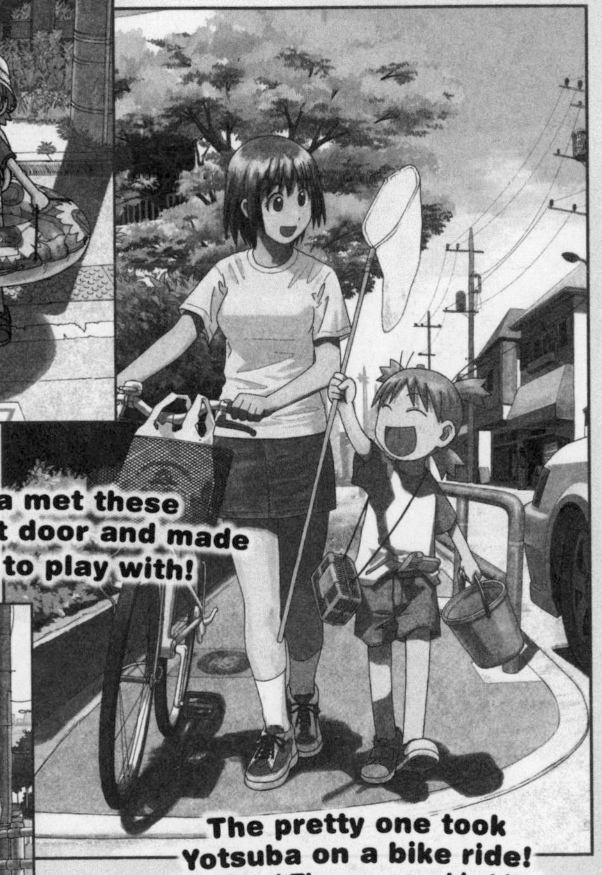

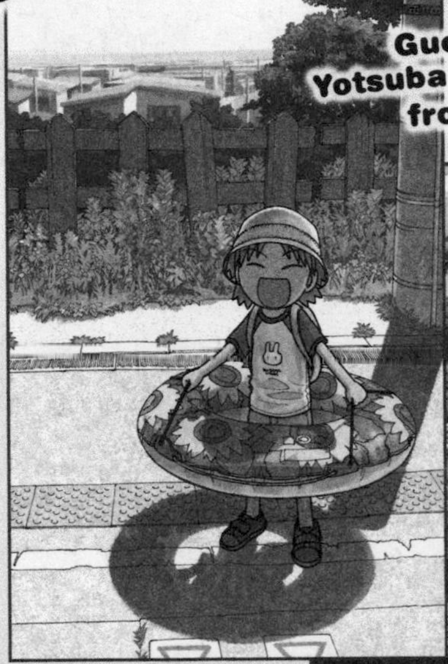

And Yotsuba met these
nice people next door and made
new friends to play with!

!

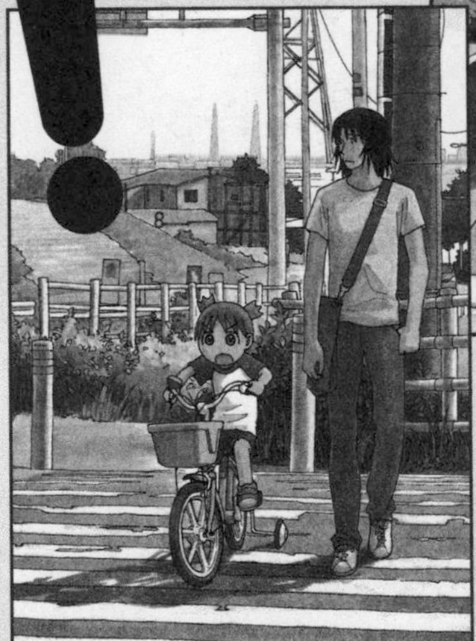

The pretty one took
Yotsuba on a bike ride!
(Whoooa! There was a big hill!)

And Ena's a good drawer!
(Almost as good as Yotsuba!)

And their mom always
gives Yotsuba ice cream!
(Yummy!)

And...
And...
OHHHH!

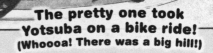

A POLAR BEAR IN LOVE 1

Koromo

TRANSLATION: Taylor Engel ❤ **LETTERING:** Lys Blakeslee

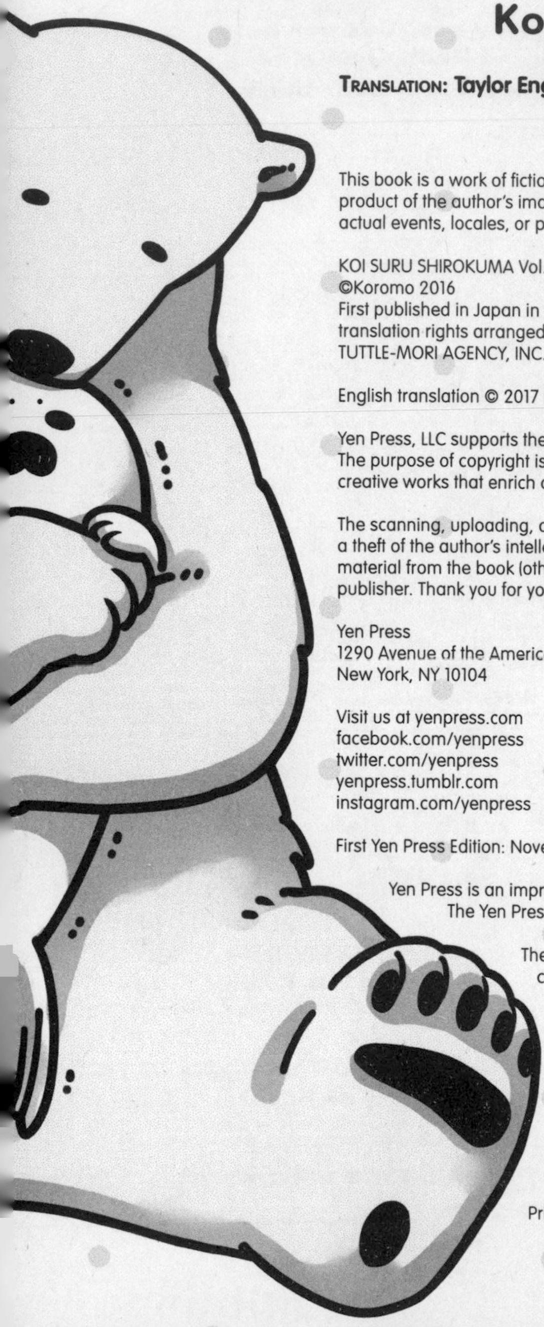

This book is a work of fiction. Names, characters, places, and incidents are the product of the author's imagination or are used fictitiously. Any resemblance to actual events, locales, or persons, living or dead, is coincidental.

KOI SURU SHIROKUMA Vol.1

First published in Japan in 2016 by KADOKAWA CORPORATION, Tokyo. English translation rights arranged with KADOKAWA CORPORATION, Tokyo through TUTTLE-MORI AGENCY, INC., Tokyo.

Yen Press
1290 Avenue of the Americas
New York, NY 10104

Visit us at yenpress.com
facebook.com/yenpress
twitter.com/yenpress
yenpress.tumblr.com
instagram.com/yenpress

First Yen Press Edition: November 2017

Yen Press is an imprint of Yen Press, LLC.
The Yen Press name and logo are trademarks of Yen Press, LLC.

The publisher is not responsible for websites (or their content) that are not owned by the publisher.

Library of Congress Control Number: 2017949438

ISBNs: 978-0-316-44171-1 (paperback)
978-0-316-44172-8 (ebook)

10 9 8 7 6 5 4 3 2 1

BVG

Printed in the United States of America